THE JAPANESE
IMPERIAL INSTITUTION
IN THE
TOKUGAWA PERIOD

STUDIES OF THE
EAST ASIAN INSTITUTE
COLUMBIA UNIVERSITY

HERSCHEL WEBB

THE JAPANESE
IMPERIAL INSTITUTION
IN THE
TOKUGAWA PERIOD

1968

COLUMBIA UNIVERSITY PRESS

NEW YORK AND LONDON

Herschel Webb, author of *An Introduction to Japan* and *Research in Japanese Sources: A Guide*, is Associate Professor of Japanese at Columbia University.

Copyright © 1968 Columbia University Press
Library of Congress Catalog Card Number 68-11912
Printed in the United States of America

THE EAST ASIAN INSTITUTE
OF COLUMBIA UNIVERSITY

The East Asian Institute of Columbia University was established in 1949 to prepare graduate students for careers dealing with East Asia, and to aid research and publication on East Asia during the modern period. The faculty of the Institute are grateful to the Ford Foundation and the Rockefeller Foundation for their financial assistance.

The Studies of the East Asian Institute were inaugurated in 1962 to bring to a wider public the results of significant new research on modern and contemporary East Asia.

To my mother and father

PREFACE

THE JAPANESE MONARCHY survived a thousand years of neglect and the atrophy of its political functions to emerge in the nineteenth century as a powerful instrument of state. From the Meiji Restoration of 1868 until the adoption of the 1946 constitution the emperor was described as the ruler of the country, or at least as the head of its government. The Restoration, almost universally acknowledged as the dividing point between traditional and modern Japan, comprised a variety of changes in the different social spheres; one of the most basic of these was the creation in the political sphere of a new kind of monarchic government which tended to centralize and strengthen the state.

The purpose of the present study is to shed light on the origin of this new conception of the monarchy by examining the last, most obscure, and feeblest phase in the history of the imperial institution before its reemergence. During this period, when the effective central government of Japan was headed by shoguns of the Tokugawa house, the emperors were not only politically impotent, they were virtually imprisoned. Imperial weakness was not a new condition, for the strong, Chinese-style imperial office of early times had already begun to atrophy in the ninth century. However, the process of atrophy was not fully accomplished for many centuries. Power clung to the emperor's office for years after it had left his person; imperial influence persisted in the capital when it had disappeared in the provinces. Even in the fifteenth and sixteenth centuries, a period of extreme political fragmentation and factionalism, the enfeebled emperor continued to maintain some share of power in the enfeebled central government, if only on account of the personal influence which he was able to bring to bear on more powerful political figures. The Tokugawa period, which followed, was a new phase in the relations between the throne and the government, because then for the first time the imperial institution was almost totally isolated from every governing office. This isolation began in the years of reunification immediately preceding the establishment of the Tokugawa shogunate. It was fully instituted within a generation of the shogunate's establishment, and it persisted until the closing years of Tokugawa rule.

The duration of this phase of the imperial institution defines the primary chronological limits of the present study. An introductory chapter gives a brief account of the origins of the imperial office and of the various stages of its development before the Tokugawa period. I had originally planned to describe as well the transition from the late Tokugawa period to the Meiji Restoration in more than cursory detail within the compass of this volume. It soon became apparent that this was not practical. The Tokugawa government did not fall until the Meiji Restoration of 1868, but as early as 1858 the imperial institution commenced a series of changes so profound and so rapid as to require of the historian a very different treatment from that of the earlier period. In fact, I realized that in order to do justice to the transition it would be necessary to accord it a length scarcely shorter than that of the present study. As a result I decided to end the narrative of this book at a historical moment when the emperor and his court had emerged sufficiently from their obscurity to be recognized once and for all as figures of national politics. Such a moment occurred in 1858 with the governmental crisis occasioned by the shogunate's acceptance of a commercial treaty with the United States. I intend to treat later events in the transition to the Meiji monarchy in a study now in progress, "The Japanese Imperial Institution in the Meiji Restoration."

I have been generously assisted in the preparation of this study by grants from the Council for Research in the Humanities of Columbia University and the Guggenheim Foundation, which I gratefully acknowledge. I should like also to express my appreciation to my colleagues at Columbia, particularly Professor Wm. Theodore de Bary of the Department of East Asian Languages and Cultures and Professor James Morley of the East Asian Institute, for many acts of kindness that eased the work. In addition I wish to thank, for their friendly advice and encouragement, Hans Bielenstein, Professor Minamoto Ryōen, Professor Mori Katsumi, Ivan Morris, Edward and Marleigh Ryan, Michael Solomon, David Titus, and Paul Varley.

HERSCHEL WEBB

New York City
October 16, 1967

CONTENTS

THE JAPANESE
IMPERIAL INSTITUTION
IN THE
TOKUGAWA PERIOD

It is the glory of God
To conceal a thing:
But the honour of kings
Is to search out a matter.
The heaven for height,
And the earth for depth,
And the heart of kings
Is unsearchable.

Proverbs 25:2,3.

That government is best of which only
the existence is known.

Lao Tzu, *Tao Tê Ching*

I

ORIGINS

✳ IN 1690 the German physician Engelbert Kaempfer arrived in Nagasaki to take up employment in the Dutch East India Company's factory there. His journey to the East had been packed with marvels, which he observed sympathetically and reported with fastidious detachment.[1] He had seen a Russia emerging into the world of Europe under Peter the Great. He had helped forge the initial links of scholarship binding modern Europe with the Middle East when he observed and described ancient Mesopotamian writing, for which he coined the word "cuneiform." [2] Kaempfer's learning and curiosity were boundless; he had unusual linguistic skill; he sought new adventures courageously. But the greatest of his gifts, one that was to lift him far above the average level of diarists in exotic territories, was the rationalism of his mind. He was never content to treat the wonders he observed merely as inexplicable, but was always concerned to detect in them their regularities and their similarities to phenomena which he and his European readers would know and understand. Both his correct and his mistaken observations show a passion for reducing the world of nature and man to a single, orderly, and comprehensible whole. Are the Japanese

[1] Kaempfer, *Amoenitatum Exoticarum Politico-Physico-Medicarum Fasciculi V, Quibus Continentur Variae Relationes, Observationes, & Descriptiones Rerum Persicarum & Ulterioris Asiae.* (The journal of Kaempfer's travels in the Middle East.) Kaempfer, *The History of Japan, together with a Description of the Kingdom of Siam, 1690–92.*

[2] See *Encyclopaedia Britannica,* 1963 ed., *sub* "Cuneiform"; Kaempfer, *Amoenitatum Exoticarum,* pp. 331–34.

descended from the Chinese, he asked. Obviously not, for the languages, religions, and customs of the two countries are nothing alike. But surely the Japanese must have come from somewhere? Yes, they came from Babylonia, taking the overland route through southern Siberia. They are therefore our cousins, he seems to say, and we may learn from them, their customs, and their institutions the common patterns of human behavior that we see without noticing in our own society.

Kaempfer's great *History* makes the Japan of his day vivid and helps us to resolve the paradoxes about it that native sources have produced. One of the confusing features of Japanese life in the Tokugawa period which Kaempfer helps to make less confusing is the system of "dual monarchy," by which one hereditary officer governed the country from the capital at Edo and another of a quite different family somehow possessed still greater prestige reigning in his own capital at Kyoto. The former monarch was to Kaempfer the "Secular Emperor" of the country; he was, of course, the official whom we know as the shogun. The other monarch to him was the "Ecclesiastical Emperor," whom he described as a sort of Pope or head of the state church. This is the figure whom the Japanese refer to as *tennō*; Kaempfer sometimes employs contemporary periphrasis in talking about him, calling him Mikado (Palace Gate) or Dairi (Palace), and one customarily refers to him in modern English as the Emperor of Japan. He enjoyed ascriptions of sanctity that to Kaempfer were consistent with his being a religious, but not at all a political, personage.

He [the tennō] thinks that it would be very prejudicial to his Dignity and Holiness to touch the ground with his feet; for this reason, when he intends to go any where, he must be carried thither on Men's shoulders. Much less will they suffer, that he should expose his Sacred Person to the open air, and the Sun is not thought worthy to shine on his Head. There is such a Holiness ascrib'd to all the parts of his Body, that he dares not cut off, neither his Hair, nor his Beard, nor his nails. However lest he should grow too dirty, they may clean him in the Night, when he is asleep, because they say, that what is taken from his Body at that time, hath been stolen from him, and that such a theft doth not prejudice his Holiness or Dignity.[3]

As for the relations between the secular and ecclesiastical thrones, Kaempfer makes it clear that the first provides the economic means for the support of the second, though in a somewhat niggardly way.

However, they still keep up their former grandeur and magnificence, and it can most truly be said of this Court, that it is remarkable for a splendid poverty. The great ones run themselves in debt, and the inferior officers and servants, whose allowances are far from being sufficient to maintain them, must work for their livelyhood.[4]

The ecclesiastical emperor's courtiers had elaborately graded ranks which signified to Kaempfer titles of ecclesiastical offices, though they were at the same time vestiges of political titles from the period when the ecclesiastical emperors had been secular rulers as well.

All titles and degrees of honour, whatsoever, are conferr'd . . . by the Mikaddo, and by him alone. When the Secular Monarchs took the Government of the Empire into their hands, the Dairi reserv'd to himself, along with the supreme authority, this considerable branch of the Imperial prerogatives. Hence whatever titles the Secular Emperors intend to bestow on their Favourites and Prime Ministers, must be obtain'd of the Mikaddo.[5]

Finally, Kaempfer deals with the question of the potential threat to the secular authorities from this sacrosanct churchly institution.

[3] Kaempfer, History, vol. 1, pp. 260–61.
[4] Ibid., p. 265.   [5] Ibid., p. 263.

The Secular Monarch constantly keeps a strong guard of Bugjos[6] and Soldiers at the Dairi's Court, as it were, out of tenderness and care for the preservation and safety of his sacred person and family, but in fact to put it out of his power, ever to attempt the recovery of the throne and the supreme authority, which he took from him.[7]

There are inaccuracies in Kaempfer's account. For example, all evidence indicates that the emperors did bathe themselves. Yet despite its misstatements, his description of the imperial institution is remarkably just, doing great credit to the objectivity of his Japanese informants and to his own powers of analysis. The imperial institution in the Tokugawa period was indeed a kind of state church, though it had overtones of a political nature owing to the fact that it had earlier been a secular government. The effective government of the time permitted the throne to retain certain ceremonial prerogatives, but the emperors had no true powers of state. The government provided the material support of the imperial court, but also maintained a close military guard over it lest its members seek a restoration of its long-vanished political authority and overthrow the effective government.

Kaempfer's distinction between imperial and shogunal functions is especially valuable to us because it uses terms that relate them to Western experience. Native writers customarily described the two thrones with different sets of contrasting terms, which are less likely to make immediate sense to those unacquainted with the usages of the Japanese state and society. The most common pair of terms used for the shogunal and imperial

[6] *Bugjo* (*Bugyō* in standard romanization): A class of high shogunal officials, frequently called "administrators" in English, and corresponding to ministers of executive departments of the central government or to mayors of the principal cities in the shogunal domain. Kaempfer probably refers here to the *Kyōto machi bugyō*, the "city administrators" or "mayors" of the imperial capital, though there were only two officers of this title at any one time.

[7] Kaempfer, *History*, vol. 1, p. 268.

institutions were *bu* and *kō*, elements of Chinese derivation that have acquired the not entirely satisfactory association with the English words "military" and "public." The imperial institution was also sometimes associated with another element, *bun*, which was the opposite of *bu*, and is therefore usually translated "civil." Here are a few examples. The aristocratic caste which furnished the military, police, and administrative personnel of the effective government was called *bushi*, "military nobles." The word is substantially the same as "samurai." *Buke* and *bumon*, literally "military families," referred to the bushi caste in general. By contrast, the hereditary caste of courtiers attached to the imperial court in Kyoto as retainers of the emperor were known as *kuge* or *kugyō* (*ku* is a variant of *kō*), "public families" or "public nobles."

In contemporary parlance the Tokugawa shogunate was a particular instance of *buke seiji* or *bumon seiji*, that is, "military government." In general, that expression meant government by soldiers, or at least by officials whose titles implied military command. It suggested the philosophic sense of a government which relied for its control on force or the threat of force. The opposite terms were *bunji* and *bunji seiji*, "civil government." In a philosophic sense these referred to the classic Confucian ideal of government which had no need for military or penal sanctions but relied entirely on the example of a virtuous ruler to maintain order. It was also used for those activities of any government, such as ritual and the codification of law, that were conceived of as having exemplificative or morally instructive purposes. In historical contexts *bunji* tended to be used of the institutional usages pertaining to the emperor's throne, as opposed to the military and penal arms of the government subordinate to him. When used of periods after the political functions of the imperial institution had become atrophied, the word might be applied to the entire system of offices and functionaries headed by him.

These usages should make certain implications clear. First, while the term *bu* continued to retain to a considerable degree its original associations with warfare and soldiery, it also came to be applied to things more aptly described in English as aspects of the civil administration. that is, the term *buke seiji* referred to both the military and civil arms of the effective government of the country, and a bushi administrator as often as not was charged with essentially civilian responsibilities as a bureaucrat, a judge, a clerk, or even a teacher or physician.

The element *kō*, which in other contexts almost always pertains to public or governmental affairs, was not applied to the institutions and usages of the effective government. Furthermore, the associations of the element *bun* were rather far removed from those of the English word "civil," lying for the most part entirely beyond the realm customarily thought of as political. *Bun* had connotations, apparently, of two sorts. One related to social ideals as opposed to social actualities, the "ought" as opposed to the "is." The other related to that side of life in a society of high civilization which makes it civilized: its arts and letters, its philosophy and learning, and its material technology. One may even detect in the element *bun* a certain emphasis on the purely decorative or aesthetic aspects of civilization, as opposed to those which serve mundane practical needs.

These connotations help to explain the associations which writers of the Tokugawa period intended when they applied the elements *bun* and *kō* to the emperor's office. It was not a government at all in the usual sense, for it did not govern anyone other than its own functionaries. Yet it looked like a government, because its members had titles which seemed to imply political functions, and they were organized into an elaborate hierarchy of offices which resembled a chain of administrative command. The imperial court was a pseudo-government. To call it a government was a means of setting forth clearly the analogy and contrast with the institution of the shogunate, which was a true government.

The administration of the shogun was "military" in two different senses. First, its founder had been a soldier and it had been brought into being by force of arms. Second, even after the shogun became more civilian bureaucrat than soldier, then more figurehead than civilian bureaucrat, the instruments of shogunal rule continued to be instruments of restraint. Government theorists of the Tokugawa period, most of them spokesmen for the political system which they described, nevertheless implied when they used expressions like *buke seiji* that shogunal rule was a deviation from an ideal. For those theorists were partisans of a Confucian ideology which regarded the use or threat of force by a ruler as evidence that he lacked sufficient personal virtue to maintain virtue in his subjects. That the same flaw mars all modern governments and most of those recorded in history would not have ruffled dedicated loyalists to the Confucian ideal. They would have granted the fact freely and asserted boldly that human imperfection in no way tarnished the validity of the ideal.

To speak of the emperor's throne with terminology that contrasted sharply with that of the effective government—in fact to use political terminology of it at all—was a means of saying that it was an image of an ideal state. It differed from the ideal in the all-important respect that it was not a government at all, performing none of the functions for which governments are organized. It bore somewhat the same relationship to a government that a picture of a horse does to a horse. When one says of a painting that there is a horse in it, or that the horse is running, one is not telling an untruth. However, it is essential to realize that the words "horse" and "running" in that statement are not to be understood in the usual sense. Similarly, when men of the Tokugawa period said of the imperial institution that it performed functions analogous to those of the shogunate but that the means by which it did so was the ruler's virtuous example rather than instruments of restraint, one should be aware that each term in the statement must be accepted as symbolic rather than literal.

A picture of a horse is not a horse. A concept of a virtuous ruler is not a virtuous ruler. An ideal of a perfect institutional system is not a perfect institutional system. These cautions are necessary correctives to too literal an understanding of the statements which Tokugawa period writers made about the imperial institution. They are all the more necessary because those writers are our best source of information on what the institution was and why it was maintained.

Contemporary Japanese thought of the imperial throne as an image of the ideal state. Yet the thing of which the image was a depiction was still more than that. The perfection that was associated with the emperor and his court was such as might be desired in every human collectivity—hierarchical organization, moral excellence in the presiding person, a division of functions in the lower orders, and a proper performance of his duties by every inferior person, each one emulating in his own way the excellence of the superior. The institution, to those who described it articulately, was no mere static symbol of moral perfection. It was concrete and complex, like a work of art. Its parts filled space and moved in time. The medium, the raw material out of which the depiction was made was not inert matter but flesh and blood, living persons like the commonalty of mankind. The institution was like a work of art, and more particularly like a work of dramatic or theatrical art.

This simile will be developed further in the present study, one of whose aims in fact is to show that it may be more than a simile. For the moment, one may sum up the foregoing discussion by saying that, whereas Engelbert Kaempfer regarded the imperial throne as ecclesiastical and the shogunate as political, his Japanese contemporaries typically described both offices in political terms. Kaempfer noticed the quasi-political features of the imperial institution but wrote them off as historical vestiges. Japanese writers, on the other hand, treated them as intrinsic to the purpose of the institution. On closer inspection, however, the native writers appear to have admitted with Kaempfer that the shogunate was political and the imperial institution was something else. It was a quasi-aesthetic token of a moral ideal.

· 2 ·

The earlier history of the imperial institution explains the peculiar position which it occupied among the institutions of Tokugawa Japan, and helps to account for the particular mixture of political and nonpolitical characteristics which the throne came to assume.

The antiquity of the institution is its most striking feature. It is probably the oldest hereditary office in the world, and if any nonhereditary offices are older, they are most likely limited to certain sees of Roman and Greek Catholicism. The exact age of the Japanese imperial throne is indeterminable. Japanese mythology assigns an exact date, February 11, 660 B.C., to the accession of the first emperor, but the consensus of modern scholarship is that nothing at all can be known about Japanese history at so early a time. The source for that date is the *Nihon shoki* of 720, Japan's oldest history in Chinese language and style, the historicity of whose early sections is very questionable. The same work provides a list of 33 or 34 sovereigns up to A.D. 600, with specific reign dates for all of them. The specificity of the *Nihon shoki* chronology is itself grounds to doubt its reliability. Japan lacked a written language until the fifth or sixth century. Before then her history and mythology were preserved orally. Similarly, accurate calendration and the recording of exact dates seem to have been imported from the mainland then or later. The more native and primitive *Kojiki* of 712 duplicates the *Nihon shoki*'s king list but differs in many points on dates of imperial reigns. Its whole chronology is much more vague (and believable) than that of the other work. Minute study of these two books, which are the earliest native documentary sources, has produced a reasonably reliable record of the imperial institution after about 500, as well as sound grounds for belief that it had existed for several generations before that date.[8] Attempts to pinpoint further the origins of the institution have not been satisfying. Statements by various scholars to the effect that the institution was already in existence by, say, A.D. 200 or 300 are no more than guesses.[9]

The institution is therefore prehistoric in origin. Given so long a continuous history, it might well be expected to have changed so profoundly since the beginning that almost nothing of its original character has lasted to the present time. Still it is tempting to examine it in its earliest known state for possible features that have continued to characterize it. Japanese theorists have posited the continuous existence of several features. These they describe as parts of the "unchanging essence" of the monarchy and as main ingredients of national polity. They will be discussed at their proper places in this study. For the present, one may specify two noteworthy features of the institution that appear to have existed at the beginning of Japanese recorded history and that have continued to exist ever since.

The first of these continuing features is the respect shown in theory and in fact for absolute dynastic legitimacy in determining an emperor's right to his title. That this feature is sufficiently rare to be noted requires some explanation. Of course,

---

[8] See the discussions in Sakamoto, *Nihon-shi gaisetsu*, pp. 42–46; Wakamori, *Kokka no seisei*, in *Shin Nihon-shi taikei*, vol. 1, pp. 158–60.

[9] For an interesting discussion of the mythological and historical considerations that have guided the dating of the origins of the Japanese nation see Nihon-shi Kenkyū-kai (comp.), *Nihon no kenkoku*.

monarchic institutions tend to be hereditary in most societies, but most other societies have admitted the concept that a monarchic office might continue to exist and continue in general to be transmitted by heredity even though from time to time it should pass to members of a different family. In both Eastern and Western societies theorists of monarchic legitimacy have labored hard to justify this sophistication of the dynastic principle and to define its limitations. The monarchy of imperial China was dynastic for the most part, but there were numerous changes of dynasty in its two-thousand-year existence. Furthermore, the main tradition of political legitimacy in China asserted clearly that such changes might be justified. Mencius's influential doctrine that a popular revolution signified a transference of legitimacy from one ruler to another was only one instance of a universal pattern of Chinese political thought which held that the first criterion for a monarch's right to govern was something other than heredity. In this respect the Chinese monarchy was not much different from the kingly institution of France, which survived the transference of title from the Merovingian to the Carolingian to the Capetian house, nor from that of England, traceable back through several dynastic houses to a Saxon kingship that was in theory elective. Even the throne of the Holy Roman Empire, which remained elective until it was abolished, was no more than an extreme case of the same type, a monarchic institution which tended to be passed on by blood descent but whose continuity was regarded as independent of the fragile hold on power of a single family.

From first to last Japanese theory on the imperial dynasty has asserted a definition of legitimacy which is of the opposite emphasis from the Chinese and European. All theorists have insisted that an emperor must be a member of a certain family, and they have further asserted that all Japanese emperors have in fact met that primary test of legitimacy. All of the dynastic disputes in Japanese history have centered around which of two members of the imperial family had the right to rule, and every idea advanced by Japanese thinkers as to the mechanism by which an emperor should be chosen, the personal qualities he should have, or the tokens by which the true emperor might be recognized has first presupposed that there should be no choice of claimants outside the imperial family.

The ideas the Japanese hold of blood heredity in the imperial family are more extreme than those that are applied to other Japanese families. Japanese society has accorded great importance to hereditary rights in general. For example, until the modernization of the system of land tenure in the 1870s there were legal restrictions against alienation of a farm family's real property. Furthermore, intangible rights, such as membership in a certain trade or occupation or eligibility to hold prestigious ranks or titles of office, have tended to be treated as the inalienable property of a family much in the same way as are its material goods. The Japanese family is not only a biological or domiciliar unit serving the usual social purposes; it is a corporate entity charged with the responsibility of maintaining its physical and intangible possessions indefinitely. But it is precisely because of the extraordinary pressures which Japanese society places on the individual family to perpetuate itself that an exceptionally easy mechanism for adoption has become institutionalized. The typical Japanese corporate or legal family has continued to exist because it has had unusual freedom to bequeath its estate to an outsider whenever the blood line died out. The imperial family could not adopt heirs from outside its own membership. If the same practices had applied to the imperial family as to ordinary ones, the imperial throne would have come closer to resembling the monarchies of China or the West as described above.

Japanese attitudes toward the imperial family's hereditary rights are similar to the ideas held toward hereditary rights in general, but in order to explain the intensity of the attitudes in the one particular instance, it is necessary to adduce a cause of a different order. This is the folk belief, associated with the indigenous religion of the Japanese people, that blood descent from a god confers the unique power to communicate with the god. The Sun Goddess, Amaterasu Ōmikami, chief divinity of the Shinto pantheon, was the progenitrix of the imperial line, according to the origin myth of the Japanese people as it appears in the *Nihon shoki* and *Kojiki*. Primitive Japanese as well as great numbers of their more recent descendants believed that ministrations to that most awesome personage were of potent efficacy in ordering the affairs of agriculture, warfare, and the governance of society. A man who was not of the imperial line not only lacked the power to make use of the god's higher power, but he also risked incurring an awful curse if he presumed to do so.

There is a telling allusion to that dread in Japan's greatest literary work, the *Tale of Genji*. One important episode in the novel relates to a certain prince, the son of Genji and the Empress, who is brought up by the Emperor as his own son and actually attains the imperial throne. The event has baleful consequences in the shape of portentous disorders, though only Genji, the young Emperor's true father, knows their cause.

The Palace was frequently visited by the most disagreeable and alarming apparitions, the motions of the planets, sun and moon were irregular and unaccountable, and clouds of baleful and significant shape were repeatedly observed. Learned men of every school sent in elaborate addresses to the Throne, in which they attempted to account for these strange manifestations. But they were obliged to confess that many of the reported happenings were unique, and of a very baffling character. While speculation thus reigned on every side, Genji held in his heart a guilty secret which might well be the key to these distressing portents.

The young Emperor eventually comes to know the secret of his birth. He is overcome with shock and confusion. He confides in Genji his desire to abdicate immediately, indicating as his reason a foreboding that "calamity of some stupendous kind" is at hand. For solace he conducts research to find if ever before there might have been other such unfortunate cases as his.

He threw himself with fresh ardour into the study of history, reading every book with the sole object of discovering other cases like his own. In China, he soon found, irregularities of descent have not only in many cases been successfully concealed till long afterwards, but have often been known and tolerated from the beginning. In Japan he could discover no such instance; but he knew that if things of this kind occurred, they would probably not be recorded. . . .

Soon thereafter, he abdicates.[10]

This extraordinary episode does more than indicate the awe with which the Sun Goddess's legacy was regarded. If ever so subtly, it gives the observant reader grounds to suspect that the exact lines of descent of the Japanese imperial house may be unprovable. For though one can scarcely build a historical case on a work of fiction, one may at least surmise that its author was aware of the principles of good fiction, which include plausibility. Notwithstanding this qualification, the fact remains that the overwhelming majority of Japanese have believed that the hereditary character of imperial legitimacy has always been, and must by the very essence of the case always remain, absolute.

· 3 ·

The second characteristic of the imperial institution that existed at the dawn of history and that has continued to exist ever since has already been hinted at. It is the tendency to accord primacy to those functions of the emperor that derived from his unique powers to ministrate to his divine ancestors. These func-

10 *The Tale of Genji,* by Murasaki Shikibu, translated by Arthur Waley, pp. 371–78.

tions will be referred to here as sacerdotal or religious. They may be roughly subdivided into acts of potent magic, calculated to effect beneficial change in nature or society (for example, prayers for rain or for a change of heart in rebellious subjects), and oracular acts, intended to communicate between the divine progenitrix and ordinary men (for example, reports to the god about secular events, and relaying the god's advice about how secular issues should be resolved). Only the emperor was thought capable of making these acts effective, and they were therefore regarded as the most essential part of his job. Another group of functions, which one may call secular, were performed either by the emperor or by the administration over which he presided. These may be specified as all those ordinary acts performed by political society (warfare, punishment, taxation, public works, and so forth) on which divine descent conferred no particular power or efficiency. Even in very early Japan this second set of functions was thought of as less essential to the imperial office than the first, and in later periods it slipped away entirely from the competence of the emperor.

The words "religious" and "secular," as used here, are only shorthand terms for the sphere of unique imperial power and the sphere of its absence. One should not assume that the "religious" sphere was exclusively concerned with the hereafter, with eternal things, nor with that realm which sophisticated cultures call the "supernatural." Primitive Japanese had no clear understanding of the difference between natural and supernatural events. To them the power to induce rain by means of ritual imperial acts was not categorically different from the power to control flooding by means of a dam. That is, the only difference perceived to exist between them was that one act required the agency of the emperor whereas any number of people could perform the other with equal efficacy.

Despite this qualification, the sphere of unique imperial power had characteristics that permit us to apply the word "religious" to it. It consisted in the main of two areas of human experience that have been the specific concern of religions in all societies. One area is phenomena which ordinary human understanding cannot comprehend and ordinary human skill cannot control. When human ingenuity devised dams to control flooding, that phenomenon ceased being a matter of "religious" concern; the rainfall that was the ultimate cause continued to be. The other area to which unique imperial power pertained was the ascertainment of universal principles for correct human conduct. As the magic acts performed by the emperor had as their purpose the control of phenomena that were beyond ordinary human means, the oracular acts existed to disclose moral truth.

Instructive comparisons may be drawn between the traditional monarchies of the East and West on the basis of the interplay within them between secular and sacerdotal functions. The imperial thrones of China and Japan and kingly institutions of the Western Christian tradition have all, of course, had governmental functions, or when completely impotent in a practical political sense, have at least been conceived of as having an intimate relationship with the institutions which did govern. In addition, the thrones of all three civilizations have shared at least the characteristics that they have all had carefully defined positions among the religious institutions of the society. Every religion tends to describe the interaction between the human and the divine in its own way, so it is not easy to formulate general terms in matters such as these that will be equally applicable to religions as diverse as Western Christianity and the state cults of China and Japan. The attempt must still be made to find some minimum common ground for all of them that will permit the inspection of the crucial differences among them. The first generalization that can be made is a matter of broad philosophic speculation. All three societies have conceived of a super-terrestrially ordained moral order as the

ultimate criterion for the judgment of human acts. The earthly
analog of abstract moral law is political law, and the ethical
thinkers of all three societies would have agreed in the main
that political statutes are to be adjudged good or bad accordingly
as they conform to abstract moral law. Making and enforcing
human laws is the specific function of kingly institutions. Even
in places or times when the king was not himself a lawgiver or
a ruler, society has made the metaphorical ascription of those
functions to him. Implicit in these common presuppositions on
ethics and politics is the idea that, whereas men are subject to
the king's law, kings are subject to a higher.

"It is the glory of God to conceal a thing: but the honour of
kings is to search out a matter." The Proverb formulates a
subtle relation among God, rulers, and men. It speaks of the
elusiveness of moral truth and the necessity for rulers to understand it so that their subjects may perceive it in the more in-
telligible form of earthly law. Chinese and Japanese theorists of
kingship would not have disagreed with it. In all three cultures
the king was conceived of as one who spoke with the supernatural source of morality and relayed what he learned to his
subjects as law. Herein lay both his religious and his political
roles.

One all-important distinction existed between Eastern and
Western monarchies in the way in which their religious functions were manifested. The Christian Church, an institution
standing in proud independence of Christian monarchies, was
itself an organ for the ascertainment of divine law and the moral
guidance of men. Though Western political practice has exhibited a wide variety of relationships between Church and
Throne, from the theocratic to the Erastian, it has always,
where monarchies that called themselves Christian were concerned, demanded some admission by the secular authorities of
the sacerdotal prerogatives of the Church. The minimum concession to churchly power has been to grant the Church the

ability to perform those sacramental acts that most directly betokened human intercourse with the divine. In more typical cases, the Church assumed the power to advise the king on moral matters, to judge the morality of his acts, and even from time to time to declare that an improper act of a king was without force. In the long line of Western kingly tradition, kings have tended either to share the role of earthly transmitter of moral law or else to stand subordinate to the Church in the transmission, receiving from it, and only indirectly from God, the moral sanction by which the king's laws might be judged.

In China and Japan no such independent ecclesiastical institution existed. The secular and sacerdotal powers over the whole of society were united in a single institution having the emperor as its sole head. In neither society did this mean that the acts of rulers were wholly beyond human criticism, but it did mean that in a purely institutional sense the emperor and his ministers had to rely on their own resources in determining the relevance of their acts to abstract order and morality. It was thought best for emperors to be moral men, that is to say, to govern with attention to superhumanly ordained principles, but any other man who said of an emperor that he was not moral risked the criticism that the emperor was after all in a better position than he to know what was moral and what was not.

Both in China and in Japan the religious role of the emperor could be interpreted to mean several different things. It might be taken to be a supernatural power to talk with divinities and to use potent magic to effect change in the world of nature or of men. More sophisticated men might prefer to regard the power of the ruler as residing instead in his ability to instill virtue in other men by their emulation of his own virtue. A symbolic interpretation was also possible. By it the emperor, who was the head of human society, was taken to stand for all of society, and the communion with the superhuman from which human morality arose was betokened by rites and ceremonies performed by the emperor. However one regarded his role, it demanded the performance of acts that in Western Christian tradition would normally have been considered sacramental or priestly.

This then is a defining characteristic of Chinese and Japanese monarchies: that they have not only been regarded as having something to do with the religions of those societies but have actually been accorded much the role of a state church. To call the emperors of China and Japan the Chief Priests of the national religions of those countries might bring forth misleading associations for Western readers, but it would not be totally inaccurate.

It must now be emphasized that, despite this basic similarity, the religious role of the Japanese emperor was significantly different from that of the Chinese emperor. In very early Japanese history, before acquaintance with Chinese practices caused the Japanese to describe the native institution with foreign terminology, the difference is particularly striking. One way of describing it is to say that, whereas in the Chinese monarchy there was a total union of secular and sacerdotal functions in the person of the emperor, in Japan there tended to be a division of labor, so to speak, whereby the emperor discharged the religious functions of his office, since he alone had the power to make them efficacious, but delegated to others the secular functions, which did not depend on his unique powers.

This is of course a generalization which does not apply to all cases. There was a disparity among powers and roles of different rulers of the same country on account of the personal differences between individuals. Weak Chinese emperors might perform the sacrifices of their office yet allow others to govern in their name. Strong-willed Japanese emperors might wield real political power. Yet the individual differences should not cloud the fact that Japanese society in the earliest period known to historians did not really expect the emperor to be the functioning senior administrator of the national government, as contemporary Chinese society did. Some concrete illustrations of the way in which the early Japanese imperial institution operated will clarify the point made here and may then permit speculation as to the particular way in which early Japanese society conceived of the superhuman ordination of earthly power.

All students of Japanese history have noticed the tendency for royal power to devolve upon the monarch's subjects. Once a man had achieved an office or title, it was often regarded as an inheritable possession. In this way the political power that devolved on a king's subject might be perpetuated in a dynasty of rulers who continued generation after generation to rule without a kingly title. The Soga, Fujiwara, Taira, Minamoto, Hōjō, Ashikaga, and Tokugawa are all examples of families who transmitted political power by blood inheritance, masking their rule behind a variety of offices, none of which literally signified kingship. Of these families only the first, the Soga, lived before the wholesale modification of the Japanese imperial institution along Chinese lines, and even the Soga ruled a Japan which was in touch with China and beginning to acquire the coloration of a Chinese-style state. The history of that family is one of our best sources on the usages of the imperial institution before foreign influences changed them, but only because there is so little earlier evidence. It is one of the chief irreducible problems in the study of very early Japanese history that, because the art of history was itself a culture trait which the Japanese took from China, we must make out the shape of native institutions as best we can through spectacles manufactured outside Japan.

One must keep this caution in mind if one is to understand the way in which Japan was governed in the late sixth and early seventh centuries. The picture which the *Nihon shoki*[11] paints

11 *Nihon shoki (Kokushi taikei*, vol. 1), pp. 135–68. Translated by W. G. Aston as *Nihongi, Chronicles of Japan from the Earliest Times to A.D. 697,* London, George Allen & Unwin, 1956, Part 2, pp. 121–56.

is confusing in several respects. There is a strong presumption in the text that under normal circumstances the emperor ruled, for a special point is made of the fact that in the reign of the first female sovereign, the Empress Suiko (r. 593–628), most of her powers were assumed by her regent, Prince Shōtoku. This would all be clear enough if the same text did not disclose that another dominant figure in the government (so far as military, fiscal, and similar affairs were concerned) was the Great Imperial Chieftain (Ō-omi), Soga Umako.

In the reign of Suiko there were three persons all of whom could by some definition be called "rulers." The text is disappointingly vague about what division of functions there was among them, but some points are clear. Most of the personal acts attributed to the Empress are of three kinds: acts of Shinto ceremony such as the sovereign always performed in person; pronouncement and receipt of communications with foreign states; and the issuance of statements to the people representing the official policy of the government. Acts of the latter two classes indicate that the sovereign continued as before to stand as the personal embodiment of the government in all its public dealings with those outside it. The Regent, it is said, "had general control of the Government, and was entrusted with all the details of administration."[12] Yet most of the acts specifically associated with him in the text have to do with one or the other of the two state cults of the time, Shinto or Buddhism. Where these were concerned it is implied that he had the power to make decisions. He seems to have undertaken on his own more acts of a political or semi-political character than the Empress, for his name, not hers, is associated with such decisions as the adoption of the Chinese calendar in 604, the drafting of the seventeen-article "Constitution" (actually a code of general ethical precepts rather than of specific administrative or penal statutes) in the same year, and the consecration of the Hōryū-ji

[12] *Nihongi*, Part 2, p. 122.

monastery as a center of Buddhist worship for the Japanese state (607).

The text is downright evasive when it comes to the behavior of Soga Umako. In some places it would appear that authors of the *Nihon shoki* held him and his works in anathema. He had first of all assassinated Suiko's predecessor, the Emperor Sushun. On another occasion he clashed with imperial will by making the unusual request of the Empress that the district in which the Soga family had originally resided be made their permanent fief (that is, withdrawn from the administrative and fiscal control of the Empress's government.) Umako's son, Soga Emishi, and grandson, Soga Iruka, also perpetrated great outrages against imperial authority, and thereby stimulated the reaction in favor of the prerogatives of the imperial house that culminated in the great Taika Reform (645). The text as a whole leaves the reader with the impression that the Soga's acts were unprecedented and unjustifiable. Yet other details suggest a slightly different picture at least of Umako's relations with the throne and the historians' view of his role. A character sketch appended to the *Nihon shoki*'s notice of his death is not unfriendly. "He had a talent for military tactics, and was also gifted with eloquence. He reverenced deeply the Three Precious Things."[13] (That is, he was a pious Buddhist.) The Empress's speech in which she refused Umako the fief which he had requested is as concrete a statement as there is as to what Umako was and what he did.

We are sprung from the Soga family. Moreover the Ō-omi [Umako] is Our uncle by the mother's side. Therefore the words of the Ō-omi, if spoken at night, [are carried into effect by us] before the night has given way to morning; if spoken in the daytime, [they are carried into effect] before the day has become dark. What speech of his have We not attended to? But if now in this Our reign, We were rashly to part with this district, future sovereigns would say, 'A foolish woman ruled the Empire, and rashly lost this district.' Not only should We be accounted unwise, but the

13 *Ibid.*, p. 154.

Ō-omi would be thought disloyal. Such would be Our ill-fame in ages to come.[14]

The text suggests that the tension between the throne and the Soga family stemmed from their unusual arrogance and from their actual mistreatment of the imperial family. It implies, however, that there was nothing especially untoward about the fact that the Empress received orders from Umako and carried them out. Precisely because the text on this point is so vague— because it specifies only Umako's acts of mayhem and arrogance, alluding only indirectly to his secular power—the supposition seems probable that the "deputation" of a subject to wield the sovereign's nonreligious functions was a regular feature of the imperial system in pre-Taika Japan. In other words, the evidence suggests that in the reign of Suiko there was a twofold delegation of the Empress's powers. In the first place there was a not-exceptional delegation of some of the normal powers of government to the Soga family, and in the second a more unusual delegation of most of the remainder to Suiko's nephew and regent, Prince Shōtoku.[15]

There are hints in the two earliest histories that much the same devolution of power on families of nonroyal officials had occurred as a more-or-less regular institution before the time of the Soga. Before the introduction of Buddhism in the middle of the sixth century the Mononobe family had had great power. With their allies the Nakatomi (later Fujiwara), they made themselves the defenders of the native faith against the growing influence of Buddhism, which their successors the Soga advocated. The Mononobe had supplanted a short-lived "dynasty" of

[14] *Ibid.*
[15] Ishii, *Tennō*, pp. 1–54, discusses the relative importance of secular and sacerdotal functions of the early Japanese monarchy with great subtlety. See also the following general discussions: Maki, "Hōsei-shi jō ni okeru Tennō," in *Shin Nihon rekishi: Tennō-shi*, pp. 1–19; Kawakami, "Kōi no hatten to shisei seido," in [*Iwanami kōza*] *Nihon rekishi*, vol. 5, pp. 3–45; Higo, *Tennō-shi*, pp. 33–43.

ruling officials of the Ōtomo family in the first half of the sixth century. Legendary haze still further obscures events before about 500, but the chronicles speak, for example, of an Ō-omi, Heguri no Madori, who "usurped the government of the country and tried to reign over Japan" shortly after the death of Emperor Ninken (498); of the conduct of government by various Ō-omi and Ō-muraji (Great Deity Chieftains) in the reigns of Hanzei, Ingyō, Ankō, and Yūryaku (ca. 433–89); and the domination of a whole line of legendary emperors (Keikō, Seimu, Chūai, Ōjin, and Nintoku) by a certain Takeuchi no Sukune, whose assigned dates are so vast that they may plausibly be considered to refer to a dynasty of officials rather than to a single person.[16]

These are indications that the performance of secular functions of state by nonroyal persons, of which the Soga family's rule was a notorious instance, had long roots in native Japanese practice. Ishii Ryōsuke's reconstruction of the earliest condition of the imperial institution makes use of documentary and philological evidence to assert that the cultural and religious community of the Japanese people existed before the autonomous clans (uji) had been welded together into any sort of political union; that the imperial clan was acknowledged by other uji to have common religious functions over all of them that in no way originally implied political hegemony; and that therefore the office of the emperor was a priestly office before it came to be associated with state power.

· 4 ·

If much of the foregoing argument rests on slender evidence, there can be no question that the changes wrought in the imperial institution in the seventh century due to the imitation of contemporary Chinese practices represented a strengthening of the political character of the emperor rather than a weakening

16 Ishii, Tennō, pp. 38–39.

of it. The Taika Reform was not only an assertion of greater control by the central government over the provinces; it was an assertion of the imperial family's political primacy within the central government. Native accounts of course would call the Reform a *reassertion* of national and of imperial centralism, with the implication that the earlier assertions of imperial power that had undoubtedly occurred prior to Soga dominance had been on the same order as the new case. In fact they were not commensurable, but the reasons for the discrepant terminology may be deferred till later. It does not affect the fact that before the Taika period the throne not only served religious functions; it served primarily religious functions. Even for a time after the Taika Reform the sacramental and ceremonial duties of the sovereign were regarded as so important that they seemed to justify his yielding most of the effective powers of government to others. Only with the accession of the Emperor Tenji (668) did there appear anyone who combined in his own person substantial secular powers and the title of tennō.[17]

The case of Tenji illustrates the reluctance with which the Japanese came to associate the title with the power. He was a co-conspirator with Nakatomi (Fujiwara) Kamatari in the coup d'etat of 645. Both men wielded secular authority behind the titular sovereigns Kōtoku and (Empress) Saimei. Kamatari was ineligible for the imperial office, but the future Tenji was not. Still, he refused the imperial title for over twenty years after the coup. At the beginning of Kōtoku's reign he accepted the title of Crown Prince. When Kōtoku died (654), it would have been natural for him to have become emperor, but he did not. When Saimei died (661), Tenji behaved in an unprecedented manner by continuing to rule as Crown Prince, no successor to the imperial title being appointed for seven years.

All of these examples, especially those of Suiko and Tenji, seem to indicate that there was a widespread feeling in Japanese

[17] See *ibid.*, pp. 58ff.

court society of the early period that it was inappropriate for a reigning emperor to trouble himself with practical political concerns. In the course of the seventh century greater conversance with the political institutions of China taught the Japanese that a reigning priest-king need not be a political figurehead but might simultaneously occupy the position of a senior administrator. The resulting modification of Japanese monarchic usages is probably visible from the time that Tenji assumed the imperial office, and it had almost certainly taken place by the reign of Tenji's brother Temmu (r. 672–86).

The imperial reigns from Temmu to Kammu span the years from 672 to 806. In almost every way this period was the apogee of Chinese cultural influence in Japan. Through its assimilation of Chinese philosophy, arts, and material culture, Japan attained membership in a distinctive Far Eastern civilization. Systems of political and social organization came in the train of the more easily assimilable areas of Chinese culture. Native institutions in general held out against them but in the end were modified by them. With the imperial institution the modifications were most pronounced in the realm of intellectual formulations of its nature and function, but these also altered the manner in which the institution actually performed its work in the state system of the time.

Emperors from Temmu to Kammu presided over a state apparatus whose externals and nomenclature closely resembled those of Sui and T'ang China.[18] Contemporary edicts and historical accounts describe all acts of the government as proceeding from the imperial throne. Powers of appointment to the other competent organs of state were the emperor's, in a legal or theoretical sense. But not only in that sense, for all the evidence of the main historical sources for the period, the *Nihon*

---

[18] Wada, *Kanshoku yōkai*, pp. 16–25; pp. 33–254, is an excellent description of the *ritsu-ryō* offices. The following are useful treatments in English: Reischauer, *Early Japanese History (c. 40 B.C.–A.D. 1167)*, Part A, p. 53; pp. 87–105. Sansom, *A History of Japan to 1334*, pp. 67–70.

shoki, Shoku Nihongi, and *Nihon kōki,* indicates that at least the more strong-willed of the sovereigns of the time, Temmu, Shōmu, Empress Kōken-Shōtoku, and Kammu, were real rulers, perhaps the only ones in the whole long history of the imperial institution. During the same period the earliest true histories were written. The same Chinese viewpoint that assigned effective powers of state to contemporary holders of the imperial title was anachronistically reflected backward on earlier epochs to create the belief that the emperor's secular rule had always been the norm of Japan's political life. The state apparatus of eighth-century Japan no longer functioned as it was intended to from early in the ninth century; four centuries later it had ceased to function at all. However, the same viewpoint persisted for all this time and for further centuries that the Chinese-style usages represented an ideal of government by which any other form might be judged.

The legal formulations of the eighth century administrative structure were the Taihō *Ritsu* (Penal Code of the Taihō period) and Taihō *Ryō* (Civil Code of the Taihō period), both completed in 701, and the revision of the latter of 718, which is known as the Yōrō Ryō. The system which resulted will be referred to here as the *ritsu-ryō* system, in accordance with the practice of Japanese historians.

When one looks at a diagrammatic representation of the ritsu-ryō system, the most striking things about it are its centralism and its symmetry. All responsibility and all power pertain to the sovereign, and they are channeled through a complex hierarchy of offices, each of which is essential to the neatness and balance of the whole. Immediately subordinate to the sovereign is a single official, the Prime Minister (Dajō Daijin), who is titular president of the central administration, or Great Council of State (Dajō-kan). Lest one make the mistake of assuming that the office of Prime Minister was merely a new version of the old organs with similar sounding names that had connoted de facto rule, it should be understood that the office was nearly always unfilled. From Tenji's reign to Kammu's it was filled only twice. The first holder was Tenji's son and heir-apparent Prince Ōtomo, who was Prime Minister briefly in the year-and-a-half before Tenji's death.[19] The second holder was the Priest Dōkyō, Prime Minister and Master of Buddhist Meditation (Zenji) from 765 to 770. The case of Dōkyō was regarded as highly exceptional even at the time. He was not of the imperial family nor of any of the other aristocratic houses that monopolized political power at that time. The Empress Shōtoku, for reasons of sexual attraction, Buddhist piety, or both, offered Dōkyō the Prime Ministership as a prelude to offering him the imperial title in 769. Ministers opposed to Dōkyō obtained an oracle saying that disaster would follow if the throne went to an outsider. On account of this and other machinations their faction emerged victorious on Shōtoku's death, whereupon Dōkyō was demoted.[20]

In both the above cases the office of Prime Minister seems to have been regarded as a stepping stone to the imperial office itself, a different thing entirely from the older unitary offices of state that had permitted the emperor's secular authority to be deputized to them as a regular and permanent usage. Those who wished to preserve the personal power of the sovereign had good reason from earlier experience to avoid creating any single office immediately subordinate to the throne, and they therefore devised the expedient of relegating the office of Dajō Daijin to fiction.

The Great Council of State was therefore an organ which in normal times had as its sole presiding officer the sovereign. The Great Council was subdivided into two large branches, the Controlling Board of the Left (Sabenkan) and the Controlling

[19] Nihongi, Part 2, pp. 294ff. See also Reischauer, Early Japanese History, Part A, pp. 153–54.
[20] Shoku Nihongi (Kokushi taikei, vol. 2), pp. 324–80. See also Reischauer, Early Japanese History, Part A, pp. 204–09.

Board of the Right (Ubenkan), headed by Ministers of the Left (Sa-daijin) and Right (U-daijin). Subordinate to the Great Council and independent of the Left and Right branches were some other high ranking officials: the Minister of the Center (Nai-daijin) and several Major Counselors (Dainagon), Middle Counselors (Chūnagon), Minor Counselors (Shōnagon), Senior Secretaries (Dai-geki), and Junior Secretaries (Shō-geki). These, together with the Ministers of the Left and Right, comprised a small secretariat for carrying out all of the emperor's personal decisions.

Each of the two Controlling Boards (Left and Right) was charged with more specific executive functions. In addition to parallel rosters of central officials for each Board, each consisted of four Ministries (shō) that corresponded to executive ministries or departments of modern governments. The names and most important functions of the eight ministries were as follows.

CONTROLLING BOARD OF THE LEFT

Ministry of Central Affairs (Nakatsukasa-shō): governance of the Empress, palace ladies, and imperial attendants; custody of the palace library and collections; divination.

Ministry of Ceremonial (Shikibu-shō): education; bestowal of ranks.

Ministry of Civil Administration (Jibu-shō): ceremonial music; affairs involving Buddhism and aliens; imperial tombs; mourning and burial.

Ministry of Popular Affairs (Mimbu-shō): taxation.

CONTROLLING BOARD OF THE RIGHT

Ministry of War (Hyōbu-shō): functions obvious from title.

Ministry of Justice (Kyōbu-shō): punishments.

Ministry of the Treasury (Ōkura-shō): metal work, lacquer manufacture, and weaving.

Ministry of the Imperial Household (Kunai-shō): palace provisions, equipment, and upkeep; government slaves; public works.

Each ministry might be subdivided into many or a few Bureaus (Ryō) or Offices (Shi or Tsukasa), charged with specific work. Only on these lower levels of the system was there any departure from the bilateral symmetry of the whole.

Lesser offices attached to the Great Council of State performed some other functions. These were a Board of Censors (Danjōdai); Headquarters of the Gate Guards (Emonfu), Palace Guards (Ejifu), and Military Guards (Hyōefu); various other offices with military or security duties; and offices for the housekeeping and maintenance of the palaces of other members of the imperial family.

The city of Nara was oriented to the north, where the emperor and court resided. Its parallel and perpendicular streets formed perfectly balanced rectangles, a visible counterpart of the symmetrically balanced administrative system. The city government appropriately comprised Divisions of the Left and Right, each managing commercial affairs through its Eastern, or Western, Market. (Left, in a geographic reference, meant East, that is, the left side of the sovereign, who confronted his people from his palace in the northern part of the city.) Provincial governments were also symmetrically organized and headed by imperially appointed Governors (Kami), Assistant Governors (Suke), and so on.

The above description has concentrated on the formal, or aesthetic, features of the ritsu-ryō system. A historian or political scientist whose aim was to describe the government of the Nara period would have to say much more about it than this, for he would be interested primarily in the way the system worked. It did function for a time as the effective government of Japan, and an administrative structure planned according to similar principles served the purposes of state power in China for a much longer period. The dynamics of political life in the Nara period depended in part on the personal strengths and weaknesses of officials, factional alignments and oppositions, systematic or casual means of communication among various organs of state, and so on, all matters that resist reduction to a formal scheme. However, the symmetries of the system are all-important to our purposes here, for these lasted. It is hoped to show that the reason they lasted is that later generations of Japanese accorded to them a value that was completely independent of any pragmatic purposes which the ritsu-ryō system had ever served.

To help explain what that value was, let us take a simple and familiar analogy from the aesthetic paraphernalia of the American government. The United States Capitol in Washington is elegant and symmetrical. Its north and south wings are identical in size and external appearance, though the Senate and House of Representatives, which the two wings house, are of very unequal size. The architects have apparently ignored functional considerations in order to *symbolize* a political truth: that the powers of the two Houses are equal and that in every other practical respect they are balancing terms of a symmetrical structure. No political scientist describing the American government would linger long over a description of the Capitol building, because it is no more than an attractive image of political realities which can be described more easily with different terms.

The symmetries of the ritsu-ryō system were also symbolic, and in the Nara period part of what they symbolized was actual balance and parallelism in the distribution of state power. To that degree the historian of the Nara period would do better to search behind the symbol for the political reality which it represented. However, there is more to the external symbolism of the ritsu-ryō structure than that. The above description of the system should be sufficient to indicate that even in the Nara period there were some aspects of the formal structure that could scarcely be said to have represented political realities. For example, what functional reality could ever have been represented by the neat eight-fold division of ministerial responsibilities, or the careful distribution of the ministries into a pair of fours? The form of the structure symbolized more than the way it worked; it symbolized an elaborate conceptualization of the timeless ethical precepts for ordering human society.

The Japanese, as the Chinese before them, looked to a natural order beyond the world of men to justify the order of political society. They saw the natural order as marked by perfect balance and symmetry in all its parts. In all the universe only man was capable of disturbing the balance, but morality enjoined him from doing so. Political society existed in order to bring men into harmony with nature. The parts of the state structure should be balanced and symmetrical, because in that way they could better perform their functions in accordance with the orderliness of nature. In other words, they were contrived as devices for making society moral. But even if they failed to perform their ethical function in a direct way by imposing order on the processes of effective government, they might still perform them in an indirect way, by acting as a reminder to people that a balanced and harmonious natural order existed and that human behavior too should be harmonious and orderly.

When the ritsu-ryō system was adopted, it made the emperor a secular ruler as well as a chief performer of the rites of the national religion. However, it also added something else to his role that was of more lasting importance. It made his office the central term in a symbolic representation of natural moral order. In the Nara period the sovereign was the source of law; then and thereafter he symbolized the source of ethics.

· 5 ·

Historians usually date the next fundamental change in the functioning of the imperial institution from the middle of the ninth century, when there commenced what amounted to a hereditary dictatorship or regency by heads of the Fujiwara family and a termination of the personal rule of the sovereign. There can be no doubt of the vast importance to Japanese institutional history of the onset of Fujiwara rule, but it should be pointed out that about fifty years earlier there had occurred a significant departure from the features that characterized the monarchy in the Nara period, and one which foreshadowed certain aspects of the Fujiwara regency. This took the form of a divorcement of the emperor from the regular offices of the ritsu-ryō state structure and the creation of new ad hoc bodies through which the personal acts of the sovereign were administered.

The Emperor Kammu, who founded the city of Kyoto, had been in every sense head of the government and had conducted his administration through the regular offices of the ritsu-ryō system. Three of his sons reigned in succession from 806 to 833. The eldest, Emperor Heizei, ruled from 806 to 809, when he abdicated on account of extreme illness. His younger brother, Emperor Saga, accepted the throne but soon found himself in conflict with Heizei, who had recovered from his illness and wanted to reassume the imperial title. Saga suspected that some of the regular ministers and ministries of state were in league with Heizei. As a consequence he set up a personal private secretariat (Kurōdo-dokoro) that in effect removed from certain of the regular offices their administrative powers. This event occurred in 810, the year following Saga's accession to the throne. Similarly, in a later act of the same year, Saga created eight extraordinary adviserships (sangi) for the conduct of provincial government.[21]

As the personal relationship between the emperor and his new appointees was close, their appointment to powers theoretically vested in the more impersonal ritsu-ryō bureaucracy had the temporary effect of strengthening the emperor's control over

21 Reischauer, Early Japanese History, Part A, pp. 232–33.

the government. Ironically, the ultimate significance of the new development was precisely the opposite. That is, the substitution of ad hoc for regular offices led to a withering away of the emperor's normal means of administrative authority and the substitution of new instruments of control that might or might not be subject to the influence of the emperor. The rationale of the ritsu-ryō system demanded not so much the one-man rule of the emperor as it did government by the "emperor-in-the-court," analogous to the doctrine of British monarchy by which the sovereign of the country is the "Queen-in-Parliament." Under normal circumstances the emperor's decrees suffered no diminution of force by being channeled through the ritsu-ryō offices, but on the contrary gained effectiveness by being shown to be the prime movers in a massive and powerful administrative organism. The creation of the kurōdo-dukoro and sangi accustomed Japanese society to the idea that the older system was not necessarily the effective government of the country. From the acceptance of imperial government outside regular court channels, it was no great step to the acceptance of effective government without emperor or court, the state of affairs that came about with the reduction of emperors to puppets of their Fujiwara ministers.[22]

The ancient pedigree of the Fujiwara and their history of distinguished service to the throne had already made them powerful political figures long before they took the remaining leap to absolute rule. Kamatari, the first of his family to bear the name of Fujiwara, had been one of the architects of the Taika Reform and was a leading figure in the importation of Chinese institutions by Japan. Having helped frame the ritsu-ryō system in the seventh century and made good use of it in the eighth and ninth, the Fujiwara proceeded then to render it fictitious.

Fujiwara dominance came about partly because of their politi-

[22] Ishii, Tennō, pp. 77–84.

cal skill and partly through their manipulation of the institutional system. It is the second aspect of their rise to power that is significant to the subsequent history of the imperial institution. The main institutional devices used by the Fujiwara in their control of the government are as follows:

Imperial marriages. The domination of a young and impressionable emperor by his maternal grandfather was an old stratagem. For example, the Soga family in the period of their greatest power had seen to it that heirs to the throne were chosen from imperial children of Soga consorts. Before the middle of the ninth century many Fujiwara women had been imperial consorts. The mother of the Emperor Montoku (r. 850–58) was of the Fujiwara, and Montoku was influenced by his uncle Fujiwara Yoshifusa to select as his heir a child by Yoshifusa's daughter Akiko. When that child came to the throne (Emperor Seiwa, r. 858–76), Yoshifusa took advantage of the relationship to dominate the imperial institution. The stratagem was repeated many times by later Fujiwara family heads. Perpetuation of close relationships between the Fujiwara and imperial families was ensured in the tenth century, when the custom was institutionalized of limiting the principal consorts of an emperor to Fujiwara daughters.

Regency for Minor Emperors. Control of the throne through maternal relatives was as precarious as any power that depends on bonds between persons rather than regular institutions. Fujiwara Yoshifusa first achieved an institutional justification for his power over Seiwa through the office of Regent (Sesshō). The office had existed from time to time in the past, as in the case discussed above of Shōtoku Taishi, the regent for his aunt Empress Suiko. Earlier regents, however, had invariably been members of the imperial family itself, that is to say, persons related to the sovereign through masculine lines of descent. It has already been stated that Prince Shōtoku, as regent, enjoyed great and exceptional deputized powers, since he undertook in his name all the imperial acts that did not for religious reasons require the actual participation of the sovereign. The holder of the title sesshō was assumed to have the power to perform some of the emperor's own acts for him. It was therefore the practice that the office should be filled only during reigns of sovereigns who were literally incompetent (because of minority, illness, or as in Suiko's case the frailty of her sex).

The Civil Dictatorship. Yoshifusa's successor Mototsune occupied the office of regent for the minor emperor Yōzei (r. 876–84), but wished to remain in power in the next reign, that of the 54-year-old Kōkō (r. 884–87). To this end a new institution was devised, the office of Civil Dictator (Kampaku). Although the two offices of sesshō and kampaku were very similar in functions and powers, they differed greatly in the legal theory by which these were justified. A kampaku was not to govern by his own will, but was merely an intermediary through whom the intentions of the emperor were made known to the court and society. In other words, the office depended for its efficacy on a certain personal dominance exerted by the kampaku over the emperor. Yet, under any circumstances, it was an office of great *potential* power, and the fortunes of the Fujiwara were greatly enhanced in the late ninth century when the institutional provision became accepted that there should always be a kampaku whenever the office of sesshō was not filled, and that both offices should be the property of the head of the Fujiwara clan.

The House Secretariat. The personal political skill of several members of the Fujiwara family in the ninth and tenth centuries created a state system in which the kampaku's job of "relaying" imperial commands was tantamount to ultimate authority. The Fujiwara rulers often, for example, used their influence to ensure that a successor to an abdicated or deceased emperor be a minor, for whom the Fujiwara clansman would rule as sesshō. Then, by the time the majority of the emperor required the termination of the regency, the pattern of personal domination of the elder over the younger man would already have been established, enabling the Fujiwara, as kampaku, to continue his absolute rule. One remaining institutional feature was needed to place Fujiwara control on a basis of permanent firmness. This was a family secretariat, somewhat similar to the personal secretariat (kurōdo-dokoro) of Saga's reign, which usurped most important administrative functions from the regular offices of the ritsu-ryō system. By the early tenth century it was already inconvenient and difficult for any emperor, however forthright, to return administrative work to the organs that had officially been established for it, and by the end of that century it had become completely impossible.

The process by which the Fujiwara regularized their rule and rendered it more durable was not finally accomplished until about the time of the great Regent Michinaga, who dominated the government from 996 to 1017. In the meantime, the devices for rule described above had not been applied continuously or consistently. The Emperor Uda (r. 887–97) was not the child of a Fujiwara mother, and to a degree he escaped domination by Fujiwara ministers. Sometimes there was no sesshō or kampaku. Uda, for example, seems to have tolerated rule by the kampaku Motosune until the latter's death but had sufficient freedom of action to avoid appointing another Fujiwara to succeed him. From 890 until the death of Uda's successor Daigo (930) there was on the surface at least a return to the personal rule of the emperor. The same circumstance was repeated two reigns later under Emperor Murakami (r. 946–67). In fact, however, a study of the actual state of affairs in these reigns shows that Fujiwara family heads maintained considerable authority even without titles implying dictatorship. Michinaga, greatest of his family, dispensed with the titles until shortly before his death, apparently satisfied that his strength of character and personal authoritativeness were sufficient to ensure for him absolute power.

This slow development of a hereditary dictatorship by a non-imperial family has been anathematized by Japanese historians as a perversion of native ways of government, a cancerous growth on the political body that thwarted the natural operation of Japanese institutions. It must of course be conceded that the development of new offices of control, the sesshō and kampaku, as an overgrowth upon the ritsu-ryō structure, was alien to the intentions of the framers of that system. The Fujiwara dictatorship was utterly different from the ideal pattern of administration envisioned between the seventh and early ninth centuries.

Yet looked at in a somewhat broader historical perspective, the Fujiwara dominance may be seen as a return to a more native way rather than a deviation from it. For the ritsu-ryō system was itself an alien implantation in Japan, and its workings were contrary to age-old Japanese political instincts precisely because they implied the involvement of the throne in active politics. It is a matter for speculation just why such a reversion to the throne's earlier condition occurred. Certainly the unequal struggle for power between emperors and their Fujiwara ministers is an important factor. Still, it must also be assumed that the long-ingrained attitude of the Japanese that it was inappropriate for the emperor to have too close a contact with political affairs had lingered after the creation of Chinese-style instruments of state, and that that attitude made it easier for society to accept the atrophy of the ritsu-ryō institutions.

But if the Fujiwara dictatorship was a development justified by native tradition, why then should there have been such misgivings about it on the part of later historians? The question is an important one in describing attitudes toward the throne in Tokugawa times. It will be dealt with in greater detail in a

later section of this book. For the moment one can say simply
that by the middle of the Heian period the Japanese embraced
two different ideals as to the proper structure and operation of
government. The older of them satisfied better the requisites
of native Japanese religion by elevating the emperor to a position above politics, and in addition it provided in pragmatic
ways for reasonably efficient administration of governmental
affairs. The newer, Chinese, ideal had seemed at first to be
better suited to the needs of a more centralized and tightly
organized state, a state in other words like the China of the
T'ang which Japan wished to emulate. Even when that superficial attraction proved illusory, when the ritsu-ryō system was
shown to be far too cumbersome and complex for Japanese
needs, something about the Chinese system continued to appeal
greatly to Japanese sensibilities. That appeal that transcended
the practical might at first glance appear to be religious or ethical, since it grew out of the Chinese belief that the institutions
of man ought to be true reflections of a harmonious and orderly
universe, in order that mankind might achieve morality. It seems
to the present writer, for reasons to be described later, that the
appeal to the Japanese of the Chinese system ought rather to be
called aesthetic. It satisfied their sense of what was pleasant,
beautiful, or emotionally attractive, rather than their beliefs
about what was conducive to just and moral behavior among
men.

The institutions of Fujiwara control no doubt offended later
Japanese in part because they were ad hoc bodies that appeared
to mar the elegance and symmetry of the T'ang official system.
At this crucial moment in ninth century Japan, when practical
needs of administration and native habits of action combined
to create the pattern of non-imperial rule that was to persist for
a thousand years, a tension arose between two sets of values.
One cannot overstress its importance, for it was to be one of
the central themes of Japanese political thought.

· 6 ·

It is not the purpose of this book to relate in detail the history of pre-Tokugawa political institutions or of the attitudes held at various times toward them. However, some patterns of historical development are important for understanding the throne in Tokugawa times.

One of these was the tendency for administrative bodies outside the ritsu-ryō system to become accepted as regular. It has already been shown how Fujiwara Yoshifusa's dominance of the throne soon became legitimated by means of the old title of sesshō. There were no ancient precedents for the office of kampaku, but that, too, soon came to be regarded as a regular part of the system of court titles. Although the twin offices were vacant for many years in the ninth and tenth centuries, from the time of their reestablishment in 967 they were permanent fixtures. Thereafter they were vacant only during what must be accounted as disruptions of the normal administrative processes. (Michinaga behaved like a sesshō from 995 to 1016, when he actually assumed the title. There were brief interregnums in two other periods of crisis, the transition from the Kamakura to the Ashikaga shogunate, and the rule of Hideyoshi.) The most obvious means by which a title achieved fully legal status was a patent of appointment bearing the emperor's signature. This legal attestation was then made a matter of public record by having it recorded in the official roster of imperial appointments, *Kugyō bunin*.

Though regularized through the devices of imperial patent and public registration, the offices of sesshō and kampaku were not regarded as having modified the ritsu-ryō system but as merely having been superimposed on top of it. One can see this clearly in the many books written from the tenth century on purporting to describe the "regular" administrative structure.

The earliest of these was the *Engi-shiki* ("Institutes of the Engi Period") finished in 967, the very year in which the offices of sesshō and kampaku were reestablished on a permanent basis.[23] Here there is no mention of these offices, but the title of the work fully accounts for the omission. The Engi Period (901–923) was in the reign of the Emperor Daigo, when the formalized offices of the Fujiwara dictatorship were temporarily vacant. The *Engi-shiki* was the prototype of later accounts of court organization, and these too customarily omit mention of the two new offices. The conclusion that may be drawn is that although they were fully legal, they functioned outside the ritsu-ryō system that was presumably the "real" government of the country.

This pattern was repeated over and over again. Whenever the institutional structure lost its effectiveness, new offices appeared. These existed for a time on a temporary or emergency basis then came to be considered as more-or-less regular parts of the institutional system, but remained separate from the old structure whose functions they assumed.

The Fujiwara family began to lose their position of absolute control in the eleventh century. The family which succeeded them as heads of the effective government was the imperial house itself, but this revival did not mean a return to the procedures of the Nara period. Instead, it was accomplished by the devolution of power on a new office, the Ex-sovereign's Private Secretariat (In-no-kurōdo-dokoro).[24] This development brings to mind the way in which the Emperor Saga had used a new institution outside the regular structure to strengthen his personal control. The Emperor Go-Sanjō (r. 1068–72; d. 1073),

---

[23] *Engi-shiki* (*Kokushi taikei*, vol. 26), is a good modern scholarly edition. On the compilation and character of the work see Kurita (comp.), *Sōgō kokushi kenkyū*, vol. 1, pp. 472–73. See also Reischauer, *Early Japanese History*, Part A, p. 64.

[24] Wada, *Kanshoku yōkai*, pp. 214–28. Sansom, *A History of Japan to 1334*, pp. 199–203.

who in the Record Office (Kiroku-jo) of 1069 created the institutional forerunner of the new system, is generally considered
one of the most able of all Japanese sovereigns. Certainly his
innovation was a remarkably ingenious use of the peculiar
strengths and weaknesses which Japanese administrative habits
imposed on the imperial family. Even if it was inappropriate
for a reigning emperor to concern himself with politics, no such
inhibition applied to an ex-emperor. Domination of the sovereign by his maternal relatives was a time-tested means of political control, so paternal lines of relationship might have been
expected to be still more efficacious. Finally, the creation of a
small, personally-controlled administrative body served the same
purposes as with the sovereign's private secretariat of Emperor
Saga or the house secretariat of the Fujiwara. That is, it enabled
the effective ruler to bypass the complex lines of authority called
for in the regular structure and to make his decisions known
through the intermediation of men with closer personal ties to
himself. As with the Fujiwara offices, the Ex-sovereign's Private
Secretariat neither replaced the older system nor was it really
integrated with it, but was merely superimposed on top of it.

The *insei*, or "government by ex-sovereigns," remained a semi-
regular part of the Japanese institutional system long after it
had ceased to be the effective government of the country. From
about the middle of the twelfth century the government again
devolved on other families than that of the emperor. From that
time until 1333 three aristocratic houses successively governed
Japan. All of them initially achieved power through military
strength and the control of provincial lands, but, as was usual in
Japanese practice, their power was later regularized through in-
corporation into the institutional system, which the emperor
headed. However, the particular institutions which were used
were different in all three cases.

The first family, the Taira, adopted the simple expedient of
ruling through certain top offices in the ritsu-ryō system. Taira

Kiyomori was Minister of the Center in 1166 and Prime Minister briefly in 1167. His sons Shigemori and Munemori at later times held the title of Minister of the Center.[25]

The Minamoto family, who were ancestral enemies of the Taira, made war against them and defeated them. In doing so, they appeared to have committed a grave crime against the established order. That this thought occurred to Minamoto Yoritomo, head of the family, is shown by the extraordinary lengths to which he went to demonstrate that his acts were occasioned by imperial loyalty. The legal face he put on his campaign against the Taira was that the latter had betrayed the emperor's trust through their misrule, and that the emperor had commanded him to destroy them.[26]

The specific commission Yoritomo received from the emperor on this occasion was of the greatest importance to the future development of Japanese institutions. Its title was *Sei-i Taishōgun*, "General-in-chief for Barbarian Subjugation." It was not a new title, for it had been held before by noblemen of the early Heian period who had enjoyed supreme authority in the provinces during a campaign against the northern aborigines. Implicit in the title were emergency powers in provincial areas too remote for the emperor's influence to reach. The shogunate was not just another new office fixed on top of all the old ones; it was an entire government located at its own capital, Kamakura, and it soon attained a degree of structural complexity rivaling that of the older system in Kyoto. A key element in the shogunal system was the fact that all of the officials in the Kamakura bureaucracy were personal vassals of the shogun, and that their sole connection with the Kyoto court was through him. Yoritomo always carefully fostered the legalism that he was an imperial appointee, and he succeeded in giving perma-

[25] *Kugyō bunin* (*Kokushi taikei*, vols. 53–57), vol. 53, pp. 455; 462–63; 486; 498.
[26] See the discussion in Shinoda, *The Founding of the Kamakura Shogunate*, pp. 82–83; 101–2; 112–13.

nence to the institution he founded by gaining society's acceptance of the principle that the office of shogun should always be filled and that its occupant should be the head of the Minamoto clan. This device did not achieve its planned end of perpetuating the rule of Yoritomo's dynasty, but it did have the result of limiting future holders of the shogunal office to men who really belonged to the Minamoto family or men who could plausibly claim to.

From the time of Yoritomo's sons, the actual power of state devolved upon yet another military family, the Hōjō. These made use of yet another institutional device for gaining and keeping control. This was an office of the Kamakura shogunate known as *shikken*, and it may best be described as a regency for the shogun.[27] As before, the Hōjō made no attempt to abolish older offices which had once connoted authority, or even to replace the families which had been regarded as having hereditary rights to them. The years from 1213, when the Hōjō regency was established, to 1333, when it was overthrown, witnessed the extreme high point of Japanese institutional complexity. The emperor presided over a hierarchy of officials of the ritsu-ryō system, which remained on paper much as it had been at its inception. At the head of the imperial court stood twin offices of sesshō and kampaku, which had once been irregular but were now regarded as legal and permanent. The holders of these offices, and of many in the ritsu-ryō system as well, continued to be limited to descendants of the great Fujiwara dictators of the ninth, tenth, and eleventh centuries. The actual governance of the Kyoto court was in the hands, not of the reigning emperors nor of their regents, but of ex-sovereigns maintaining private organs of control. None of these institutions actually governed the country; the effective government was located 300 miles away in Kamakura. Its titular head was a shogun, who was

[27] Wada, *Kanshoku yōkai*, p. 281. Sansom, *A History of Japan to 1334*, pp. 371–85.

always the head of the Minamoto clan. The real head of the Kamakura government and the ruler of Japan was a regent for the shogun, and he was the head of the Hōjō family.

It was inevitable that at some point a new aspirant to power should make an attempt to sweep away this clutter of meaningless institutions and start over again with something simpler. The attempt was made upon the overthrow of the Kamakura shogunate and Hōjō regency by the reigning emperor of that time, Go-Daigo (r. 1318–39). This was the famous Kemmu Restoration,[28] which later imperial loyalists of a radical persuasion looked back to as the model for their own program. Once again it is appropriate to the present discussion to concentrate on the purely formal aspects of the Kemmu government, ignoring the other military, economic, and social bases for Go-Daigo's power, because his rule was short-lived and nothing remained after its demise to influence later generations but a memory of its institutional features.

Go-Daigo's first action to strengthen imperial control was to abolish the system of government by ex-sovereigns. This he did in 1321, when his father, the ex-emperor Go-Uda, relinquished the headship of the family. Go-Daigo was then the senior member of his own branch of the imperial family. By not abdicating, he was able to retain the ritual functions of the imperial office, at the same time assuming the headship of the imperial family that had formerly been taken by ex-sovereigns. In a second step, during the same year he reduced the power of his Fujiwara ministers by asserting direct control of the tax-free lands of the

[28] McCullough (trans.), *The Taiheiki: A Chronicle of Medieval Japan*, is a translation of the portions on Go-Daigo of this work. Though the historical reliability of the *Taiheiki* has been severely questioned by modern historians, it was traditionally regarded as one of the main sources on the Kemmu Restoration. Webb, *The Thought and Work of the Early Mito School*, pp. 204–60, is a discussion of the Restoration from the standpoint of imperial sovereignty, together with a partial translation of the quasi-primary account of Go-Daigo in *Dai Nihon shi*. See also the discussion in Sansom, *A History of Japan, 1334–1615*, pp. 22–42.

Fujiwara that had been the economic base of their power. This paved the way for abolition of the offices of sesshō and kampaku in 1333. In the meantime the Kamakura government had fallen, enabling a faction of soldiers and courtiers loyal to the emperor to establish a new central government in Kyoto whose administrative institutions were once again those of the imperial court. The resulting state structure was of course substantially the same as the ritsu-ryō system as it had existed up to the reign of Kammu and then again briefly in the reigns of Daigo and Murakami. This was a case of conscious imitation on Go-Daigo's part, because he admired above all things the institutions of the Engi period as described in the *Engi-shiki*. He requested that he be given the posthumous name of Go-Daigo, which means "the Latter Daigo," in memory of the sovereign who ruled in the Engi period.

The Kemmu system functioned as a true central government for just two years. In 1336 one of the emperor's generals Ashikaga Takauji gained control of Kyoto by means of a coup d'état. He attempted unsuccessfully to force Go-Daigo's abdication, and he did succeed in causing the latter to flee with his loyal ministers southward to the mountain stronghold of Yoshino. Takauji then declared that Go-Daigo was deposed anyway and established in his place in Kyoto a rival sovereign of a related branch of the imperial house. That emperor, Kōmyō, repaid his benefactor Takauji by naming him shogun, an office to which Takauji could make plausible claim because of his descent from the Minamoto clan. Though the Yoshino government existed until 1392, its institutions died with it, and the reunified nation from that time had as its central government a collection of institutions similar to those of the Kamakura shogunate, save that the shogun governed himself without the aid of a shikken and the shogunal government was located close to the imperial court in Kyoto. Within the imperial court there had been a return to the structure of Kamakura times, with the exception that the Ex-sovereign's Private Secretariat was not reinstituted.

Thenceforth there was no real clean sweep of the institutional structure until the Meiji Restoration of 1868. In fact, many features of the ritsu-ryō system, including several of its high-sounding but empty offices of state, persisted until the organization of the cabinet system in 1885.

Though the Ashikaga family were not effective national rulers after about the middle of the fifteenth century, the institutional system over which they presided lasted on paper for another century and more. The next major chapter in Japanese political history commenced with the Ōnin War of 1467–77, when to all intents and purposes the central government ceased to govern the country. The main importance of the imperial and shogunal governments after that time was as symbols of unity and legitimate rule, which were to be achieved by military action and at the hands of new men not connected with the Kyoto aristocracy. In 1568, when the reunification of Japan may be said to have started, there existed as a prize for the reunifier a pseudo-government in Kyoto that was much the same in its formal structure as that which the first Ashikaga shogun had made use of two centuries before.

Since the ninth century the reigning emperor had lacked effective power, except for Go-Daigo's brief restoration. From the eleventh to the fourteenth century the sovereign was not even the head of the imperial family. Yet in all this time he retained the ritual and ceremonial functions of his office. Simultaneously another of its functions acquired even greater importance than before. The emperor legitimated effective power. Every real national ruler of the period derived justification for his power from the fact that he held some kind of appointment from the emperor. In the case of the Hōjō regents, the appointment was indirect, by way of the office of shogun, who was an imperial appointee. In all the other cases the emperor personally sanctioned the effective government, signifying by his own presence what was the central authority to be obeyed. In the fifteenth and sixteenth centuries the imperial name failed to save the faltering power of the Ashikaga shogunate. Its powers of legitimation were latent. History furnished ample precedents that if any government restored unity, it would call itself the emperor's government.

· 7 ·

On November 9, 1568, Oda Nobunaga, accompanied by his protégé Ashikaga Yoshiaki, the last shogun of his house, entered Kyoto, thereby completing the unification of the central provinces from Owari to the Kinai region. On March 24, 1603, Tokugawa Ieyasu received from Emperor Go-Yōzei the first patent of appointment given to a member of his family to the office of shogun, which Yoshiaki's death in 1598 had left vacant. Such were the initial and terminal events of the process by which a true central authority was reestablished, then extended to embrace the entire country, and then given the imperial sanction of legitimacy which alone might ensure its indefinite continuance in the hands of a single family. The history of the 35 intervening years is a story of military and political strategy. Provinces were conquered, local military rulers subdued, and soldiers loyal to the central authority newly established as governors of distant provincial territories. A system of soldierly house law was sharpened and refined for more effective governance of diverse classes and regions; and a complex institutional and police system was built to enforce the laws that had been enacted. No less important, there was a legitimation of power, a softening of the facts of brutal conquest and oppressive police control justifying them in terms of age-old moral and religious tenets of the Japanese people. In this aspect the emperor played an important part in the reunification of Japan.

The importance of his role lay partly in his power to bestow certain high titles of state which would make their bearers appear to govern by unassailable right even if they had attained power through military might. The emperors Ōgimachi (r. 1557–86) and Go-Yōzei (r. 1586–1611) invariably ratified the military and political faits accomplis that their subordinates had achieved, but in this limited sense at least they were active collaborators in the reunification.

At the beginning and end of the period in question the chief legitimating agent was the office of shogun, though for the years in between other state titles of an older system were used. Nobunaga was first elevated to the headship of a central, rather than a provincial, government when he succeeded in establishing his puppet and candidate for the office of shogun in Kyoto.[29] Nobunaga did not claim the title of shogun for himself. He was not of the Minamoto clan and did not claim to be. Granted the disadvantage that he lacked the title, he made the best possible use of his domination of Yoshiaki to make it appear that his rule was the extension of the legitimate rule of the Ashikaga family. For a very brief period after he came into the control of the capital, his administration bore much the same relation to the institutions of the shogunate as that of the first shikken (regent) of the Hōjō family had borne toward the institutions of the Kamakura shogunate. In other words, Nobunaga was the deputy of the emperor's deputy. However, his political temper was pragmatic; effective military control satisfied him, and he soon discovered that he could dispense with appeals to legitimacy through the office of the shogun. In 1573 he quarreled with Yoshiaki and imprisoned him. Though Yoshiaki did not formally abdicate the title, both his own reign and that of his family may be said to have come to an end at that time. There-

---

[29] On the legal basis of Nobunaga's rule see Yoshikawa, "Nobunaga no kinnō," in *Azuchi, Momoyama jidai shiron*, pp. 115–34. Watanabe, *Azuchi jidai shi*.

after when Nobunaga felt the need for some higher legitimation of his rule, he sought it directly from the emperor. In 1574 Ōgimachi granted him the Junior Third Court Rank (Jū-sammi), technically equivalent to the offices of *Sa-daiben* and *U-daiben,* Controllers of the Left and Right, which had ranked immediately under the Ministers of Left and Right. It does not seem a very impressive rank for the military commander of the central provinces to have achieved, but it must be remembered that Nobunaga was not of the Kyoto aristocracy, which usually monopolized the titles and ranks of the ritsu-ryō system. It gave him prestige that he had conspicuously lacked until then. He was simultaneously made an Imperial Adviser (sangi). In 1575 he became a Provisional Major Counselor (Gon-Dainagon) and Major Captain of the Right Inner Palace Guards (U-kon'e Taishō). The year after that he was Minister of the Center, and finally in 1577 he assumed his highest title, the relatively modest one of Minister of the Right.[30]

To a degree the same pattern of behavior persisted under Nobunaga's successors, Toyotomi Hideyoshi and Tokugawa Ieyasu. If they had chosen, both could have hidden behind someone with clearer hereditary claims to rulership than they, either of the Ashikaga or some other family, and the historical precedents for such a policy were strong. Both seem instead to have devoted themselves wholeheartedly to the attempt to establish new bases of legitimate power in their own names, which should be theirs alone to bequeath to their heirs. Neither Hideyoshi nor Ieyasu had any clear-cut claim to membership in one of the great aristocratic families which had governed Japan in the past, but both of them employed scholars to fabricate genealogies which would convince others that they had. Their contemporaries appear to have been convinced. The conclusions that may be drawn from this are, first, that these military conquerors felt the desirability of possessing pedigrees that would give their

[30] *Kugyō bunin,* vol. 55, pp. 471–73; 476.

government the appearance of legality, and, second, that so
long as their claims to legitimacy were plausible enough to satisfy
the emperor, they were good enough for his subjects.[31]

The legitimation of Hideyoshi's rule also took the form of
incorporating it into an existing but atrophied institutional system under the imperial throne. In this case, however, the system
that Hideyoshi chose was that of middle Heian times, that is,
the ritsu-ryō system plus the sesshō-kampaku offices that had
been associated with the Fujiwara dictatorship. From 1583 on,
Hideyoshi climbed the ladder of court honor, occupying succes-
cessively the posts or ranks of Junior Third Rank and Imperial
Adviser (1583), Provisional Major Counsellor (1584), and Minister of the Center (1585). Hideyoshi fraudulently claimed
descent from the Fujiwara, and the Emperor recognized the
claim when he appointed him to the office of kampaku in 1585.
Go-Yōzei, who came to the throne the following year, gave him
the additional title of Prime Minister from the ritsu-ryō system.[32] The title by which Hideyoshi is best known to history is
taikō, which signifies a kampaku who has yielded his position to
his son, as Hideyoshi did to his adopted heir Hidetsugu in 1591.
The procedure and the title were both in emulation of the
institutions of the middle Heian period. In 1592 the Emperor
obligingly named Hidetsugu Minister of the Left. Hideyoshi's
final choice of a successor was the son of his old age, Hideyori,
to whom Go-Yōzei gave the ritsu-ryō titles of Minister of the
Center (1603) and Minister of the Left (1605).[33] Such was the
Emperor's role in the attempt which Hideyoshi made to legitimate and perpetuate the rule of his family.

That attempt came to failure in the face of the competing
ambitions of Tokugawa Ieyasu for his family. For some time
after his consolidation of power in 1600 Ieyasu continued to

[31] On the pedigree of the Tokugawa see Itō, *Nihon hōken seido shi*,
p. 246.
[32] *Kugyō bunin*, vol. 55, pp. 489–91; 493.
[33] *Ibid.*, pp. 520, 523.

respect the fiction that his rule was by way of a regency for Hideyori, but ultimately the respective claims of the two men and their families were completely irreconcilable, with the result that an open clash between them occurred in 1614. At its completion in 1615 Hideyori killed himself and his faction was exterminated. The emperor's part in all of this was necessarily passive. It consisted in ratifications of the various settlements that had already been achieved rather than active help in achieving them. The last imperial act involving the Toyotomi was the withdrawal of Hideyori's court titles in 1607.[34]

Tokugawa Ieyasu made use of titles from the ritsu-ryō system, being made Minister of the Right in 1603 and Prime Minister during the last month of his life in 1616, but he did not hold the title of kampaku.[35] The explanation seems to be simply that he did not go to the trouble of establishing the claim of Fujiwara blood that contemporary society thought of as a requisite for that office. However, Ieyasu (or his genealogists) did make the claim that he was of Minamoto stock and was therefore eligible for the office of shogun.

It is not clear when the idea of founding a new shogunal dynasty first occurred to Ieyasu. Sources are preserved that relate in detail Ieyasu's habits of book collecting and reading. They mention conspicuously his devotion to the thirteenth century chronicle *Azuma kagami*.[36] That book narrates the career of Minamoto Yoritomo and the founding of the Kamakura shogunate.[37] Two aspects of Yoritomo's strategy were directly influential on Ieyasu's use of legitimating titles. First, the particular title which Yoritomo received from the emperor, that of shogun, was military in nature, implied emergency powers over areas too distant to be controlled directly from the capital,

---

[34] *Ibid.*, p. 526.
[35] *Ibid.*, p. 520; *Tokugawa jikki* (*Kokushi taikei*, vols. 38–47), vol. 38, p. 131.
[36] Kondō, *Go-hon nikki zokuroku*, in *Dai Nihon shiryō*, part XII, vol. 24, pp. 417–21.
[37] Relevant portions are translated in Shinoda, *The Founding of the Kamakura Shogunate*, pp. 149–364.

and therefore could be used as justification for unrestricted governance not only of troops but also of provincial areas and their populations. Second, Yoritomo insisted that he alone of the military aristocracy should be in a position to receive from the emperor titles suggestive of legitimate authority. That is, Yoritomo reacted against the system by which his former rivals, the Taira, had monopolized the chief titles of the ritsu-ryō system, thereby permitting the emperor a certain degree of freedom of choice to signify which of the Taira's henchmen he wished to honor. Yoritomo, on the other hand, created an entirely new system of titles and offices for members of his own feudal aristocracy. So far as that system was concerned, he, not the emperor, had absolute control.[38]

These procedures of the early Kamakura shogunate had until a generation before been the closest semblance Japan knew to a legal central authority. In other words, Ieyasu could achieve the essential advantages of Yoritomo's system without resuscitating the long-dead institutions of the Kamakura shogunate but merely by modifying the fresher and more familiar usages of the Ashikaga government. Most features of the Edo administration were closer to Ashikaga than to Kamakura equivalents, but the reverse is the case with those institutions of the Tokugawa shogunate that linked it with the imperial institution. As in the Kamakura period, the older court structure was perpetuated in Kyoto, while the effective government erected its own administration separate from the emperor's shadow-government both geographically and institutionally. Like Yoritomo, Ieyasu received his legitimating commission directly from the imperial throne, and no other member of the effective government had any position at all in the official hierarchy of the imperial court.[39]

We stress here the varying practices adopted by Japan's reuni-

[38] *Ibid.*, pp. 136–44.
[39] For general discussions of Ieyasu and the founding of the Tokugawa shogunate see Sadler, *The Maker of Modern Japan, the Life of Tokugawa Ieyasu*. Sansom, *A History of Japan, 1334–1615*, pp. 385–406.

fiers for legitimating their power to help show how the emperor's personal role in the process came to be limited as the foundations of national power became firmer. It should be apparent from the above description that the official system through which Oda Nobunaga and Hideyoshi legitimated their rule demanded more frequent and active participation by the emperor than that which went into effect with the foundation of the Edo shogunate. In addition the official appointments made by emperors before Ieyasu's time affected lower echelons of the effective government than did those which he permitted.

Imperial influence in the period of reunification did not end with the ratification of military faits accomplis and the bestowal of decorative titles on effective military rulers. By the snobbish standards of the Kyoto aristocracy the military lords of the time were low-born upstarts, and the latter appear to have shared this belief. Nobunaga and Hideyoshi took pride in their court titles, and they also cultivated personal association with emperors and the other members of the court. In other words, they did not imprison the sovereign, as the first few Ashikaga shoguns had done and as the Tokugawa shoguns were to do later; they befriended him. Ōgimachi and Go-Yōzei enjoyed personal influence of an ordinary human sort because they were intimates of the most powerful military rulers of the country.

This sort of influence was not an entirely new phenomenon. From the time of the Ōnin War central control over the country collapsed. With it the controls that customarily restrained the emperor also collapsed. This gave the sovereign certain kinds of freedom that he had lacked before, the freedom to travel about the city or the countryside and to see people from a variety of classes and regions. This increase in freedom would have been of no particular consequence to politics if the emperor had merely sunk to the level of a private person. The ancient associations of the office prevented that from happening. They protected the sovereign from bodily harm, and this was itself no slight boon in a period when rather few great personages died natural deaths. Finally, they gave his words and wishes a force that could not be accounted for by the material circumstances of his life or his physical instruments of power. Factional warfare continued until unity was actually achieved. In such a situation the active support of the emperor was a thing much sought by fighting men. Many dreamed of national unity, but the dream could become reality only if a single authority could identify itself with the most important symbol of unity, the throne. Moreover, the support of the emperor could not be won by force alone, but had to be won by an appeal to his personal choice. As a result the emperors of the period of disunity took a more active part in political strategems than the sovereigns of most other periods.

These emperors were not figures of great power because they lacked the military resources which power required in that age. Their influence was never decisive in settling a major conflict between powerful adversaries, although they could alter policies in smaller ways by giving or withholding the sanction that alone could give a contestant for power the right to call himself the emperor's soldier. The Emperor Go-Tsuchimikado (r. 1464–1500) appears to have had some independence of action when he lent his own name to the shogun Yoshimasa's campaign against his brother Yoshimi in 1469. This he did by declaring Yoshimi a rebel and ordering Yoshimasa to chastise him.[40] However, that expedient could scarcely be used against any faction which was in firm military control of the capital. From the time that Nobunaga occupied the city in 1568, the emperor no longer had any real freedom to repudiate him in favor of some other fighting man, and the later instances of the emperors' exerting their personal influence on the effective government are of a different kind.

The Emperor Ōgimachi was on friendly terms with Nobu-

40 *Dai Nihon shiryō*, part VIII, vol. 2, pp. 344–46.

naga. He appears to have accepted the latter's presence with good grace. His bestowal of titles on Ashikaga Yoshiaki and on Nobunaga himself are evidence of this. On some occasions, however, he used the power of his office to influence Nobunaga's policies. For example, in 1579 he remonstrated against a plan which Nobunaga had to destroy the Kōya-san Monastery as he had done that on Mount Hiei in 1571, and the remonstrance was successful.[41]

Hideyoshi too seems to have been on relatively good terms with Ōgimachi and Go-Yōzei, and he did not personally take a hand in reimposing the rigid patterns of court ceremony and etiquette that had acted to restrict sovereigns in the past. The most noteworthy event in the association between Hideyoshi and Go-Yōzei was the latter's visit to Hideyoshi's new city palace, the Juraku-dai, in 1588.[42] It was an entertainment on the most spectacular scale, and the Emperor was a guest in the palace for five days. Both court nobles and military lords attended. Hideyoshi had contrived the occasion for a political purpose. He required the daimyos who were assembled to take an oath of three articles, which read:

1. We weep for gratitude that His Majesty has come on this Imperial Visit to the Juraku-dai.

2. We swear for ourselves, our children, and our posterity that if there should be lawless persons who take control of imperial property or the property of imperial courtiers, we shall deal with them severely.

3. We will not contravene in the slightest any command of His Lordship the *Kampaku*.[43]

[41] *Kōya shunjū hennen shūroku* (*Dai Nihon bukkyō zensho*, vol. 131), p. 273. See the discussion in Sansom, *A History of Japan, 1334–1615*, pp. 296–97.
[42] *Juraku-dai gyōkō-ki*, in *Gunsho ruijū*, vol. 2, pp. 468–90. See also the discussion in Ishii, *Tennō*, pp. 150–51.
[43] *Juraku-dai gyōkō-ki*, p. 435. A different translation of the oath and a discussion of this event appear in Sansom, *A History of Japan, 1334–1615*, pp. 341–42.

The Emperor's presence at the oath-signing and the allusions to him and to the court in the first two articles signify that Hideyoshi consciously used the imperial name to bolster his authority over his vassals. This is one more instance of the emperor's legitimating function, the definition of where rightful government lay by reference to the presence in it of the imperial person.

The emperor's personal wishes cannot be shown to have had the slightest effect on Hideyoshi's policies. Since Nobunaga's time the foundations of central authority had become firm enough that even that slight degree of persuasive power which Ōgimachi had shown in the 1570's had disappeared. The pattern of the Tokugawa shoguns' personal relations with the emperor was still different. Personal visits of one to the other did not cease until 1634, but they had already become less frequent and more formal in the time of Ieyasu. Contests of will between emperor and shogun became more numerous for a time, and they invariably ended in the ignominious defeat of the emperor.

In summary, the emperors played a role of real importance in the reunification of the country, but the sovereign's personal intervention became less necessary and less frequent as the unification proceeded. Titles of legitimation became less numerous. So did personal meetings between emperors and military rulers, which eventually stopped entirely. Through the lifetime of Nobunaga the throne had had some freedom of action and some influence on affairs. In Hideyoshi's time it had less independence and no influence. From the time of Ieyasu it had no freedom.

· 8 ·

Tokugawa Ieyasu's treatment of the throne is a paradox. He divested the court of all of its power to interfere in the affairs of his own government. He extended the power of the shogunate even to the selection or approval of the emperor's court officials. He laid down rules of protocol that isolated the Kyoto aristocracy from all but a handful of shogunal officials. He imposed further restrictions that isolated the reigning sovereign from all but a few of his own ministers. He caused these restrictions to be codified as law, and then he declared that the law was unalterable. Despite all this he declared himself to be the emperor's most loyal subject. He lavished gifts on the court, provided permanently for its upkeep, and improved its material standard of living. He thereby enabled the emperor and the court to perform their ancient ritual acts with a grandeur that they had lost in the period of disunion. In short, though Ieyasu may be said to have constructed a prison and housed the emperors there, it was a prison that had all the dignity and splendor of a cathedral.

Two emperors occupied the throne in the years of Ieyasu's rule, Go-Yōzei to 1611 and Go-Mizunoo thereafter. Relations with Go-Yōzei were tranquil for the most part, but they were marred toward the end of his reign by a clash of wills between Ieyasu and the court. In 1609 some court ladies, including members of the Emperor's harem, had had illicit relations with various members of kuge houses. The court solicited advice from the shogunate, which returned the suggestion that the Emperor mete out appropriate punishments. The Emperor then referred the matter to the heads of the highest-ranking kuge families, who decided to impose the death penalty. When the sentence was reported to Edo, Ieyasu intervened, demanding that the punishment be mitigated to banishment. The court resignedly did so, but the Emperor was enraged and, in fact, went into a severe illness over the affair. Early in 1610 he indicated his intention of abdicating. That was a power which one would think the sovereign would have retained after all the others had been taken away, but here again Ieyasu opposed him. At about the same time one of Ieyasu's daughters, the only child of his favorite concubine O-katsu, died. In his grief Ieyasu did not wish to be bothered with the affairs of an imperial abdication and accession, and he requested postponement. Go-Yōzei waited sullenly for more than a year (until 1611) before making good his intention of abdicating.[44]

The relations between Emperor Go-Mizunoo and the Toku-gawa government were even less satisfactory, but their stormiest phase occurred after Ieyasu's death, when Tokugawa Hidetada was the head of the family. Nevertheless, in 1615, one year before Ieyasu died, he performed an act which marked the ulti-mate assertion of the shogunate's power over the court. This was the promulgation of the *Kuge sho-hatto*, or "Laws pertaining to the kuge."[45] The timing of this event is significant. Two years earlier a briefer code had been issued with similar intent. In the meantime there had occurred the final military events in the Tokugawa campaign to eliminate all their rivals for political power. The last great enemy was Toyotomi Hideyori, the only son of Hideyoshi. Hideyori had been five when his father died and ten when Ieyasu became shogun. Now he was an adult and his very eixstence was an irksome reminder to Ieyasu that Hideyoshi had ruled before him and that the Toyotomi family therefore had more plausible claims to hereditary authority than his own. In 1614 Ieyasu made war on Hideyori at the latter's stronghold, Osaka Castle. The following year the castle fell, Hideyori killed himself, and his family and supporters were destroyed. Ieyasu had been the ruler of Japan since 1600, but only from 1615 was the hereditary succession to his power by later members of his family secure. In the fall of that year he proclaimed the *Buke sho-hatto*, "Laws governing the military families," a document that was to be the cornerstone of the

[44] Based on the description in Tsuji, *Nihon bunka-shi*, vol. 5, pp. 130–33.

[45] A text appears in *Tokugawa kinrei-kō*, vol. 1, pp. 1–4. For a discus-sion see Tsuji, *Nihon bunka-shi*, vol. 5, pp. 142–51.

legal institutions of the Tokugawa shogunate.[46] Ten days later the *Kuge sho-hatto* were promulgated.[47]

In form the code was adopted upon the agreement of shogunate and court officials, and it was announced to the court as though it had been established by the court's own high officials. Three men participated in the drafting. They were the abdicated Shogun Ieyasu, his son the titular Shogun Hidetada, and Nijō Akizane, who had formerly occupied the position of kampaku and was about to reassume it.[48] The code consisted of seventeen articles, probably in imitation of Prince Shōtoku's Seventeen-Article Constitution of 604.[49] Several of the articles merely articulated procedures that were already practiced, but some others were new restrictions on the powers and freedom of the Kyoto court. As the basic law code pertaining to the imperial institution in the Tokugawa period, the *Kuge sho-hatto* deserves more detailed description here.

The first article was wholly unexceptionable, but significant. It enjoined the emperor and his courtiers to devote themselves to scholarship and the arts. It pointed out that these had always been the special province of the imperial institution and that their cultivation was essential to the state. "Only through study can one illustrate the ancient Way and one's rule achieve great peace." This sort of terminology runs through the writing about the imperial institution in every period, the Tokugawa period included. Here we see it in a document sanctioned, or rather dictated, by the shogunal authorities. The emperor was expected to "rule," but obviously not in the sense of administering the

---

[46] *Tokugawa kinrei-kō*, vol. 1, pp. 90–104. A translation and discussion appear in Tsunoda, de Bary, & Keene (comp.), *Sources of Japanese Tradition*, pp. 335–38. See also Murdoch, *A History of Japan*, Volume II, p. 703.

[47] *Dai Nihon shiryō*, part XII, vol. 22, pp. 18–26; 158–201.

[48] Ishii, *Tennō*, pp. 155–56. Tsuji, *Nihon bunka-shi*, vol. 5, p. 143.

[49] Ishii, *Tennō*, p. 155.

government. His instruments were study and art, the implements of peace, and they were devised to achieve peace.

Articles II and III defined relative court ranks as among imperial princes (members of the imperial house), present holders of the three top positions in the ritsu-ryō system (Prime Minister, Minister of the Left, and Minister of the Right), former holders of those offices, and members of the top kuge families. This angered the court, not because the shogunate was dictatorial, but because it was capricious. A number of precedents were gathered together without much logic from the Kugyō bunin (the official roster of top imperial appointments) to give certain members of the imperial family low ranks of precedence relative to some of the kuge ministers. These articles led to some incidents in later generations which were very irksome to the court.

Articles IV and V gave the shogunate effective powers to veto appointments to offices of Prime Minister, Minister of the Left, Minister of the Right, sesshō, and kampaku. They did so by demanding that holders of these offices must not only be of appropriately high-ranking families of the kuge aristocracy, but also men of "skill." It was tacitly assumed that an imperial appointee's skill should be a matter for joint consultation between the court and shogunal authorities.

Article VI perpetuated a long-established procedure that inheritance in kuge families and the imperial family should go through male lines of descent. In other words, it forbade the most common Japanese pattern of adoption of heirs by means of an arranged marriage between one's daughter and the able son of an outside family.

Article VII codified a practice which Ieyasu had decided some years earlier of maintaining strict shogunal control over all imperially bestowed ranks and titles to members of the military aristocracy. Ieyasu had initially gained imperial approval for this procedure on a visit to the court in 1605, and as a consequence the titles of honor held by bushi had already come to be separately administered from those held by kuge.[50] Most of the titles held by both orders of aristocracy were from the ritsu-ryō system. Some had once been functioning offices of the central government, and others implied provincial governorships, vice-governorships, and the like. The Kyoto aristocracy filled most offices of the system, but as early as the Heian period the court had made use of the titles as purely honorary adornments for the members of the provincial and military aristocracy whom it wished to reward. After the atrophy of the ritsu-ryō system, the titles still connoted relative social prestige among the ruling classes, and they were therefore coveted by samurai. Long before the Tokugawa unification the ranks and titles had come to be similar to ranks of the modern British peerage. A daimyo who called himself "Governor of Izu" was not likely to have any more to do with the province than, say, the Prince of Wales has to do with Wales.

Ieyasu did not do away with the use of honorific court ranks and titles by his own vassals, but he insisted that he, not the emperor or the imperial court, should have the final decision as to who should receive them. In addition he increased the number of titles available to bushi by stipulating that a kuge and a bushi might both simultaneously occupy the same pseudo-office. The legal fiction was retained throughout that the bestowal of such honors on bushi was an imperial prerogative. Through the reign of the fourth Tokugawa shogun, Ietsuna (d. 1680), the Kyoto court actually took the initiative in granting them, whereupon the Edo court decided whether or not it would permit them to be received. From the time of the fifth shogun, Tsunayoshi, Edo proposed and Kyoto approved.[51]

[50] Ishii, Tennō, pp. 158–59. Zoku shigushō, (Kokushi taikei, vols. 13–15), vol. 15, p. 4.
[51] Ishii, Tennō, p. 159. Tsuji, Nihon bunka-shi, vol. 5, p. 149.

Article VIII set forth as an imperial duty the determination of when to declare a new calendrical era (nengō). Even in times of extreme disunity this had been a function of the imperial court and a reminder of national cultural community. There was nothing unusual in the shogunate's conceding that responsibility to the Kyoto court. As will be shown in a later section, the concession was more apparent than actual, since in fact the shogunate demanded its customary veto power over imperial decisions pertaining to the calendar.

Article IX contained regulations for court costumes.

Article X defined the order of precedence among the various kuge houses.

Article XI was a penal provision calling for punishment by banishment for those contravening the commands of the kampaku, or the top shogunal officials stationed in Kyoto. Though innocent looking, this article gave the shogunate effective legal control over the behavior of court society.

Article XII stated that punishments of kuge should be in accordance with rank.

The remaining five articles of the code all concerned the *monzeki*, imperial relatives who took Buddhist vows in order to assume the headship of certain large temples, monasteries, and nunneries. The monzeki had been an institutional link between the Kyoto court and the outside world, and as such they had to be brought under the control of the shogunate. The monzeki continued to receive their appointments from within the court, but the shogunate arrogated to itself the power of approval or veto.

The promulgation of the *Kuge sho-hatto* was one of the last major acts of Ieyasu's career. When he died in the spring of 1616, the imperial institution already possessed most of its characteristic features of the next 250 years. They may be summed up as follows.

The Kyoto court had no effective powers outside its own

society, for these had been wholly assumed by the "military families," that is, the vassals of the Tokugawa shoguns. The court was self-governing to a degree, but with the important qualification that its most important governing officers had to be approved by the shogunate. The emperor had little opportunity to see persons outside his court other than certain officials of the shogunate. He had therefore lost even that small chance of influencing potential dissidents or being influenced by them that emperors had enjoyed briefly in the fifteenth and sixteenth centuries.

The emperor continued to exercise a legitimating function on the effective agencies of government. This he did by means of the commission given to the head of the military government that allowed him to call himself "Shogun." He also in theory granted honorary titles of nobility or rank to members of the military aristocracy. In fact, the so-called power of bestowal amounted to little more than a power of attestation, for the court could not decide on its own to honor any other military person with an imperial dignity if the shogunate did not want him to be so honored.

In addition to the conferral of ranks and titles, the court performed certain rituals and had certain other functions pertaining to the calendar. These were vestiges of the magic and oracular acts that sovereigns had performed at the dawn of Japanese history. Some regarded them as still charged with magic power. Others considered them tokens of the natural order which defined standards of human conduct. The ritual, the system of court offices, the physical setting in which the life of the court took place, and even the layout and appearance of the imperial city were reminders of the Nara period, the springtime of Japanese culture, when men had taken such delight in the elegant ways of an alien civilization that the Japanese of later ages were caused to regard them and their institutions with a fierce nostalgia.

II

THE EMPERORS
AND THE COURT

❋ NO SMALL PART of the charm of modern Kyoto is the sad awareness that the city is no longer what it once was. One can still make out traces of the symmetrical grandeur that Emperor Kammu planned for it, but the regularities have grown indistinct with neglect and many of the greatest monuments are gone. Even the location of the city has shifted. Its center is north and east of where it was originally placed, causing the modern city to straddle the Kamo River, which was intended to form its eastern boundary. The Imperial Palace too is northeast of its original site, and though its grounds are extensive, they are smaller than before. The streets are still broader than those of other Japanese cities, but not so broad as Kammu planned them to be. There are fewer temples than before, and fewer palaces.

Most of these changes had taken place by the beginning of the Tokugawa period. In fact they represent the permanent damage done by the ravages of war from the Ōnin period to Nobunaga's entry into the city. However, one part of Kyoto, one of the saddest, attests to much more recent destruction. This is the Imperial Park (Gyoen), an area of some 220 acres including the Imperial Palace (Gosho). The Palace is still there, as well as an enclosure formerly used by ex-sovereigns, and some other out-buildings, but these occupy the smaller portion of the enclosure. The remainder is now a public park, filled with tree-lined walks and baseball diamonds. There is scarcely any air of history about it, but it is truly a place of unique historical importance. In the Tokugawa period this was the place of residence of the kuge, some 140 families of hereditary retainers of the imperial court.[1] Here and in the palaces which the area surrounded was the setting for the lives of one of the most curious aristocratic societies in the history of the world.

When the Emperor moved to Tokyo in 1869, most of the kuge moved with him. About 1877 the governmental authorities decided to level the area, not particularly in order to provide better park facilities for the city, but in order to prevent the remnants of this social class whose interests were so rooted in the past from becoming a nucleus of discontent against the modernizing policies of the Meiji government.[2] Only one mansion was spared outside the two palace enclosures, that of the Katsura family, a cadet branch of the imperial house. Though the walls and interior garden of that residence give one some impression of what the district must have been like a hundred years ago, the house itself is recent and tells one little; the kuge quarter has been virtually destroyed.

It can never have been a place of great luxury. The ideas of royal gardens that one might derive from Versailles, Nymphenburg, or the Forbidden City in Peking are completely inappropriate to the Kyoto Gyoen. City maps from the Tokugawa period show it to have been almost entirely occupied by the walled yards of separate families.[3] These varied greatly in size. That of the Katsura family, for example, was comparatively large, measuring some 500 or 600 feet in length and some 300 feet in width. The huge majority of the lots were much smaller:

---

[1] See the enumeration in Ponsonby-Fane, Kyoto, the Old Capital of Japan (794–1869), pp. 367–72.
[2] Fujita, Heian-kyō hensen-shi, p. 146. See also Heian tsūshi, kan 9, p. 19a.
[3] See for example Fujita, Heian-kyō, map #11; also the maps in Ponsonby-Fane, Kyoto, pp. 353, 355.

Ponsonby-Fane says they were 400 *tsubo* (approximately 120 feet square) or less.[4] Countless upper-middle class establishments in Japanese cities today are more imposing. Certainly there was nothing about the smaller residences of the kuge to warrant calling them palaces. The walls around each family's residence must have entirely removed any feeling of spacious grandeur that the Gyoen might otherwise have had. Those familiar with present-day Kyoto can perhaps obtain some impression of what the area must have been like from the grounds of the great Zen Buddhist monastery Myōshin-ji. The grounds of that monastery are quite extensive, but aside from the area in the center devoted to the main temple buildings, the area is subdivided into countless small enclosures for side temples or the residences of individual priests. The effect is one of somber and dignified beauty, but hardly of luxuriousness or grandeur. Inside each small enclosure there is the beauty of nature, but pruned and restricted after the manner of a Japanese family's garden.

The Gosho, or *Kindairi-gosho*, as the imperial palace is called, is of a quite different character. The main buildings that one may see there today are recent, dating from 1855, but they replaced structures of very similar design, which had been destroyed by fire in the preceding year. In fact, the average lifetime of any particular building in the compound was not long, for construction was of wood and fires were frequent. The basic architectural style of the palace is no more recent than that of the late Muromachi or Momoyama periods, in other words, the time when Nobunaga commenced the rebuilding of the city. To be less technical about it, the architecture of the palace is simple and austere, a bit disappointing to tourists who expect a child's dream of a fine house and find instead a larger, squarer version of a Shinto shrine.[5]

[4] *Ibid.*, p. 376.
[5] For descriptions of the *Kindairi* see *Japan, the Official Guide,* pp. 681–83. Ponsonby-Fane, *Kyoto,* pp. 328–46.

The palace enclosure is over 1450 feet from north to south and about 800 feet from east to west. It is entirely surrounded by a wall about fifteen feet high, interrupted at irregular intervals by eighteen gates. The wall will seem to the tourist today to be the most awesome symbol of the emperor's extreme isolation from the rest of society, though it may have been less forbidding to the Japanese at a time when practically all institutions were fenced for security and privacy. In the Tokugawa period the gates of the palace, for which one Japanese word is "mikado," were the outsider's usual token for the august personage inside. The single large gate (Kenrei-mon) at the front (south) of the enclosure was reserved for the emperor alone. As will be seen, this is tantamount to saying that it was very rarely used.

Inside the enclosure a considerable number of buildings are distributed in an irregular pattern. The most commanding of them is the *Shishin-den* ("Purple Dragon Hall"), a structure about 100 feet wide facing the Kenrei-mon at the southern end of the enclosure. It was a ceremonial hall in which the more or less public ritual acts of the emperor were performed, acts like the enthronement and the New Year's audience which required the participation of many courtiers. Behind the Shishin-den and to the left of it was the *Seiryō-den* ("Clear Cool Hall"), which was the other main ceremonial building of the palace. The corresponding structure in the original Heian palace had served as the main residence of the emperor, but in the Tokugawa period it was a place of ritual. Here the emperor performed the private acts of worship that were regarded as central to his role, principally the ministration to his divine ancestress, the Sun Goddess.[6]

To the east of the group just described there stood in the Tokugawa period a smaller building known variously as the

[6] *Heian tsūshi, kan* 4, pp. 4b–7a; pp. 11a–15a; *kan* 9, pp. 10a–12b; Ponsonby-Fane, *Kyoto*, p. 335.

Ummei-den ("Hot Bright Hall") or *Kashikodokoro* ("Place of Awe") or *Naishi-dokoro* ("Place of the Imperial Priestesses"). Here was enshrined the sacred jewel, one of the three imperial regalia that Japanese legend has it were transmitted by the Sun Goddess to successive generations of her imperial descendants and that betokened imperial legitimacy. It was guarded by princesses of the imperial house. With the removal of the emperor to Tokyo the jewel went too, and later the building in which it had been housed was also removed.[7]

As one proceeds northward into the central portions of the enclosure, one passes several buildings, and in the Tokugawa period there were many more. These served a variety of functions: robing chambers, waiting rooms, guards' offices, an imperial lecture hall, places for small audiences or minor ceremonies, and so forth. Near the center of the enclosure is the *Otsune Goten*, or "Ordinary Palace," which was the emperor's actual residence. One is happy to discover that it is a fine Japanese-style mansion, less austere and more habitable than the ceremonial buildings of the enclosure. It adjoins a large private garden with lakes and brooks.[8]

The northern portion of the enclosure was devoted to the empress's palace, *Kōgō no Miya*. Until after the time of Ieyasu the same area was reserved for abdicated sovereigns, but a separate palace, the *Sentō Gosho*, was built for them outside the Kindairi enclosure in 1628. The Kōgō no Miya contained numerous buildings, most of which no longer exist. The two principal ones still stand. These are the *Kōgō Otsune Goten*, which was the residence proper, and the *Higyō-sha*, a place for rituals and ceremonies.[9]

A separate enclosure southeast of the Kindairi houses the

[7] *Heian tsūshi*, kan 5, pp. 1b–2a; kan 9, pp. 12b–13a. Ponsonby-Fane, *Kyoto*, p. 336.
[8] *Heian tsūshi*, kan 9, pp. 14a–b. Ponsonby-Fane, *Kyoto*, pp. 337–38. See the illustration in *ibid.*, facing p. 338.
[9] *Heian tsūshi*, kan 9, pp. 17b–18b. Ponsonby-Fane, *Kyoto*, pp. 339–40.

Sentō Gosho, alluded to above, and the *Ōmiya Gosho*. The latter was occupied at various times by imperial consorts, imperial widows, and abdicated sovereigns in times when there were more than one of them. Like the palace of the empress, these contained buildings for ceremonial functions as well as residential quarters.[10]

At some periods members of the imperial family—consorts, abdicated sovereigns, or imperial children—occupied palaces within the present Gyoen but outside the compounds of the Kindairi, the Sentō Gosho, or the Ōmiya Gosho. In addition, the Gyoen enclosure included some areas unaccounted for in the above description—gardens, grounds for playing ceremonial football (kemari), etc.

A few kuge families resided in other parts of the city. The richest and highest ranking of them might have country establishments as well as their regular city residences in the Gyoen. The outstanding example is the great palace and garden of the Katsura family, whose family name is derived from the location of the palace beside the Katsura River southwest of the city.[11] One other country place associated with the imperial court in this period remains to be mentioned. This is the *Shugakuin*, a magnificent group of pavilions and gardens splendidly situated in the hills northeast of the city. This was originally built as a pleasure resort for the abdicated emperor Go-Mizunoo about 1650. For the next eighty years it was a place of frequent retreat for ex-emperors, and after nearly a century of disuse it was restored in 1823 for the pleasure of the retired emperor Kōkaku.[12] Both the Katsura and Shugakuin estates are maintained as detached imperial palaces and as semi-public parks.

[10] *Heian tsūshi, kan* 9, pp. 20a–24b. Ponsonby-Fane, *Kyoto*, pp. 340–45.
[11] For a description see Ishimoto, *Katsura, Tradition and Creation in Japanese Architecture*.
[12] See below, p. 125. For description of the Shugakuin, see Mori, *Study on the Imperial Villa of Shugaku-in*.

• 2 •

Such was the setting of the life of the court. We now deal with
the personages of the court: the emperors themselves in historical succession, the other members of the imperial family, the
kuge, and the representatives of the military aristocracy who
resided in Kyoto.

Thirteen men and two women occupied the imperial throne
from 1586 to 1866. They will be referred to collectively as the
kinsei sovereigns. Kinsei means "modern times," but it is invariably used by Japanese historians to refer to the Tokugawa period. A note about the names of emperors is in order here. The
practice of this book is consistent with that in most Japanese
and Western language texts. That is, all sovereigns are referred
to throughout by posthumous names. These names have usually
been assigned by the court immediately after the sovereign's
death, sometimes in accordance with his own expressed wishes.
We need not be concerned with the rare instances in which a
single ruler was assigned more than one name of this kind,
since no such case happened in the Tokugawa period. At any
rate, the Japanese government and scholars now accept a single
list of posthumous names which was agreed upon late in the
nineteenth century.[13] All sovereigns of course had personal
names, but these are almost never used by historians, having
been considered by prewar Japanese to be too intimate for common purposes. All of the male sovereigns with whom we shall
be concerned had personal names ending in the element *-hito*,
which means "humanity" or "benevolence." The imperial
family of Japan has never had a family or dynastic name. Of
course the names of members of the imperial family would
always in Japanese be accompanied by titles of rank, such as

---

[13] *Teishitsu seido-shi*, vol. 6, pp. 648–57; 725–40; table, pp. 869–81.

Tennō (Emperor) or *Shinnō* (Prince). We shall frequently omit the titles here, taking full advantage of the fact that Western practice permits greater freedom of discourse about royal personages.

The occupant of the throne in the time of Nobunaga and Hideyoshi is known posthumously as Ōgimachi. His personal name was Katahito. He is called the 106th of his line.[14] His role in the reunification of the empire has been discussed in the previous chapter. He abdicated his throne in 1586, thereby restoring a practice that had fallen into disuse in the period of the warring states. The successor was his grandson, Emperor Go-Yōzei, whose father, the Imperial Prince Masahito, had predeceased him. There follows a brief outline of the history of the imperial family in the Tokugawa period in the form of biographical sketches of the fifteen sovereigns of the period, indicating for each one the circumstances of his succession and the most significant events of his life and reign.[15]

107. *Go-Yōzei* — b. 1571; r. 1586–1611; d. 1617. It was pointed out in the preceding chapter that this emperor's powers of official appointment were of use to Hideyoshi and Ieyasu in legitimating their rule. From Go-Yōzei's abdication in 1611 until his death in 1617 he remained head of the imperial family. Thenceforth there was usually an ex-sovereign to preside over family affairs at the same time that ceremonial functions were carried out by the reigning sovereign.

108. *Go-Mizunoo* — b. 1596; r. 1611–29; d. 1680. Go-

[14] The official king-list of the Japanese dynasty may be found with reign dates in the Appendix below, pp. 269–73. The first few emperors in this list were legendary or semi-historical. Reischauer, *Early Japanese History*, Part A, pp. 13–14; pp. 114ff., discusses the historicity of the list. The system of numbering reigns here is conventional. The legendary sovereigns are included, and separate numbers are assigned to each of the nonconsecutive reigns of the Empresses Kōgyoku-Saimei and Kōken-Shōtoku.

[15] The sources for the following material include *Koji ruien*, vol. 12, pp. 37–44. *Teishitsu seido-shi*, vol. 4. *Zoku shigushō*, vol. 15, passim. *Yashi, kan* 7–21.

Mizunoo was the son of Go-Yōzei. His career was marked by growing tensions between the imperial and shogunal offices, which culminated in his irate abdication of the throne to his daughter. At first he appears to have enjoyed friendly relations with shogunal officials, but these later changed to frustration and enmity because of a succession of irksome incidents in which the Edo government thwarted the Emperor's wishes.

One part of the campaign by the Tokugawa to strengthen their dominance of the imperial family was the arrangement of a marriage between Go-Mizunoo and Kazuko, the daughter of the second Tokugawa shogun, Hidetada. Ieyasu himself is said to have proposed the marriage shortly before his death, though he was thwarted by the opposition of the ex-emperor Go-Yōzei. Hidetada continued to press for the arrangement and was finally successful, forcing Go-Yōzei to agree just before the latter's death in 1617. Kazuko was taken into the imperial harem in 1620, later being given the title of Empress. It was very irregular for anyone outside the highest ranking kuge houses to attain such a title, but of course the behavior of the first three Tokugawa shoguns toward the throne was marked by many acts that were very irregular. Surprisingly, the marriage between Go-Mizunoo and Kazuko is reputed to have been happy for the two principals, though the manner in which it was concluded can only have been an annoyance to the Kyoto court.[16]

The systematic control of the imperial institution by the shogunate may be dated from 1615, when the Kuge sho-hatto were promulgated.

The circumstances of Go-Mizunoo's abdication are of significance to the development of the institution and will be discussed later in this chapter. It will suffice to say here that the emperor had finally become exasperated at being dealt with in so peremptory a fashion by the shogunate and decided rather suddenly to abdicate in 1629. None of his sons born up to that

16 Ponsonby-Fane, "Kōhi, Imperial Consorts in Japan," p. 153.

time had survived, so he chose as his successor the eldest daughter born to him and Empress Kazuko.

Though he had abdicated, Go-Mizunoo continued to preside over his family until his death. His love of learning, particularly of the Japanese classics, his relations with his son Go-Kōmyō, and his part in the succession of the Emperor Go-Sai are discussed below.

109. *Meishō* — b. 1623; r. 1629–43; d. 1696. Meishō is famous for the circumstances surrounding her accession and for the fact that she was the first female sovereign since the Nara period. Other than that, she was a nonentity, who came to the throne as a child, abdicated while still adolescent, and was dominated from first to last by her elders in the imperial family and the court. She never married. It is not clear just why she did not, but it may be surmised that for her to have done so would have entailed problems of protocol both in the treatment which was to have been accorded to her spouse and in the disposal of her children. By ordinary Japanese family law a man's wife and children belong to his family unless he is adopted by the wife's family. The imperial family employed ancient usages forbidding inheritance through female lines, and those usages had been reduced to writing in the *Kuge sho-hatto*. Accordingly, Meishō's children would not have belonged to her family but to her husband's, yet as children of an ex-sovereign they would presumably have merited some sort of special treatment that would have been difficult for theorists of imperial etiquette to work out.

110. *Go-Kōmyō* — b. 1633; r. 1643-54. Go-Kōmyō was the second of four children of Go-Mizunoo who reigned as sovereigns. He occupied the throne during his adolescence and indeed can scarcely be said to have lived into adulthood. He had advantages of sex and character over Meishō and resisted better than she domination by his father and the court. He was a scholar like his father, with whom he disagreed fundamentally

in taste. He despised the native literary classics and deplored the enervating influence which they had had on the imperial court. He thought them trivial and obscene. In their place he recommended the study of Confucian philosophy and Chinese verse. As the first imperial patron of Japanese neo-Confucianism, he has a certain importance in the history of seventeenth century thought.[17]

111. *Go-Sai* — b. 1637; r. 1654–63; d. 1685. Go-Kōmyō's illness and early death caught the court unawares. No heir to the throne had been appointed either formally or by informal understanding. The ex-emperor Go-Mizunoo selected another of his sons to succeed, a prince who had previously been adopted to head the Arisugawa, a cadet branch of the imperial family. Go-Sai had bad luck as titular sovereign. During his reign a succession of calamities occurred, the most noteworthy of which were the great fire of Edo (1657), the burning of the imperial palace (1661), the destruction by fire of a portion of the Great Shrine at Ise (1661), and a number of earthquakes in various parts of the country (1662). A Chinese theory of portents which had long been known and respected in Japan held that such disasters might be indices of imperial misrule and hence might justify replacing the sovereign. The shogunate concluded that some unspecified lack of virtue on Go-Sai's part might be at fault in this instance, and he was forced to abdicate. He had many children, but these were passed over in the succession in favor of yet another of Go-Mizunoo's sons. The remaining years of Go-Sai's life were passed in seclusion.

112. *Reigen* — b. 1654; r. 1663–87; d. 1732. There is little to report of historical interest about Reigen or his next few successors except details of succession. Reigen had a long and apparently tranquil life after his abdication and was the head of his family during the next two reigns.

113. *Higashiyama* — b. 1675; r. 1687–1709; d. 1709. Reigen's

[17] See below, pp. 150–51.

son. He abdicated on his deathbed to ensure that there would be no gap between reigns.

114. *Nakamikado* — b. 1701; r. 1709–35; d. 1737. A son of Higashiyama. The death in 1732 of his grandfather Reigen made him head of the household, a position which he retained after his abdication.

115. *Sakuramachi* — b. 1720; r. 1735–47; d. 1750. The eldest son of Nakamikado.

116. *Momozono* — b. 1741; r. 1747–62. The eldest son of Sakuramachi. During his reign there began the famous incident involving Takenouchi Shikibu and Yamagata Daiji, Confucian scholars who first taught a radically anti-shogunal version of the emperor cult. This is discussed below, in Chapter Four.

117. *Go-Sakuramachi* — b. 1740; r. 1762–70; d. 1813. The Emperor Momozono left sons, but the eldest was only four years old and was deemed to be too young to succeed to the throne. The court chose Momozono's elder sister, Go-Sakuramachi, who is the most recent Empress Regnant of Japan. Like Empress Meishō she never married, probably for the same reasons.

118. *Go-Momozono* — b. 1758; r. 1770–79. It was intended from the start of Go-Sakuramachi's reign that she should abdicate when her nephew, Momozono's eldest son, was old enough to perform the ceremonial duties of his office. That boy reigned as Go-Momozono, died rather suddenly, and thereby caused a serious problem of succession, as he was the last male left in his immediate branch of the imperial family.

119. *Kōkaku* — b. 1771; r. 1779–1817; d. 1840. The situation regarding the succession which existed at the time of Go-Momozono's death was as follows.[18] The latter had only one child, a daughter, who was born in the same year, 1779. Even if she had been older, it would have served no useful purpose to

[18] See *Koji ruien*, vol. 12, pp. 250–51. *Teishitsu seido-shi*, vol. 4, pp. 323–27. *Seishi kakei dai-jiten*, vol. 1, pp. 121–27.

have made her a kind of interim sovereign such as Go-Sakuramachi had been, because of the very strong precedents that only
blood inheritance through the male line could qualify a person
for membership in the imperial family. In other words, her
children, assuming that she had succeeded to the throne, would
not have been able to succeed her. Go-Momozono's only brother
had predeceased him. There were therefore no available claimants among the descendants of Sakuramachi. Some of Nakamikado's sons were still alive, but they were aged Buddhist
priests, unlikely to solve for long the inheritance problem. It
was therefore necessary to select a successor from among the
cadet branches of the imperial family. There were four of these,
and the family from which the heir was chosen was the Kan'in.
The first prince of this house was a younger brother of the
Emperor Nakamikado. Although the son of that man, the
second prince, lived until 1794, he was passed over in favor of
his son, who reigned as Kōkaku. There is some indication here
that the officials of the court purposely did so in imitation of
the many past cases in which a child or adolescent had been
titular emperor while his father was the real head of the family.[19] The affair in which the court attempted to give Kōkaku's
father Prince Kan'in the title as well as the duties of an ex-
sovereign occasioned much bitterness between the Kyoto and
Edo governments.[20]

Kōkaku's long reign was uneventful, but the period of his
retirement is noteworthy for considerable relaxation of the controls which the shogunate maintained over the imperial court.
Unlike his predecessors of the previous 100 years, ex-Emperor
Kokāku enjoyed the freedom to travel about the city, and many
stories are told of the pastimes of his latter years.[21]

[19] Descriptions of Kōkaku's succession appear in Tsuji, *Nihon bunka-
shi*, vol. 5, p. 305. Kuroita, *Kokushi no kenkyū, kakusetsu*, vol. 2, pp.
501–02.
[20] See below, pp. 123–25.
[21] *Shugaku-in-gokō-shi*, in *Koji ruien*, vol. 12, pp. 747–48.

120. *Kōmei* — b. 1831; r. 1846–66. A son of Ninkō. He was the first sovereign in centuries to emerge as a significant historical personage. From immediately after his accession the court was more independent in its relations with the shogunate than ever before. It was a reign of mounting national crisis because of Western pressures and the collapse of shogunal government. The role of Kōmei and his court in the history of the time is described below, Chapter Four.

On Kōmei's death he was succeeded by his son, who is known to us as Emperor Meiji. In the first year of his reign the last Tokugawa shogun turned over the headship of the effective government to him.

• 3 •

Membership in the imperial family of Japan is defined according to a complex system of rules. It is by no means sufficient to be a blood descendant of an emperor; if it were, the family would by now no doubt contain a large portion of the population of Japan. First of all, all female lines of descent are automatically excluded from the imperial family, although daughters of emperors are members of it until they are married. In earlier periods it was the practice to keep the imperial family relatively small by allowing most imperial sons to found new families of their own. The families were thenceforward regarded as noble, but nonroyal. The various branches of the Taira family traced their descent to imperial princes of the early ninth century; similarly those of the Minamoto clan were descended from the imperial family of later years. A great many other imperial sons became Buddhist priests and therefore presumably celibate. If they had progeny, they were nonimperial. These devices for limiting the size of the imperial family were conscious instruments of policy for the various nonimperial effective rulers from the Heian period on. Fewer numbers meant ease of control, a smaller budget for the maintenance of the court, and the minimization of succession disputes.[22]

It was thought desirable to allow a certain number of imperial princes to remain in the family, for only these could inherit the throne and there was always a danger that the emperor or heir apparent would die without heirs. Accordingly, a few of the younger sons of emperors remained family members. The son of an imperial prince was also an imperial prince unless the court took some special action to divest him of family membership. It might do this by granting him a patent to found his own family (as with the Taira and Minamoto above), but the more usual method from the Kamakura period on was to have the more distantly related imperial princes adopted into courtier families.

Until the fourteenth century there was no attempt to set up a cadet branch of the imperial family on a permanent basis. Every earlier collateral line of imperial princes had been allowed to die out or lose its imperial status after a few generations. During the period of the Northern and Southern courts it was decided to create a sub-clan whose heads would always be imperial princes and would therefore enjoy the right of succession to the throne. This was the Fushimi family, descended from a younger son of the Northern emperor Sukō (r. 1348–51).[23] A son of the third prince of the house succeeded to the throne as Emperor Go-Hanazono in 1428, when the main line of the dynasty came to an end. Three more cadet houses had been founded before the late Tokugawa period, the Katsura, Arisugawa, and Kan'in families.[24] These names are not true surnames but rather titles of nobility that could be held by only one prince at any one time. The second Prince Kan'in, who was the father of Emperor Kōkaku, was known in Japanese as Kan'in-no-

[22] See *Koji ruien*, vol. 13, p. 552.
[23] *Kindai teiō keizu*, in *Koji ruien*, vol. 13, pp. 559–62.
[24] *Ibid.*, pp. 563–68.

Miya Sukehito-Shinnō, which means something like "His Lord-ship of Kan'in, the Imperial Prince Sukehito."

Adoption was freely practiced among the various branches of the imperial family, including the main line. If the head of a cadet branch had no sons of his own, he usually adopted one of the emperor's sons to carry on his line. We have seen a case of the reverse kind when a son of the Kan'in house provided a successor to Go-Momozono in 1779.

The principal house of the imperial family in the Tokugawa period consisted of the emperors, their formal consorts, their sons, and their unmarried daughters. Imperial children might be very numerous. Go-Mizunoo is reported in the court genealogies as having been the father of 37 sons and daughters. He was one of 25 children of his father, Go-Yōzei. Go-Sai had 27 children. A child's imperial paternity was regarded as the all-important factor in deciding whether to list him in the official roles of family membership. Obviously, the children of the emperors mentioned above were born to many different mothers, but the identity of the mother was regarded as of no importance in determining legitimacy.[25]

The women of the emperors formed a various group, for which it is difficult to find a satisfactory term. Only a few of them should be referred to as wives, empresses, or consorts, for in our context those words had best be reserved for the women who received certain official patents of position and who ful-filled a certain ceremonial role in the structure of court society. It would be misleading to call the remainder concubines or mistresses, for the emperor's contacts with them might be casual and temporary. The term "palace women" would be inapt for two reasons: there were a great many women of the palace performing a variety of services that had nothing to do with providing imperial heirs; furthermore, some who were more

[25] See the imperial genealogies in *Seishi kakei dai-jiten*, vol. 1, pp. 16–134. *Honchō shōin jōun-roku*, in *Gunsho ruijū*, vol. 3, pp. 379–498.

intimately involved in an emperor's personal life did not live inside the palace. None of the imperial women actually resided in the emperor's personal apartments. The consorts had their own enclosed part of the Kindairi, and the others either lived with their fathers or had houses of their own. Practically all of the women were of kuge families, although there were some exceptions. Go-Mizunoo's empress, Kazuko, was the daughter of the shogun Hidetada. Some other consorts were princesses from cadet branches of the imperial family.[26]

Imperial children were born in their mothers' residences, whether inside or outside the Kindairi. The Emperor Meiji, whose mother was not a formal consort of Emperor Kōmei, was born in the small house of his maternal grandfather Nakayama Tadayasu, where he remained until his fifth year.[27] His father Kōmei had lived in his mother's residence, that of the Ōgimachi family, until he was four years old.[28] These residences were of course in the kuge quarter (the present Gyoen), but they were outside the palace enclosure. Upon moving to the palace the imperial children apparently lived with their siblings of the same sex, for the *Wakamiya Goten*, which housed them, comprised separate apartments for boys and girls.[29] An imperial son, especially one who could some day inherit the throne, might be adopted by the empress or other formal consort, in which case he would move to her palace. This was the fate of Kōmei when at the age of four he moved to the *Higyō-sha* of the Empress's palace.[30] His case indicates that the heir apparent received special treatment. When Kōmei was six, having in the meantime been named Crown Prince, he moved to his own palace, the *Hana Goten*.[31] Other imperial children eventually moved to

---

[26] See table in *Dokushi biyō*, pp. 463–68. The best secondary treatment of imperial women is Tanaka, *Tennō no kenkyū*, pp. 23–28.
[27] Watanabe *Meiji Tennō*, vol. 1, pp. 77–78; 85.
[28] Tokushige, *Kōmei Tennō go-jiseki-ki*, p. 8.
[29] *Heian tsūshi*, kan 9, p. 18b.
[30] Tokushige, *Kōmei Tennō*, p. 8.   [31] *Ibid*.

their own residences, assuming of course that they lived to maturity and were not adopted into some other family.

There were thus separate establishments for each member of the family except for the children of a certain age. This does not mean that there was no contact among the various members of the family. Ceremonial visits of respect to the emperor were an important part of the formal life of the court, and there were frequent informal visits as well. Nevertheless, there was no family life of the ordinary kind. The nearest semblance to family life that an imperial child knew was what he could remember dimly from his earliest childhood in the household of his grandfather. One supposes that maternal influence must have been quite strong and that the figure of the emperor must have seemed a bit remote even to his own children.

Readers may wonder how a polygamous family of great fecundity provided for all its children. In fact, it was not as much of a problem as one might suppose, for remarkably few of the children survived to maturity. Of the fifteen children born to the Emperor Ninkō, all but three died in infancy.[32] It is sobering to realize that even in the late nineteenth century things had not improved very much; the genealogies list fifteen children born to the Emperor Meiji between 1873 and 1897, and of these only five survived childhood.[33] In both of these examples only one of the survivors was a son.

These are extreme cases to be sure. The mortality record of earlier times is considerably better and indicates that an extreme lack of hardiness did not afflict the imperial family until some time in the eighteenth century. Of Go-Mizunoo's 37 children, 23 lived to be at least 20. One son was the Emperor Reigen, who died at 78, and one hardy daughter lived to be 93.[34]

The extraordinarily high infant mortality rate of later generations is therefore hard to account for. Medical standards were

[32] *Seishi kakei dai-jiten*, vol. 1, pp. 130–31.
[33] *Ibid.*, pp. 132–33.   [34] *Ibid.*, pp. 116–20.

low, but they do not seem to have been lower in the nineteenth century than they had been in the seventeenth. The life of the palace and the kuge quarter was confining and no doubt weakening, but there is no evidence that it had been any less so in the earlier time. One can only surmise that whatever vigor the family had once had was slowly and steadily sapped by two centuries of the most sedentary and dullest way of life imaginable.

If an imperial child did live to maturity, the possible patterns of his existence were extremely limited. He (or she) might succeed to the throne, and though that was not in itself an especially pleasant prospect, a sovereign might later abdicate and thereby achieve a way of life that was equally luxurious and far less stultifying. A daughter might leave the family through marriage to a kuge or to an imperial prince from a cadet house. A few imperial sons founded new branches of the family, and several others were adopted to perpetuate old lines that were about to die out. A few sons were adopted to head kuge families, mostly houses of the highest rank. All of these possibilities together account for less than half of the imperial children in the Tokugawa period who attained adulthood. The remainder became Buddhist priests or nuns and are known as Go-monzeki.

The practice of leaving the palace and the cares of office to devote oneself to religion has almost as long a history in Japan as the Buddhist religion itself. At an earlier time the motive may really have been to escape from worldly concern, and the life of a priestly prince may really have been contemplative. By the Tokugawa period, however, the practice had become a device to provide adequately high-ranking abbots and abbesses to head certain great temples, monasteries, and nunneries. These institutions were called monzeki. Different sources give different lists of them, probably because the exact number changed.[35] They agree that there were between 20 and 25 monasteries in the

[35] See the lists in Ponsonby-Fane, Kyoto, pp. 217–19.

Tokugawa period and 16 nunneries. About half of them were customarily headed by members of the imperial family itself, and the remainder by kuge. Before the Tokugawa period the Go-monzeki had served to maintain a degree of court control over the most important Buddhist institutions. The *Kuge sho-hatto* of 1615 provided that the shogunate should approve appointments of priestly princes, and the administrative control of the Go-monzeki from that time was nominal. They resided at their temples, most of which were in the Kansai area, but many of them also had residences in the kuge quarter.

What can one say of the imperial family in human terms? It was a blood, or biological, family, much as any other, and to an even greater degree than with other Japanese families, since one could not be adopted into its membership. On the other hand, it was not a domiciliar unit, and it could not be said to possess any of the normal economic or social functions of an ordinary Japanese family. Yet it did *symbolize* those other functions, and it did so by means of its external trappings, its formal structure, and its ritual life. The palace symbolized an ordinary family's house, and its impenetrable walls were a natural image of the protectiveness that is every human family's first obligation to its members. The Wakamiya Goten was isolated, the better to emphasize the importance of childrearing in an ordinary family. So far, symbol overlaps with fact, for these features of the imperial family's life really served similar purposes to the corresponding features of the lives of ordinary families. Certain other characteristics of the imperial family were more exclusively symbolic, for they connoted features of an ordinary family's life that differed greatly from those of the imperial family.

The most conspicuous of these is the fact that, while the imperial family was highly polygamous, it was structured to resemble the monogamous nuclear family which is the unit of Japanese peasant society. At any one time the emperor could have only one principal wife, *kōgō* or *chūgū*. She was usually chosen from one of the highest ranking kuge families, and the attainment by her of that enormous distinction conferred great honor on her family. The early kinsei emperors usually had children by their principal consorts, but most of the later kōgō were childless. Neither child-bearing nor child-rearing was the kōgō's main job, though the fiction persisted that she was the "mother" of the emperor's children. Imperial heirs by other women were usually adopted by her, and as we have seen in the case of the Emperor Kōmei they were sometimes raised in the enclosure of her palace.[36]

The ceremonial life of the kōgō was complex; she participated in some rites together with her husband the emperor, while she performed others at her own ceremonial palace, the Higyō-sha. The physical placement of that structure at the northern extremity of the Kindairi signified the kōgō's role. She was one term of a sexual polarity counter-balancing the emperor seated in his ceremonial hall of state, the Shishin-den, at the southern end of the enclosure.

Some of the other imperial women might have formal titles as secondary consorts. The generic name for these in the period in question was *nyōgo*, but there were many other ranks and titles available to bestow on them, each denoting a slightly different order of precedence or standard of treatment.[37] One means of attaining such a position was to bear the emperor's heir, and in such cases the titles were conferred after the birth of the son. There was no such ceremonial grandeur surrounding the nyōgo as with the principal consorts, and one is tempted to regard their positions as little different from the fictitious titles and ranks bestowed by the emperor on members of the kuge and bushi classes.

Finally, a word should be said about the office of Crown

[36] An overall view of the office of empress, with elaborate documentation from contemporary sources, is in *Koji ruien*, vol. 13, *kan* 19–20.
[37] See the discussion in Tanaka, *Tennō no kenkyū*, pp. 24–26.

Prince (Kōtaishi or Tōgū). The office was the formalized equivalent of an heir apparent, though an imperial child might be designated heir without ever having the title. Go-Mizunoo was Crown Prince from 1600 until his accession in 1611. Go-Kōmyō held the title briefly before his accession, but his brothers Go-Sai and Reigen never did. None of these sovereigns actually underwent the elaborate ceremony known as *ryūbō* or *ryūtaishi*, which was the ordinary investiture of a Crown Prince, for it had fallen into disuse in the time of the dynastic schism of the fourteenth century. The ceremony was revived for the future emperor Higashiyama in 1683. Later sovereigns were all formally invested as Crown Princes some time before the accession, except for Empress Go-Sakuramachi and Emperor Kōkaku, whose predecessors died suddenly without grown sons.[38]

The eldest son (chōnan) of an ordinary Japanese family is continuously trained to inherit his father's stewardship of the family. The father himself is the main teacher. The education of the crown prince was a stylized image of the common pattern. He had an official tutor (fu) who taught him poetry and philosophy at the prince's residence.[39] The tutor may have stood in place of the father-instructor of an ordinary family, but the folklore about emperors in the Tokugawa period frequently refers to the close contacts between Crown Princes and their fathers, as though the pattern for ordinary people were reproduced on the imperial level as well.[40] More will be said later about the content of a future emperor's education. Part of it was the pleasant arts of the Japanese aristocratic tradition—composition of *waka* and Chinese verse, calligraphy, and classical painting. More of it was related to "government," but that

[38] *Teishitsu seido-shi,* vol. 4, p. 202. See also the table in *ibid.,* pp. 361–66.

[39] Wada, *Kanshoku yōkai,* p. 231.

[40] See for example the works that deal in anecdotal fashion with Go-Mizunoo's relations with his children: Muro, *Kyūsō shōsetsu,* in *Zoku shiseki shūran,* vol. 6, pp. 49–51. *Shōō iji,* in *Shiseki shūran,* vol. 17, pp. 480–84.

meant Chinese and Japanese moral philosophy justifying the political order rather than the more down-to-earth concerns of an effective administration.

When one sees that the life in the Kindairi was a symbolic representation of life in an ordinary family's house, one begins to understand why the essential personages of the representation—the emperor, the kōgō, the crown prince, and the other children—were physically isolated from one another. The pedestal on which a Giorgione Madonna sits isolates her from the landscape around her, but not because the artist wishes to assert her independence of the real world that the landscape depicts. It is rather because he wants to show the unique centrality of her position in all of it. There is a diptych, a "Crucifixion" by Roger van der Weyden in the Philadelphia Museum of Arts, that illustrates perfectly the uses to which artifice and isolation of symbolic parts may be put in heightening the significance of a symbolic whole. The right side shows the dead Christ painted in literal detail against an artificial blankness of primary color. On the left side, against the same blank glow, are the literally represented figures of the adoring Virgin and St. John. The effect of the two pictures is more unified than if they were one, for the isolation of each from the other brings to one's mind with simplicity and directness the relation between them. The emotional high points of a Bach passion or a Handel opera are the set-pieces, long static pieces of artificial design, which break one's emotional involvement by stopping the pace of the surrounding drama. Here too it is the isolation that calls one's attention to the significance of each halted moment and that forces one to think out its relation to the whole. The Japanese nō theater makes much use of similar devices. The persons of the play sit apart from one another with sparse props or no props so as not to distract the viewer from the essential parts of the drama. Pauses, choruses, and dances interrupt the action and give each segment of it its full individuality.

Artifice and an isolation of its parts made the Japanese imperial family a better, because more immediately perceivable, image of the ideal Japanese family than if all of its members had lived together as an indivisible community. The discreteness of the parts made the family unfit to perform a family's ordinary functions, but that was of small account because it had few ordinary functions to perform.

· 4 ·

The kuge class did useful services of various kinds for the imperial court, but in order to explain its existence in Tokugawa Japan it is not enough to tell what it did. One must also describe how it came into being. The literal meaning of kuge is "public families," in other words, hereditary occupants of offices of state. In the Heian and earlier periods the ancestors of the modern kuge were exactly that. They were the administrators and bureaucrats of the central government, and they occupied their positions on account of birth rather than merit. They were essentially civilian, although they might have military titles, perform guard duty, or even if the occasion warranted go to the provinces to wage war. They were also an urban class in a time when the only city was the capital. When some of their number left the city to become territorial magnates, they ceased to be kuge, though they did not cease to be aristocrats. In the Kamakura period there were two orders of aristocracy, the kuge and the buke, and the defining characteristics of the kuge, as before, were that they were not soldiers and that they lived in Kyoto. Then they were no longer a governing class, for the government was run by military men and Kyoto was not its seat.

The kuge and buke classes of the Kamakura period were not much different in their family origins. The same family names —Fujiwara, Minamoto, Taira, and the rest—are to be found in both orders of aristocracy. The almost racial distinction of the kuge came about later. The military lords had greater power, but they also ran greater risks. In the centuries of turmoil following the demise of the Hōjō Regency, almost all of the old families of provincial nobility lost out to new families that gained their territorial bases through prowess at arms. Among the great dynasties of provincial rulers of the Kamakura period, only one, the Shimazu, was still a great family in the Tokugawa period. Through all this time the kuge survived. Few or no outsiders infiltrated the caste. One of its marks of definition was imperial favor, ratified over and over again by titles of nobility, and that favor could not be won by force. Another of its marks was its pattern of behavior, that is, the practice of civilized skills that required leisure for their mastery and a code of manners so complex that no adult could learn it.

For official purposes the kuge called themselves by the surnames which their ancestors had had in the Heian period. They thereby perpetuated the fiction that they were a small number of joint or extended families, each made up of a main branch and several collaterals. In fact, clan membership as such counted for little or nothing in the family life of the kuge. The domiciliar and property units were nuclear families, each of which had a distinctive name. Early in the seventeenth century a number of new houses had been created from the collateral lines of old ones, but thereafter the number was very rarely added to. As with the imperial family, the younger sons of kuge were adopted to perpetuate dying houses, or they became priests.[41]

Of the 137 kuge houses at the time of the Meiji Restoration, 128 belonged to just five of the great medieval clans. The majority, 96, were of the Fujiwara clan, and there were 18 houses of Minamoto descent, six of Sugawara, five of Taira, and three of Kiyowara.[42] Of far greater importance than clan mem-

[41] An excellent brief description of the kuge caste is in *Ishin shi*, vol. 1, pp. 21–24. Another is Wada, *Kanshoku yōkai*, pp. 272–81.
[42] Ponsonby-Fane, *Kyoto*, pp. 367–72. Wada, *Kanshoku yōkai*, pp. 277–78.

bership was the stratification of the houses into six ranks which determined the title or office to which the house could attain and also bore a rough correspondence to its income.[43] The top stratum consisted of just five houses, the Konoe, Kujō, Nijō, Ichijō, and Takatsukasa. These were all descended from Fujiwara Tadamichi (1097–1164), and they were the senior branches of the Fujiwara clan. They were known collectively as *go-sekke*, "five regency houses," signifying that they alone could fill the offices of sesshō or kampaku. The formal consorts of the emperors were often from these families. The go-sekke were the richest of the kuge. One indicates the relative wealth of court families in this period by the evaluation of the lands set aside by the shogunate for their maintenance. The unit of value was the *koku*, actually a unit of volume (approximately five bushels) representing the amount of bulk rice which a piece of agricultural property was estimated to produce in one year. An attempt will be made below to explain concretely what a certain income expressed in these terms meant. Here we shall merely indicate the relative wealth of families of certain grades. The go-sekke derived their basic hereditary income from lands ranging in evaluation from 1500 to 2860 koku. Their primacy of prestige made other forms of income available to them through their marital or other associations with daimyo families. They had estates in the Gyoen that were much more elaborate than those of ordinary kuge, and in fact were comparable to the palaces of cadet branches of the imperial family. In other respects as well, these five families lived more like princes of the blood than they did like other members of their own class. Most of the other kuge houses were attached to one or another of the go-sekke in much the same way as the kuge class as a whole paid court to the emperor. The younger sons of sekke houses might become go-monzeki. More significantly, when the blood line of a sekke house died out, the adoptive heir was likely to come from the

[43] *Ishin shi*, vol. 1, pp. 21–27. Ponsonby-Fane, *Kyoto*, pp. 367–72.

imperial house itself rather than from some other kuge family.[44]

The second rank contained nine families known as *seika*. Their names were Imadegawa, Sanjō, Saionji, Tokudaiji, Kazan'in, Ōimikado, Koga, Hirohata, and Daigo. Only families of the top two grades could hold the top pseudo-military titles of the ritsu-ryō system, and the senior civilian offices of that system (Prime Minister, Minister of the Left, Minister of the Right) were also mostly reserved for them. The Imadegawa was the richest seika house, with 1350 koku. The others ranged from 300 to 700 koku.

The next three families were the third rank, *daijin-ke*. Their names were Ōgimachi-Sanjō, Sanjō-Nishi, and Nakanoin. The name of the class implies that these might become heads (daijin) of the executive ministries of the ritsu-ryō system. Their wealth ranged from 200 to 500 koku.

The remaining houses were grouped into three ranks, the *urin-ke, meika,* and *banka,* plus some special classes that were less numerous. These differed in respect to the highest ranks or offices each could receive and in other matters of precedence. Only a few were rich; the Hino, Hagiwara, and Fujinami had wealth of over 1000 koku. Six families had 700 to 1000 koku; eleven families had 300 to 700 koku; 23 families were in the 200 koku range; 44 were in the 100 koku range. The remaining 30-some families had lesser incomes, and most of them were granted no land at all for their maintenance but were paid stipends (okura-mai) of 30 koku of bulk rice annually from the lands of the imperial family.[45]

The stratification of the kuge houses enabled the court to assign ranks and offices in a more or less mechanical way. Since only the go-sekke could achieve the offices of sesshō and

---

[44] See Yabe, *Konoe Fumimaro,* p. 4 *et seq. Koji ruien,* vol. 13, p. 553.
[45] *Ishin shi,* vol. 1, pp. 26–27. See also Teishitsu Rinya-kyoku (comp.), *Go-ryōchi shikō,* pp. 248–59.

kampaku, inferior families did not vie for that distinction. Nevertheless, there were always several persons at any one time whom the court could select to fill a certain office. It was apparently the practice to rotate the highest offices among a number of families, and the shogunate made use of the built-in flexibility of appointment procedures to ensure that the governance of the court would be by persons more or less amenable to Edo's control.

Offices and titles assumed by the kuge were of two classes. Most of them, including all those of the ritsu-ryō system, must be regarded as ornamental or ceremonial. A few other titles connoted real powers, though of course the powers were effective only within the Kyoto court. We need not be concerned here with the titles of purely ceremonial significance; they will be referred to in the section below dealing with the ritual life of the court. The other titles designated the officers who administered the internal affairs of the court and who intermediated with the outside world.[46]

The chief effective offices held by kuge were sesshō and kampaku. In this period the distinction between the two was only nominal. If one was filled the other was vacant, and the age of the emperor at any particular time determined which of the two was filled. The province of the sesshō-kampaku was everything that pertained to the emperor and the court. He advised the emperor on all things and relayed the latter's wishes to everyone else. Proximity to the sovereign gave him an advantage over everyone else in the kuge class, and he had other advantages that made him a more influential figure than the sovereign. For one thing, his physical freedom was greater, since he could travel outside the kuge quarter and have personal dealings with a comparatively broad segment of kuge and military society. Second, he was usually of mature years and of greater experience than the sovereign, who was most often an

[46] *Ishin shi*, vol. 1, pp. 24–25. See also Wada, *Kanshoku yōkai*.

adolescent or young man. Under normal circumstances there was only one member of the Kyoto court who could contest the sesshō-kampaku's domination over it. This was the abdicated sovereign, but he too lived in great seclusion and was prevented by court etiquette from having the broad personal associations that would allow him to assert himself in the court at large.[47]

The sesshō-kampaku's power was limited by the procedure—from custom, habit, unwritten constitution, or call it what you will—that his term in office be limited to a certain number of years. After he had resigned, he continued to be an imperial adviser on all matters for which the joint advice of the senior kuge was needed. In fact the heads of the five sekke houses were always figures of real influence in the court, whether or not they had ever been sesshō or kampaku.

A second permanent and central office of the court that had important administrative powers was that of *gisō*, the "memorializing officers." There were four or five of these at any one time, and they were selected from families of seika, urin-ke, and meika ranks. They were charged with the preparation of memorials to the throne and the communication of the throne's response to the court. These duties made the gisō a bureau for the drafting of legislation to be acted upon by the sovereign and the sesshō-kampaku.[48]

One other kuge office was of the first rank of importance, the *buke densō*, "officers for transmitting memorials from the military houses." Two officials held this title simultaneously, and they were usually from families with high rank and income. As the title indicates, the buke densō were the kuge officials charged with conducting relations with the institutions of the shogunate. They were the counterparts on the courtier side of the *shoshidai*, who was the shogunal deputy in Kyoto. The

[47] *Ibid.*, pp. 29–33. A list of the sesshō and kampaku with their dates of office appears in *Dokushi biyō*, pp. 152–253.
[48] Wada, *Kanshoku yōkai*, pp. 270–71.

customary route by which information or commands were circulated from Edo to Kyoto and back to Edo again was as follows. The Shogunal Council of Elders (Rōjū) sent the communication to the shoshidai, the shoshidai relayed it to the buke denso, and the buke denso to the kampaku. When the kampaku had solicited the emperor's opinion, the gisō confirmed it. An answer then proceeded from the kampaku to the buke densō to the shoshidai to the rōjū.⁴⁹

Other offices had responsibilities of more particular relevance. The *shokuji-kata* ("personnel officers") and *shitsuji-shū* ("stewards") handled administrative details concerning such matters as court ceremonial and official appointments.⁵⁰ Other kuge were attendants or functionaries in the palaces of the abdicated sovereign, the consorts, and the imperial children. Still others were attached to the cadet branches of the imperial family or to the Go-monzeki.⁵¹

The official life of the kuge consisted of the governance of its own tiny community of some hundreds of individuals, plus court ceremonials. Much leisure time was left over, and the manner in which they whiled it away has an important bearing on the role of the caste in Tokugawa society.

Many of the families regarded themselves as hereditary custodians of the various arts and pastimes that had given the court of their Heian period ancestors its stamp of rare aesthetic refinement. Two families specialized in Japanese ceremonial football (kemari). Others learned to play various musical instruments, the *shō*, *biwa*, and *wagon*, or to perform traditional dances, thereby preserving from extinction the arts of *gagaku* and *bugaku*, the classical music and dance of ancient Japan. Several families were specialists in waka, the classical Japanese verse

⁴⁹ *Ibid.*, pp. 269–70.
⁵⁰ *Ishin shi*, vol. 1, pp. 24–25.
⁵¹ *Ibid.*

form, and others in calligraphy, flower arrangement, wrestling (sumō), and boxing.[52]

Other house specializations lay in the field of scholarship and writing. Particular subjects of study included Shinto lore, Buddhism, Confucian classics, Chinese portent theory and calendration, and Chinese and Japanese history. The kuge class preserved the records of its own past greatness and that of the imperial institution, as in the standard history of the Heian palace, *Daidairi zukōshō*, compiled as a family specialty by a member of the Uramatsu family.

The specialties of some families were akin to hereditary priesthoods. The Fujinami family maintained the office of *Jingi daifuku*, charged with communicating between the imperial court and the Great Shrines at Ise. The Great Yoshida, or Urabe, family resided outside the kuge quarter near the Yoshida Shrine. They were hereditary chief priests of the Ise Shrines and preservers of the teachings known as Yoshida Shinto.[53]

The kuge were not only preservers and practitioners of the traditional arts and disciplines; they were also teachers of them. Their students might be other kuge, members of the imperial family, members of daimyo families, samurai, or Kyoto townspeople. The motives for which a courtier transmitted his art to outsiders were usually economic, for this was one means of supplementing the fixed stipendiary incomes that was not demeaning.[54] One side of the exchange was monetary, but the other was the dissemination of a priceless cultural treasure. In 1600 the bushi were not a refined, or even a universally literate class. The kuge, with certain Buddhist priests, were not only the cultural pattern-setters for the country; they were virtually its only cultured people. With peace the bushi too felt the need

[52] *Ishin shi*, vol. 1, pp. 25–26. See also Ponsonby-Fane, *Kyoto*, pp. 367–72. Wada, *Kanshoku yōkai*, p. 279.

[53] *Seishi kakei dai-jiten*, vol. 3, pp. 6487–88.

[54] Tanaka, *Tennō no kenkyū*, pp. 24–26.

for the marks of civilization, and they sought them in Kyoto. The diffusion went on, from the daimyos to their samurai retainers, from the bushi to rich townsmen, and from the great cities to the remote provinces. It still goes on, and when a troupe of court musicians performs under the auspices of the New York City Ballet, or when a Japanese lady gives lessons in flower arrangement to housewives in a New York City department store, they increase the debt which the modern world owes to the Kyoto aristocracy of the Tokugawa period.

The enormous prestige which the culture of the Kyoto court held cannot be overemphasized. Even today the dialect of Kyoto conveys to Japanese a sense of elegance that the standard language of Tokyo cannot equal. This present survival is the merest token of the graciousness with which society, especially bushi society, invested the speech, the arts, the learning, and the manners of the kuge. No better evidence of this exists than the employment of kuge both by the shogunate and by the feudal domains (*han*) as trusted advisers on the finer things of life. The Shogun Ienobu (r. 1709–12) brought the former kampaku Konoe Motohiro (1648–1722) to Edo to lecture on the *Nihon shoki*, the *Tale of Genji*, and court ceremonial and etiquette. The Shogun was spurred by two considerations. His Confucian adviser Arai Hakuseki, who was himself a man of unusual cultural attainments, recommended closer relations with the Kyoto court as a means of improving the tone of the shogunal palace. The choice of Konoe was probably dictated by the fact that he was the Shogun's friend and father-in-law.[55]

The Tokugawa family had a tradition of arranged marriages with kuge ladies, and this again indicates that Japan's ruling family sought to heighten its prestige by association with Kyoto. Of the fifteen Tokugawa shoguns, five took their first consorts, or principal wives, from kuge families. The consorts of seven

[55] Tsuji, *Nihon bunka-shi*, vol. 5, pp. 236–39. Kurita, *Arai Hakuseki no bunji seiji*, pp. 581ff.

others were imperial princesses.[56] What dignified the shogunal family was likely to do still more for a daimyo's. The shogunate attempted to forbid contacts of a marital or even social kind between kuge and bushi other than those of the Tokugawa family, but the interdiction was not really effective after the first few years of the Tokugawa period. Only a few of the greatest daimyo families—Shimazu, Mōri, Ikeda, and a few others—commanded sufficient prestige of their own to make them attractive employers or spouses of the kuge, but these families made the most of their opportunities.[57]

References have been made above to various ways by which the kuge supplemented their official incomes. We shall conclude this section with some general remarks on the economic condition of the kuge. Japanese historians have made much of the poverty of the class, and they have left the impression that economic debasement was at the root of the dissident movements among the kuge in the last years of Tokugawa rule. We reserve for a later chapter the examination of the validity of this assertion, treating here only the question of what the poverty or wealth of the kuge amounted to.

If we considered the official base incomes alone, our first conclusion would be that the richest kuge, the house of Konoe (2,860 koku), was much less well off than the poorest of the 270 or so daimyos of the bushi class, and in fact considerably poorer than many samurai who were not of daimyo rank. A daimyo, according to one permissible definition, was a feudal person with a fief of more than 10,000 koku, who was not the retainer of another daimyo. The largest han had samurai retainers whose fiefs were actually larger than those of the poorest daimyos. In the Chōshū domain, for example, there were eight families of Elders (the highest class of samurai retainers in the

---

[56] *Dokushi biyō*, pp. 473–74.

[57] For genealogies of daimyo families (through the eighteenth century) showing marital connections see *Kansei chōshū sho-kafu*.

han) with fiefs ranging from 16,000 to 5,000 koku. In the same han there were 61 families with fiefs of from 5,000 to 250 koku, and 661 families in all with more than 100 koku. Of a total of 5,675 samurai families in the domain, 1,674, or nearly one-third, had fiefs or stipends of over 40 koku.[58] As we have seen, just nine of the kuge had incomes of more than 1,000 koku; fewer than half had 200 or more; nearly 30 houses subsisted at about the 30 koku level.

So stated, the figures are highly misleading. The fief of a daimyo, which after all went to support a territorial government, should not be compared with the income of a kuge any more than the city budget of Los Angeles should be compared with the income of a movie star. The same qualification applies to the fiefs of the highest ranking samurai retainers, for these too had to support establishments that did real administrative work. In other words, the main reason that the kuge incomes were incommensurable with the largest bushi fiefs stemmed from the fact that the bushi were a governing class and the kuge were not. Only if we ignore the "richest" bushi can we find a level of samurai income that may meaningfully be compared with that of the kuge. If we do this, we see that the richest of the kuge had base incomes which alone would have enabled them to live like very rich samurai even if the base incomes had not been supplemented by other means. Furthermore, the bottom level of kuge society, the 30 or so families with less than 100 koku, were still rich enough to qualify among the better-off families of the samurai class. This is not to deny that the kuge were poor. There can be no absolute standards for things of this kind. Everyone who believes that he deserves more sustenance than he gets is poor in a sense. The kuge were poor by that definition, for they were convinced along with the rest of Japanese society that they were the loftiest social stratum in the country. The most telling mark of their poverty was that they felt constrained

[58] From Craig, *Chōshū in the Meiji Restoration*, pp. 101–2.

to find other sources of income than that which the court provided them.

It is impossible to know what the real increment from outside sources was. Part of it was in the form of gifts from the shogunate or other military houses, and the value of these is difficult to convert into similar terms with the official stipendiary emoluments.[59] The income derived from work is an even more shadowy subject, primarily one assumes because the very idea of working for pay was shameful to the kuge.[60] The evidence suggests that the richest houses sometimes stood the chance of adding considerably to their incomes in the form of dowries or other gifts but that such occasions were irregular. The poorest families—those that really went to work in order to enlarge their incomes—must have got much less for their trouble, but the supplementary income was no doubt more dependable.

The palace community included another hereditary caste beside the kuge. These were the *jige*, described as inferior "officials," but actually retainers or servants. New families were sometimes added to this group, which at the time of its greatest number totaled about 460 households.[61]

There was still another group residing in Kyoto who had an important bearing on the workings of the imperial institution. This was the office of the *Shoshidai*, or Shogunal deputy, and the various other offices through which the Tokugawa government oversaw the affairs of the city and the court.

Kyoto and the surrounding countryside were in that portion of Japan known as the *tenryō*, the territory governed directly by the shogunate rather than by daimyos. The shogunal officer in charge of the ordinary affairs pertaining to the governance of the city was known as *Kyōto machi bugyō*, "city administrator," or "mayor." He was always a shogunal vassal of less than daimyo

[59] See Tanaka, *Tennō no kenkyū*, pp. 14–16.
[60] *Ishin shi*, vol. 1, pp. 26–28.
[61] *Nihon hyakka dai-jiten*, 1926 ed., sub "Jige." *Ishin shi*, vol. 1, pp. 23–24.

rank, that is, a *hatamoto,* and he was subordinate to the *Rōjū,* or Shogunal Council of Elders.[62]

The shoshidai was an officer of far greater eminence in the shogunal administrative system. He was always a *fudai* or *shimpan* daimyo of intermediate rank.[63] In theory he was responsible directly to the shogun, but especially in later years the rōjū also supervised his duties. Those duties were of two kinds; he imposed whatever physical restraints were necessary from outside in order to maintain order in the courtier community, and he acted as the shogun's personal representative in all the latter's dealings with the court. From 1600 to 1868 there were 57 holders of the office, indicating an average term for each of about five years.[64]

The shoshidai resided in a palace, the Sembon *yashiki* (mansion), located in the western part of the city. Nearby was the main architectural symbol of shogunal authority in the capital, the Nijō Castle, which was the official Kyoto residence of the shogun. This place, which is one of the glories of the modern city, was mostly unoccupied in the Tokugawa period, as no shogun visited Kyoto between 1634 and 1863.[65]

· 5 ·

A routine of perpetually recurring rites and ceremonies filled the lives of the kinsei sovereigns. Some were Shinto practices dating in their original forms from prehistoric or early historic times. A greater number of them had in the beginning been patterned after the institutions of Han or T'ang China; these came into Japan before the Heian period. Numerous textbooks of ceremonial were used by the court in our period. The principal one was also the earliest, the *Engi-shiki* of 967.[66] That book de-

---

[62] Wada, *Kanshoku yōkai,* p. 332.　　[63] *Ibid.*
[64] Names and dates of office of the shoshidai appear in *Dokushi biyō,* pp. 226–53.
[65] *Koji ruien,* vol. 16, p. 557.　　[66] See above, pp. 34–35.

scribed the institutes of the Engi period (901–923), during which the secular authority of the imperial office had been briefly revived. It had been one of the throne's periods of temporal greatness, and by implication seemed also to represent a high point in the correctness of its ritual practices. Ever since the Heian period there had been a tendency that when the court was rich and the country at peace the ceremonies had also been enacted in a proper fashion, but in times of imperial neglect and national turmoil the rituals tended to be neglected.

The increasing disorder of the Muromachi period caused many of the lesser everyday procedures to fall into complete disuse, and even some of the more momentous ones, such as the ceremony of elevating an imperial son to the office of Crown Prince, came to be ignored. The physical surroundings of the Muromachi period emperors were not an appropriate setting for elaborate ceremonial, especially after the near ruin of the city following the Ōnin War. The ceremonies required the participation of many trained courtiers, and in that time of turmoil few had the leisure or the training to take part in them. Some ceremonies required expensive costumes and properties, and there was no money to provide them.

The reunification of Japan permitted the revival of the ancient court rituals.[67] Nobunaga had commenced the rebuilding of the palace; Hideyoshi continued it; and Ieyasu by 1614 had finished the work of fashioning in it a fitting stage for the ceremonial life of the court. One after another the old practices were restored. There was further elaboration of usages in every generation, and the maximum complexity was not reached until the closing years of the Tokugawa period. The ceremonial life of the Kyoto court has an important claim on our attention, for it comprised the whole of the official work of the emperor and the kuge.

Prior to all other ceremonies in the reign of an emperor were

67 See Kuroita, *Kokushi no kenkyū, kakusetsu,* vol. 2, pp. 318–19.

those of accession (*senso*) and enthronement (*sokui*). The first marked the actual beginning of the reign, and the second was a formal notification to the Shinto deities and the people that the accession had taken place. In very early Japan one ceremony fulfilled both functions, but long before 1600 the enthronement had become a separate ceremony which followed the accession by a longer or shorter period.[68]

There is a reluctance on the part of Japanese students of the institution to consider a man truly to have been sovereign unless he underwent both ceremonies. Yet, paradoxically, as soon as the enthronement had taken place, the man was recognized to have been emperor since his accession. The reasons for this paradox are not clear, but they seem to have been related to the idea of a two-level compact—with "Heaven" above and the people below—that pervades the theory behind the institution. A man was sovereign as soon as he entered into a certain relationship with that vague embodiment of the natural order known in Japanese thought as Heaven. At that time he became Heaven's token or exemplar in the world of men. The relationship was accomplished, more than just exemplified, with the accession ceremony. The second stage of the compact bound the people to a single sovereign, and through him to Heaven's order and morality. It was accomplished with the emperor's enthronement. Other men, including ministers and historians, waited until the enthronement to recognize the legitimacy which Heaven had already conferred in the accession.[69]

If the accession was regarded as Heaven's disposal, it was nevertheless admitted to be the result of man's proposal. Ideally the proposer should be the preceding sovereign, who by naming an heir left no doubt as to whom Heaven should select.

More frequently than not during the Tokugawa period a new

[68] *Koji ruien*, vol. 13, pp. 191–92.

[69] This and other theoretical aspects of the institution are discussed in the following chapter.

reign began with the abdication, not the death, of the preceding sovereign. In such cases there was a single ceremony for both abdication and accession, called *juzen*. Of the sixteen accessions between 1586 and 1867, eleven were of this kind. Abdication ensured that there would be no gap between reigns, a condition much commended by those who believed in the existence or desirability of a dynastic line that was literally unbroken. In the other cases, those in which a new reign commenced with the death of the predecessor, a short interregnum resulted. The longest of these for any kinsei emperor was 67 days between the death of Go-Kōmyō and the accession of Go-Sai, and the shortest six days between Momozono's death and Empress Go-Sakuramachi's accession.[70]

The accession of Go-Sai in 1654 was unusual in that the emperor had never been designated heir to the throne. Go-Kōmyō's death caught the court unawares, and there was no Crown Prince to succeed automatically. Fortunately, the abdicated sovereign Go-Mizunoo (Go-Kōmyō's and Go-Sai's father) was alive, and the appointment of a successor could be made on an appropriately high level within the imperial family.[71]

Go-Sakuramachi and Kōkaku succeeded under somewhat different circumstances. Neither was considered an automatic heir to the predecessor, for Go-Sakuramachi was a woman and Kōkaku was the nine-year-old child of a cadet branch of the family. In both cases a hasty decision regarding the succession was made by the senior kuge officials while the previous sovereign lay dying.[72] Kōmei and Meiji also succeeded on the deaths of their predecessors, but both had been named Crown Prince earlier.[73]

---

[70] See the table in *Teishitsu seido-shi*, vol. 3, pp. 79–80.
[71] *Zoku-shigushō*, in *Koji ruien*, vol. 15, p. 126.
[72] *Zoku-shigushō*, in *Koji ruien*, vol. 12, pp. 250–51; pp. 301–02. *Jūsanchō kibun*, in *ibid.*, p. 251. *Chion kyōki*, in *ibid.*, p. 301.
[73] Tokushige, *Kōmei Tennō go-jiseki-ki*, pp. 8–9. *Teishitsu seido-shi*, vol. 3, pp. 217–18.

It would have been appropriate for the accession ceremony to take place in the Clear Cool Hall (Seiryō-den), for it was related to the emperor's compact with the Sun Goddess. As we shall see, the juzen ceremony did take place there, but the other accessions—those that followed the death of the preceding sovereign—occurred in some other building of the palace. When used for this purpose, the other building was called *Seiryō-den-dai*, or "Substitute for the Clear Cool Hall." Contemporary comments explain that the real Clear Cool Hall was the place of the deceased sovereign and therefore, by implication, taboo for a time after his death.[74] This reminds one of the practice that existed before the Nara period, when there was no permanent capital. The entire palace and court were moved at the beginning of every reign in order to avoid the defilement that was associated with the previous emperor's death.

The accession ceremony consisted of three essential parts, the bestowal of two of the regalia, the jewel and sword, on the new sovereign, the token acceptance of the third, the mirror, by means of an act of worship by a courtier in front of the Place of Awe,[75] and the announcement to the court that the emperor had acceded. The preliminaries took place in the middle of the night, when the *naishi*, the ladies who guarded the regalia, brought the jewel and sword out of the Place of Awe in readiness for the presentation to the emperor.[76] Only one of the three genuine regalia, the jewel, figured in the ceremony, but replicas stood in place of the true sword, which was kept at the

[74] *Chion kyōki*, in *Koji ruien*, vol. 12, p. 231.

[75] The following description is abstracted from the accounts of various accessions in *Koji ruien*, vol. 12, pp. 226–35: *Oyudono no ue no nikki. Tadatoshi Sukune-ki. Chion kyōki. Sukeyo kyōki.* For a description in English of the ceremonies of accession and enthronement as they were performed in post-Meiji times see Holtom, *The Japanese Enthronement Ceremonies*, pp. 55–94.

[76] There were four women of this title at any one time. They were appointed from kuge families and served as personal attendants or servants to the emperor. Wada, *Kanshoku yōkai*, pp. 203–4.

Atsuta Shrine in Nagoya, and the true mirror, which was at the Ise Shrine.[77]

At about eight o'clock in the morning the main ceremony began with the gathering of the leading kuge officials in the courtyard south of the Seiryō-den-dai. The jewel and sword were now guarded by pseudo-soldiers, that is, kuge who bore the empty titles of military command from the ritsu-ryō system of court titles. A procession took place from the courtyard inward toward the Seiryō-den-dai. "Military" guards headed it, followed by others who bore the regalia. Next came the kampaku and after him a number of other "officers of state." The procession halted before the southern stairs of the building. Major Captains of the Left and Right Headquarters of Inner Palace Guards stood by the steps at either side. The kampaku and the bearers of the regalia yielded their treasures to the naishi, who took them into the inmost chamber of the building, which served as a substitute for the yoru-no-ma of the Seiryō-den, which in turn was the symbolic "sleeping quarters" of the emperor. Here the emperor received the regalia.

Soon thereafter the emperor came forward from the yoru-no-ma into the hiru-no-ma, his "daytime quarters." There he received the kampaku and customarily "reappointed" him to his office. The kampaku then retired to the steps outside, where he made various announcements for the emperor, including the rescript of accession.

Other parts of the ceremony involved the above-mentioned obeisance to the replica mirror before the Place of Awe, acts signifying the acknowledgement by the kuge officials of the emperor's accession, and the consumption of ceremonial food and drink by the emperor.

The enthronement ceremony was of a more public character.

[77] On the transmission and location of the true regalia and the replicas see Ponsonby-Fane, "The Imperial Family and Shinto," pp. 59–72; 120–53. Holtom, *Japanese Enthronement Ceremonies*, pp. 1–54.

There was no fixed time for it, but it always took place within a year or two after the accession. The imperial court decided the exact date on the basis of portent theory and the convenience of those who participated.[78]

Shogunal officials were involved in several peripheral functions at the time of the enthronement, but they do not appear to have taken part in the ceremony itself. Edo's part in the festivities was usually played by the shoshidai, though on a few occasions higher officials came from the shogunal capital to participate. The celebrants in Kyoto at the time of Empress Meishō's enthronement in 1630 included Sakai Tadayo and Doi Toshikatsu, who as *tairō*, or chief councillors, were the highest advisers to the Shogun Iemitsu. At the time of the enthronement of Go-Mizunoo in 1611, the abdicated shogun Ieyasu was present.[79]

The shogunate's participation in the affair took the form of the bestowal of gifts on the emperor, the abdicated sovereign, and other members of the imperial family by the shogun or by heads of collateral branches of his family.[80] This had a certain importance to the economic life of the court, and it also shows the public character of the ceremony. It was a notification to the world outside the Kyoto court, whereas the accession had served the purpose of private attestation to the inner circle of the court that the sovereign's reign had commenced. As with other ceremonies touching on the compact between the sovereign and his more remote subjects, the role of the subjects was taken by rulers of the military government.

The enthronement ceremony took place in the Shishin-den ("Purple Dragon Hall"). All of its essential parts were of the nature of "announcements" of the reign to the various important figures or groups that made up the emperor's world. Prior

---

[78] *Gyokkai*, in *Koji ruien*, vol. 12, p. 194.
[79] *Gyokuro-sō, kan* 8, in *ibid.*, p. 434. *Tokugawa jikki*, vol. 38, p. 544.
[80] *Gyokuro-sō, kan* 8, in *Koji ruien*, vol. 12, p. 434. *Tokugawa jikki*, vol. 40, p. 335. *Ibid.*, vol. 42, p. 596.

to the ceremony proper specially commissioned kuge messengers were dispatched to the Ise Shrine with a *hōhei,* a slip of paper symbolizing the new emperor's report to the Sun Goddess. Other messengers were sent with similar reports to the Kashiwabara Shrine (the tomb of the first emperor, Jimmu) and other imperial tombs. At the ceremony itself the leading officials assembled in the forecourt of the Shishin-den facing a throne which had been specially erected inside the building for this occasion. The emperor entered from the Seiryō-den to take his place on the throne. In the course of the ceremony two "archivists" (officials of the Bureau of Books and Drawings) burned incense in a ceremonial oven placed in the courtyard. The smoke rising to Heaven symbolized the submission of a report of the new reign to the Shinto pantheon. Later a specially commissioned official read the emperor's rescript of enthronement.

It is interesting to conjecture the exact status which contemporary theory accorded to an emperor who had undergone an accession ceremony but had not been enthroned. Definite statements are impossible, as no complete formulation of the case exists. Nevertheless, the evidence of events suggests that a sovereign's powers were in some sense limited until his enthronement had confirmed his credentials in the eyes of the ancestors, the gods, and his subjects. The Emperor Nakamikado acceded upon the abdication of his father, Higashiyama, in 1709. Two days later, more than a year before Nakamikado's enthronement, a rescript was issued in his name raising Higashiyama to the position of *Dajō-tennō.* While the bestowal of the title occasioned no special comment in contemporary documents, it has been remarked on by Meiji writers as a unique reversal of the normal order, according to which an act of that sort was performed by emperors who had already been enthroned.[81] The evidence is inconclusive, for the case definitely proves that a sovereign had the authority to perform the act even before his

[81] *Koji ruien,* vol. 12, p. 448.

enthronement. On the other side one has only an unproved suggestion that there was something irregular about it.

History records earlier instances in which sovereigns named their heirs before being enthroned, and in a few cases they even abdicated without an enthronement ceremony ever taking place.[82] There were no cases of these kinds during the Tokugawa period. In sum, it may be surmised, but without total conviction, that an emperor was not regarded as having come into his full authority until he had been enthroned.

There was a third ceremony that was supposed to take place near the beginning of a new reign. This was the *Daijō-sai*, or Great New Food Festival.[83] It was inaugurated in the reign of the Emperor Temmu, in 673. There were a few brief reigns of pre-Muromachi times when it was not performed, and it went out of practice altogether from the reign of Go-Kashiwabara (acceded 1500) until the revival in 1687 (Higashiyama's reign). It was, and still is, always performed in the eleventh civil month. The fact that that now corresponds exactly with Gregorian November may obscure part of the original significance of the festival. The eleventh civil month of the lunar calendar is the month of the Winter Solstice, and the ceremony was one of countless festivals in countless cultures of the Northern Hemisphere signifying the return of the sun from its southern journey. The calendrical placement of the festival suggests spring, just as its name suggests the autumn harvest. It was therefore preeminently the symbol of the agricultural year and of the economic foundations of Japanese society. As with so much of the imperial symbolism, it also suggests the processes of human

[82] *Ibid.*, pp. 448–50.
[83] The following is abstracted from accounts of various *Daijō-sai* ceremonies in *Koji ruien*, vol. 6, pp. 943–51, as follows: *Suezure Sukune-ki. Daijō-kai zatsuji-roku. Tamesue-ki. Yukiatsu-ki. Bunsei-do Daijō-kai chōshin bukki. Mibu keki. Sukeyo kyōki.* Holtom describes the ceremony as it has been performed in the twentieth century in *Japanese Enthronement Ceremonies*, pp. 95–140.

generation and therefore links the emperor with every family and with the perpetuation of human society.

During those years of the Tokugawa period in which the Great New Food Festival was performed, it took place in the forecourt of the Shishin-den.[84] A special enclosure was constructed in the court and two small buildings were placed inside it at the east and west. The two were identical and identical ceremonies took place within them. They were called *yuki-den* and *suki-den* respectively. The etymologies are obscure, but an old tradition has it that *yuki* means "consecrated and purified" and *suki* "secondary." Modern scholars have glossed this interpretation by saying that, whereas both pavilions were consecrated and purified, the yuki-den was the place of the first part of the ceremony and therefore the suki-den was at least in a temporal sense "secondary."[85]

Each pavilion contained an outer and an inner chamber. The inner room of each was fitted out with identical implements and properties of several kinds. One of the most conspicuous was the *shinza*, or "god's bed," a couch of ancient design equipped with several talismanic articles. The shinza did not figure in the ceremony itself, and its significance is a mystery. Holtom notes the presence among the attached articles of a woman's comb and suggests that the bed may represent the presence of the Sun Goddess.[86] No one so far as I know has suggested that the shinza may signify a marriage bed.

Preparatory to the ceremony rice was procured from specially designated fields in two different provinces. One province provided the yuki rice and the other that for the suki. In the Tokugawa period the two provinces were always Ōmi and Tamba, respectively. The ceremony commenced late in the

[84] *Koji ruien,* vol. 6, pp. 1002ff.
[85] Holtom, *Japanese Enthronement Ceremonies,* pp. 117–18.
[86] *Ibid.,* pp. 122–24.

evening and lasted most of the night. Several courtiers participated in the preliminaries, which consisted of the preparation of the rice and rice wine and the procession of the emperor, the kampaku, and attendants into the outer chamber of the yukiden. Later the emperor went into the inner chamber, accompanied only by two court ladies selected for this purpose (uneme). The ladies brought the food and wine in to him, and he presented part of it to the gods by placing it on ceremonial tables. Then he performed the heart of the ceremony, which was to partake himself of the ceremonial food and drink. When the ceremony in the yuki-den was completed, the exact steps were repeated in the suki-den.

One very ingenious theory about the duplication of the ceremony in identical settings is that the two pavilions represent the palaces of the old and new sovereigns. If so, the progression from one to the other is one more indication that the essential meaning of the Daijō-sai is natural regeneration and historical continuity.[87]

The final ceremonial act of most kinsei sovereigns was abdication. At the heart of Japanese dynastic theory was the belief that the act of abdication had to be voluntary to be legitimate. The forced abdication of Go-Daigo in 1336 at the hands of the first Ashikaga Shogun was enshrined in the national memory, and with it the conviction that Go-Daigo had continued to reign as legitimate emperor until his death. Whatever restraints hedged the power of the emperor, the idea was fixed in Japanese thought about the institution that no other person had the right to deny a sovereign's identity.[88]

Though the evidence of theory bespeaks absolute freedom for an emperor to remain emperor, the evidence of facts contradicts it. It has already been noted that of ten imperial abdications between 1611 and 1840 two were admitted by contemporaries

[87] *Ibid.*, pp. 145–46.
[88] See Webb, *The Early Mito School*, pp. 209ff.

to be other than voluntary. The sovereigns in question were both children of Go-Mizunoo, first the young Empress Meishō, who was requested to abdicate in 1643, and Emperor Go-Sai, who was actually forced off his throne in 1663.

Both decisions seem to have been made jointly by the Kyoto court and the Edo bureaucracy. Kanzawa Tokō's *Okina-gusa*[89] describes Meishō's abdication as follows: "The Empress had reigned for thirteen years. Both the civil[90] and military lords thought it time for her to retire. Sakai Tadakatsu and Matsudaira Nobutsuna[91] went to Kyoto to discuss the matter, whereupon the Empress abdicated."[92]

Between the lines of this terse account one may perceive evidence of some tension of wills between the two capitals, but it is difficult to guess what issue was involved or what position each side took. *Yuge monogatari*[93] contributes the further explanation that the bad relations that led to Go-Mizunoo's abdication in 1629 continued through Meishō's reign and that the Shogun Iemitsu had conferred many times with Go-Mizunoo on his visits to Kyoto in order to recommend that Meishō abdicate. These sources suggest the following reading of the events.

1. The Edo court had been unhappy from the start about Go-Mizunoo's choice of Meishō as his successor, even though she enabled the Shogun Hidetada to fulfill his desire of becoming a sovereign's grandfather.
2. The campaign to remove her from the throne was initiated on the highest level of the Edo bureaucracy, as indicated by Iemitsu's personal consultation with Go-Mizunoo.

[89] In *Koji ruien*, vol. 12, pp. 560–61.
[90] Civil lords: officers of the Kyoto court.
[91] Sakai Tadakatsu (1587–1672) and Matsudaira Nobutsuna (1596–1662) were leading *fudai* daimyos in the court of the third Tokugawa shogun, Iemitsu. Sakai was tairō, "senior councillor," one of two officers next below the shogun in the shogunal official hierarchy, and Matsudaira was a *rōjū*, "elder."
[92] *Kan* 9, in *Koji ruien*, vol. 12, pp. 560–61.
[93] In *Koji ruien*, vol. 12, pp. 560–64.

3. Even within the Kyoto court there was opposition to Meishō, probably due to continuing anti-feminist prejudice.

4. The Kyoto court nevertheless resented greatly the arrogation by the shogunate of a power which was deemed to be the inalienable property of the throne.

5. The most efficient means by which the court could assert its rights was to delay matters and then, at a certain time, to decide on abdication as though it were a free and spontaneous act.

6. The twenty-year-old girl who was at the center of the dispute did as she was told.[94]

In the case of Go-Sai's abdication, *Okina-gusa* describes the ill omens that accompanied the Emperor's reign, then adds: "Many thought that the Emperor ought to abdicate. In 1662 there were numerous earthquakes in the capital, continuing for months. Everyone rumored it about that it was on account of a lack of imperial virtue. . . . Even the military lords concluded that he should abdicate."[95]

These events seem to disprove utterly the contention that a reigning sovereign was free to abdicate or not to abdicate. However, when one compares them with the case of Go-Daigo, cited frequently as positive evidence, some real differences appear. Unlike Go-Daigo, neither of the kinsei sovereigns is known to have offered the slightest resistance to the suggestion that he abdicate. In that sense the acts themselves may be called "voluntary." Presumably an emperor independent enough in mind to have refused would have continued to reign whatever his mentors of the civil or military aristocracy might have wanted him to do.

A power of the reverse nature was the freedom to abdicate

[94] See also the discussion in Ponsonby-Fane, "Abdication in Japan," p. 193.

[95] *Koji ruien*, vol. 12, pp. 564–65. Ponsonby-Fane, "Abdication in Japan," pp. 193–94. See also Tanaka, *Tennō no kenkyū*, pp. 33–34.

against the wishes of the Kyoto or Edo ministers. That such power existed is attested by another seventeenth century abdication, that of Go-Mizunoo in 1629. The irregularity on that occasion, from the standpoint of court tradition, was the fact that neither of his sons had survived infancy and hence there was no possible successor among his children other than his daughter. In a private audience with two leading retainers of the Nakamikado and Ano families, the Emperor signified his intention of abdicating. Two others, Saionji and Kazan, were consulted and agreed. When the abdication took place, the Edo government and even the majority of the Kyoto court were taken by surprise. Yet despite the shogunate's disapproval, it was forced to regard the abdication as legitimate.[96]

The other instances of imperial abdication in the period seem to be in accordance with earlier precedents and with the procedures informally laid down by the Tokugawa government. Higashiyama (1709), Nakamikado (1735), and Sakuramachi (1747) abdicated because they were ill and did not expect to live much longer.[97] They thereby ensured a transfer of sovereignty without any interregnum. The abdications of Go-Yōzei (1611), Reigen (1687), Go-Sakuramachi (1770), and Kōkaku (1817) were of a still more ordinary sort. All of them had acceded as children or adolescents, served terms regarded as properly long, reached ages at which their desire for freedom might carry weight with their associates, then disburdened themselves of the ritual onus.

The abdication ceremony was similar in most essentials to the accession ceremony as described above except that the accession proper took place in the Seiryō-den and the relinquishment of his position by the old emperor in his new palace.[98] Twin

---

[96] *Tokiyoshi kyōki*, in *Koji ruien*, vol. 12, pp. 537–38.
[97] Ponsonby-Fane, "Abdication in Japan," pp. 194–95.
[98] Based on *Kan'ei-ki*, in *Koji ruien*, vol. 12, pp. 466–67; 488–89. *Go-shōdan-ki*, in *ibid*., pp. 494–97.

rescripts, of abdication and accession, were announced at this ceremony.

One specimen of an imperial rescript of abdication, that of Go-Yōzei in 1611, will illustrate the chief characteristics of the arcane, uninformative rescript form as it was used in the Tokugawa period.

Herewith the rescript spoken by the god manifest and heavenly sun sovereign of the great country of many islands. Let it be heard by the imperial and non-imperial princes, the ministers and officials, and all the people in the land. Though of mean qualities, we received the heavenly sun succession and have occupied the throne for many years. Being without virtue we feel sorrowfully that we can no longer endure this estate. We have resolved to resign the imperial office. In the heart of one who yields correct demeanor is revealed; in the heart of one who feels compassion benevolence is made manifest. The proper conduct of affairs of state is in accordance with law. Thus we have chosen an auspicious day and season, and today we have selected the Imperial Prince Masahito to be Crown Prince. We bestow on him the heavenly sun succession and the affairs of the high throne. We desire that the government of all the provinces of the land be performed in peace and order. May all display benevolence and may there be good will everywhere. May everyone come to the aid of the sovereign's court. May everyone hear the sovereign's command.[99]

Between the accession and the abdication an emperor participated in hundreds of other ceremonies. Some were daily and some monthly, but the most important were annual. The Japanese term for the calendar of court ceremonials is *nenjū gyōji*. The same term is used for written works enumerating or describing the various annual ceremonies. Several contemporary writers in and out of the court provided works of this kind that dealt with the Tokugawa period, and these enable us to generalize on the character of the ceremonial life of the court.[100]

[99] *Shōchoku-shū* (in *Ressei zenshū*), vol. 3, p. 34.
[100] *Go-Mizunoo-in nenjū gyōji*, in *Shiseki shūran*, vol. 27, pp. 191–239. *Kaei nenjū gyōji*, in *Kojitsu sōsho*, vol. 3, pp. 345–489.

Not only the individual ceremonies of the calendar but also the larger pattern of the nenjū gyōji itself was symbolic. The Chinese and Japanese civil calendar of premodern times was an almost perfect symbol of human society in the world of nature.[101] The natural solar year from one Winter Solstice to the next symbolized nature. Just as the solar year provided the pattern to which the activities of an agricultural society must conform, nature in a larger sense was the orderly arbiter of human morality. The civil calendar symbolized human society. For the sake of efficiency it deviated considerably from the solar year. It was an artifice like all human institutions. The fixed points of the civil year did not correspond to fixed points in the solar year, because the civil year contained whole numbers (twelve or thirteen) of months, each of which was the period of the moon's cycle from new moon to new moon. Yet the naming of the fixed points of the civil year was the means of restoring some correspondence with the year of nature. The lunation that included the Winter Solstice was always the eleventh month of the civil calendar. Other civil months were designated according to fixed zodiacal points of the solar year. About one civil month out of 30 contained none of the twelve principal zodiacal points. Such a month was not given a proper number but was designated as intercalary. Intercalation was the natural symbol of all those adjustments and rectifications which society must make from time to time in all its expedient institutions in order to bring them back into conformity with nature's regularity.

Most of the annual ceremonies of the imperial court were scheduled for fixed dates of the civil year. A few others took place at fixed times in the solar year. As might be expected, those fixed at solar dates were of agricultural significance, and those fixed at civil dates were more particularly associated with the affairs of a family or of the polity.

[101] For a description of the old Japanese lunar calendar see Webb, *Research in Japanese Sources: A Guide*, pp. 15–20.

A preponderance of the annual rites were in the early part of the year, particularly at New Year's. One modern tabulation of annual ceremonies of the court in the Tokugawa period lists 181 separate events, of which 71 occurred in the first civil month.[102] The New Year's rites commenced early the morning of the first day of the year with the Worship of the Four Directions (Shihō-hai) in the courtyard east of the Seiryō-den.[103] This was a formal act of obeisance to nature itself, as symbolized in the four directions to which prayers were directed, and to the imperial ancestors, to whose tombs an additional prayer was offered. It was also regarded as the central propitiatory rite of the New Year, for there were prayers against disorders and disasters. The Morning Felicitation (Chōga), which followed the Worship of the Four Directions, was the formal greeting by the emperor and empress to the officials of their court.[104] It took place in the main hall of the Shishin-den. The Lesser Morning Worship (Kochōhai) was the token obeisance by the court to the emperor.[105] It took place in the Seiryō-den, which was too small to accommodate all the officials, so only the main ones attended. The Feast of the First Day (Ganjitsu Sechie) was performed in the Seiryō-den in the presence of the regalia.[106] This was like a communion feast, for the emperor and his leading ministers partook of food and drink together.

There were many other rituals of the New Year's season. In some of them the imperial princes, the go-sekke, the other kuge, and various palace officials paid formal calls on the emperor, much as the members of any ordinary Japanese family pay social calls on one another during the New Year's. Other ceremonies were in commemoration of aesthetic or cultural pastimes. There were poetry reading festivals, ceremonies to witness the emperor's first handwriting of the year, dances by the imperial

[102] Dokushi biyō, pp. 657–712.
[103] Kaei nenjū gyōji, in Koji ruien, vol. 1, pp. 717–18.
[104] Koji ruien, vol. 1, pp. 730–32.   [105] Ibid., pp. 762–63.
[106] Ibid., pp. 787–88.

musicians, and some others. Other New Year's ceremonies were acts of Buddhist or Shinto ritual, usually in the form of readings of Buddhist texts or the token worship of the great national shrines of the Shinto religion.[107] The calendar of events proceeded through the year, but most of its latter pages were empty. Even this feature of the nenjū gyōji may have symbolic importance. The calendars of annual administrative events of the Chinese court show a similar preponderance of events in the early days of the year, the early days of a month, and the first few months of the year. This was a reflection of the feeling that a well-run government settled its affairs early and then sat back serenely to watch events take their natural course.[108] There was nothing in the Kyoto court ritual that had real administrative importance. Furthermore, there was next to nothing that even symbolized political affairs in any obvious way. Perhaps the spacing of events in the nenjū gyōji was the last vestige of the administrative character that the court calendars of China and early Japan had had. At least this is one more illustration that this institution, which was not a government, was purposely dressed out to look like a government.

Some of the emperor's acts of official business were of irregular occurrence and do not appear in the nenjū gyōji. One group, the bestowal of honors and titles of office, may be disposed of briefly. The *shokuji-kata* and *shitsuji-shū* handled the paper work involved in the conferral of all patents issued by the court, but of course the actual decisions as to who should be honored or appointed were made by others. Processes of appointment to kuge offices are not well documented, but one may guess that they were decided upon at the highest level of kuge society or else by kuge, the abdicated sovereign, and the emperor (if adult)

[107] *Kaei nenjū gyōji, passim.*
[108] Based on a private communication from Mr. Hans Bielenstein regarding his researches on administrative usages of early China.

in concert.[109] Honors and titles given to bushi were decided upon by the Edo bureaucracy. The emperor's essential part in the conferral of a title was to affix his personal signet on the document by which the appointment was effected.[110]

The other matter of practical importance to the nation with which the imperial court was directly involved was the promulgation of the civil calendar. This involved the publication every year of an edict stating whether the civil months were to be 29 or 30 days and whether there was to be an intercalary month or not. These matters required no particular decisions, as they were normally predetermined by mathematical formulas that were widely known. The yearly imperial edict merely gave them legal force.[111] Two other matters pertaining to the calendar sometimes necessitated governmental decisions. The first was *kaigen*, the decision to start a new calendrical era (nengō). Changes of era were frequent in the Tokugawa period. The longest eras of the period lasted only twenty years. A decision to change the era name might be made for a number of reasons. The most common were to commemorate a new imperial reign, to commemorate the auspicious years (the 58th and the first) of the 60-year cycle, and to signalize some felicitous or disastrous event.[112]

A less frequent matter for decision was calendar correction. If the formulas by which the calendar was determined were found to be untrue to the motions of the heavenly bodies, the government thought it necessary to revise them. Four times in the Tokugawa period there were such corrections, in 1684, 1754, 1797, and 1842.[113] Calendar revision in China had been a very

[109] *Ishin shi*, vol. 1, pp. 24–25. Ishii, *Tennō*, pp. 158–62.

[110] Descriptions from numerous contemporary sources of the emperor's part in naming shoguns are in *Koji ruien*, vol. 16, pp. 588ff.

[111] The Tsuchimikado were a kuge house with the family specialty of recording calendrical matters, but in the Edo period they received the yearly calendars from officials in Edo and had nothing to do with the work of calculating them. *Koji ruien*, vol. 32, p. 308.

[112] Morimoto, *Nihon nengō taikan*, pp. 7–13.

[113] Naimu-shō (comp.), *Sansei sōran*, pp. 381ff.

serious matter, and it had been accomplished by means of elaborate astronomical observation and mathematical calculation. It was usually much easier in Japan, for the Japanese merely adopted the results of the work that had been done in China. In 1684, for instance, the Japanese simply imported a Chinese set of formulas that had been worked out by astronomers of the Yüan Dynasty and adopted in 1335.[114] The 1754 reform represented some work by Japanese scholars. That is, it was based in part on information which the Japanese learned independently from Western textbooks of astronomy.[115]

All of these matters were in theory the province of the imperial court, but in fact the shogunate interfered in various ways. The four corrections of the calendrical formulas were actually shogunal decisions, although they were ratified by imperial proclamations. A decision to change the era name was sometimes initiated by the Kyoto court, but the shogunate reserved the right of final approval.[116] In some instances Edo actually initiated the motion for kaigen. The Genna era (1615–24), which was the first to be proclaimed after the foundation of the Edo shogunate, is a case of this kind. The occasion for the change of era at that time was the destruction of Hideyori's forces at Osaka Castle. According to the seventeenth century *Kaigen monogatari*,[117] Ieyasu made the decision himself. He gave as his reasons that the rituals of state had fallen into neglect since the Ōnin War and that now the coming of peace again enabled them to be restored. The name Genna means "the peace of former times." It brought forth memories of T'ang China, for the same era name had been used in China from 806 to 811.[118]

Cycles of ceremonies, attestations of appointment, and calendrical affairs were the whole "national" business of the emperor

114 Araki, *Nihon rekigakushi gaisetsu*, pp. 136–43.
115 *Ibid.*, pp. 155–58.
116 Morimoto, *Nihon nengō taikan*, pp. 24–44.
117 In *Koji ruien*, vol. 1, p. 582.
118 Morimoto, *Nihon nengō taikan*, p. 270.

and his court. Governance of kuge society was another part of the court's work. The affair of the palace women in 1609 is indicative of the way in which punishments were handled. The Emperor Go-Mizunoo was personally concerned with the matter, so Edo left the matter up to him for decision. However, *he* referred the disposal of the case to his top kuge advisers. Under normal circumstances the emperor does not appear to have been especially involved with everyday questions of law and order among his courtiers.

The remainder of the emperors' time could be spent in recreations and amusements. What we can document of them seems earnest and sober. Emperors composed verse in the Chinese and Japanese languages. They practiced calligraphy. They studied Chinese and Japanese history and the Confucian classics. They read Japanese fiction. Even in these activities there was a tincture of duty, for the first article of the *Kuge sho-hatto* had enjoined emperors to study so that they might "illustrate the ancient Way and their rule achieve great peace."

The ceremonial life and recreation of the kinsei emperors took place almost entirely within the precincts of the Kindairi. The imprisonment of reigning sovereigns within that area was a cardinal feature of the system by which Japanese society—the shogunal government and the military caste—controlled the imperial institution. As such it will be discussed in greater detail below. The policy was unique to the Tokugawa period. Former emperors, though they were not noteworthy travelers by other than Japanese standards (they rarely left the capital and still less frequently left the Kinai region) nevertheless made frequent trips to other parts of the city or to its environs. So frequent were imperial progresses, in fact, that they occasioned no more than perfunctory mention by court historians.[119] The first

[119] Formal Chinese-style histories of Japan like *Dai Nihon shi*, *Dai Nihon yashi*, and *Zoku-shigushō* almost invariably devoted much attention to imperial acts and affairs, even those of no demonstrable importance to history. Imperial progresses (*gyōkō* or *miyuki*) were noted in them when-

kinsei emperor, Go-Yōzei, is recorded to have made two famous
visits abroad in the city, in 1588 and 1592. Both were to the
Juraku-dai, the city palace of Hideyoshi.[120] In 1626 Go-Mizunoo
was entertained for four days at the Nijō Castle.[121] The festivities were in honor of the promotion of the recently retired
shogun Hidetada, by the emperor's command, to the rank of
dajō daijin (Prime Minister), the highest civil title of state.
With Iemitsu's personal reign as shogun (1632), the long imprisonment of reigning sovereigns also began.[122] In 1863 it came
to an end, but the description of the emperor's trip in that year
to the Kamo Shrine to pray for the expulsion of the foreigners
from Japan belongs in a later chapter of this book.

· 6 ·

Closely related to the matter of what the emperors did is the
question of the controls which the effective government exercised over them. Much of the foregoing discussion attests to
the fact that the powers and freedom of the man who occupied
the imperial throne were minimal, and hence, conversely, that a
maximum of force was applied continuously to prevent him
from acting in ways other than were expected of him. The
means by which the force was shown were as benign as human
society permits. That is, neither physical force nor threats of

---

ever they were known. The rare progresses of the Hideyoshi and early
Tokugawa periods were described at book length. (See following note.)
Thereafter the record stops until 1863.

[120] *Juraku-dai gyōkō-ki*, in *Gunsho ruijū*, vol. 2, pp. 468–90. *Juraku-dai
ryōdo gyōkō-ki*, in *Zoku-Gunsho ruijū*, vol. 4 jō, pp. 102–03.

[121] *Kan'ei gyōkō-ki*, in *Koji ruien*, vol. 1, pp. 648–50.

[122] On a few occasions, fires required the emperor and his court to take
residence at temporary palaces in or near the city. For example, a fire of
1788 forced the Emperor Kōkaku to flee to the Shōgo-in, a temple in the
east of the city, where he resided for two years. Such movements, which
were not regarded as true imperial progresses and are therefore not treated
in the works cited above (note 119), are the only apparent exceptions to
the rule of total seclusion for emperors between the dates mentioned *Zoku
Tokugawa jikki*, vol. 1, (*Kokushi taikei*, vol. 48), pp. 58–60.

physical punishment were used. The training of imperial children bred in them habits of docility and rigidly patterned behavior. The removal to other agents in the court and government of all the effective means of decision accomplished the remaining restrictions on a sovereign's personal freedom to act.

In general, the restrictive forces diminished as distance from the throne—geographical or hierarchical—increased. One might even claim that the one nearly sufficient force of control was internal to the sovereigns themselves. Positively, it was their breeding and self-discipline, and negatively, their isolation from and ignorance of practical affairs. Leaving aside this intangible "force" for control, restrictions may be categorized as administered (1) within the Kyoto court itself, (2) by the office of the shoshidai, or (3) by the bureaucracy in Edo. For reasons of efficiency the government in Edo rarely interfered with the decisions of the shoshidai when those were sufficient to keep the emperor in check. Similarly, the office of the shoshidai customarily left to the court's own officials all possible decisions relating to the emperor's treatment and behavior—all those, that is, that sufficed to maintain control.

It is clear that when one speaks of the throne in Tokugawa times, one must make a sharp distinction between the powers of the emperor and the powers of the court. One must be especially on guard against falling into an error, fostered by the surface meaning of contemporary accounts of the matter, of speaking of "imperial decisions" where one means decisions made by the emperor's ministers inside the court. When imperial powers under the ritsu-ryō system had waned in the ninth and tenth centuries, the court had fallen heir to them. The slender authority that remained after the establishment of military government was kept by the court, not returned to the emperor. On the other hand, there had been a persistent legal fiction that the court's decisions emanated from the emperor. This was true even if the emperor was a child. As a consequence, contemporary commentators almost always described the acts of an emperor's subordinates within the court, not as having been delegated to them by the throne, but actually as having been performed by the sovereign.

The most striking restrictions on imperial freedom were imposed within the court. The court decided to have Meishō abdicate, and later it acquiesced in the deposition of Go-Sai. The court selected successors to Go-Kōmyō and Go-Momozono as they lay on their deathbeds. These were all instances in which the reigning sovereign was not allowed or not able to speak for himself. Under other circumstances the emperor might be considered a member of the court. In other words, he was one of a group whose collective power was far greater than that of any single member of it.

Restriction at the level of the shoshidai was not a matter of making ad hoc decisions but rather of continuously maintaining the physical walls and institutional barriers between the emperor and the outside world. The Kindairi had a wall, which was guarded by shogunal troops. The kuge quarter was also surrounded by a fence with guards. The ostensible purpose of all of this was to keep the kuge and the imperial family from bodily harm, but it also served the shogunate's basic aim of preventing the court from having the slightest influence over political policy.

When the court wished to take some action that was unprecedented or unusual, it notified the shoshidai, which referred the matter to Edo for decision. The power of the shogunate was brought into play only infrequently, but when it was, it was absolute. One of the most famous incidents in the later Tokugawa period of the exertion of the shogunate's will over the emperor occurred in 1790 and concerned the emperor Kōkaku's attempt to bestow the title of Dajō Tennō (Great Abdicated Sovereign) on his father, Prince Kan'in.[123] The father had never been emperor, and as a mere imperial prince he was outranked

---

[123] See the accounts in Tsuji, *Nihon bunka-shi*, vol. 5, pp. 318–28. Kuroita, *Kokushi no kenkyū, kakusetsu*, vol. 2, pp. 501–4.

by the high kuge officials of the court. The situation was anomalous, but not unprecedented. Emperors Go-Horikawa (r. 1221–32) and Go-Hanazono (r. 1428–64) had both had living fathers without imperial titles at the time the sons came to the throne. In both cases the title of dajō tennō was given to the fathers.[124]

The de facto head of the shogunal government in 1790 was Matsudaira Sadanobu, a man noted for his friendly relations with the Kyoto court and for his reverence for the emperor. Yet his response to the court's request in this case was unfriendly. A somewhat similar case had come up in the shogunal court just prior to this. This concerned the treatment to be accorded to Hitotsubashi Harunari, the father of the child Shogun Ienari (r. 1786–1837). A faction in the shogunate proposed that Harunari be given the honors customarily reserved for abdicated shoguns, but Sadanobu refused. The grounds for his refusal were phrased in abstruse Confucian language, but what it amounted to was this: that the young shogun had left the household of his birth at the time that he became the shogunal heir and that his filial duties should be directed toward his deceased predecessor of the shogunal line rather than his real father of a collateral line. Sadanobu was well aware that the logic of the situation dictated a similar decision in the case of Kōkaku and Prince Kan'in, but he was reluctant to offend the emperor by giving a flatly negative reply to his request. He temporized, hoping that the Kyoto court would independently decide to drop the matter.

The emperor's courtiers, however, sided with the emperor. To be sure, one of them, the Minister of the Left, Takatsukasa Masahiro, privately opposed Kōkaku's plan, but he went on record as believing that the emperor should decide the matter as he pleased. Kyoto's request was sent again to Edo in 1791 and in 1792. Finally Sadanobu was convinced that he could temporize no longer and he made a formal refusal of Kōkaku's request.

[124] Tsuji, Nihon bunka-shi, p. 319.

There are several general deductions to be made from this story. First, it indicates the great reluctance on the part of the shogunal authorities to contradict the emperor's will openly. Second, it shows that the opinion of the court was a force independent of the emperor's will, for Sadanobu had hopes in 1790 that a negative decision by the kuge would settle the matter for good. The most important observation to be made about the affair is simply that Edo arrogated to itself the final power of decision over matters that after all related to the private relations among the members of the imperial family.

Shogunal power over the court extended into areas that are seemingly even more trivial. In 1823 the court petitioned Edo as to whether the retired Emperor Kōkaku might be allowed to visit the long disused country villa, the Shugakuin. After a delay of several months Edo allowed Kōkaku his outing, having in the meantime found it necessary to restore the villa to a condition worthy of the pleasure seeker's eminence.[125] On Kōkaku's death in 1840 the shoshidai consulted Edo on a still more innocuous matter. Would it be all right if his late Majesty were awarded a posthumous name of the Chinese style, one that is befitting his dignity and virtue? Emperors up to the Heian period had been known by such names, which are formed of two Chinese characters generally signifying desirable moral qualities. With a few exceptions the later emperors are known by less formal posthumous names, usually taken from their places of residence or entombment. Edo's answer in this case was affirmative; it was accompanied by a letter of explanation which justified the return to the past usage in terms of the long reign of the sovereign in question. He is therefore known to us as Kōkaku, "Shining Rule."[126]

On closer inspection, perhaps neither of these instances was

[125] Shugakuin gokō-shi, in Koji ruien, vol. 1, pp. 747–48.
[126] Sanehisa kyōki, in Koji ruien, vol. 13, pp. 67–70. For the probable causes of the event, see below, p. 232.

really trivial. Both decisions were departures from recent precedents and hence had to be examined for possible signs of more sweeping changes to come. The Shugakuin incident was particularly significant. It liberated retired emperors from nearly a century of imprisonment within the kuge quarter, and what is more important, it gave the residents of Kyoto their first glimpse in that many years of a man who had been their sovereign. A contemporary account says that the event was splendid. "Multitudes of people worshipfully filled the streets shouting 'Banzai' in their joy."[127] Shogunal officials were gratified by the display, for popular demonstrations of affection for the imperial institution redounded indirectly to the credit of the shogunate. The system of shogunal controls may be said to have existed to ensure that such demonstrations would always remain worshipful and joyous.

The shogunate provided the base of the court's material support. It did this by maintaining within the tenryō (shogunal domain) lands known as goryō (fisc lands), the income from which was apportioned among the emperor, the imperial family, the go-monzeki, and the kuge.[128] Fisc lands had a long history before the Tokugawa period, but by the middle of the sixteenth century they had become minuscule. When Hideyoshi came to power, the imperial goryō was 3,000 koku, but he increased it to 7,000. The Tokugawa shoguns made further increases, first to 10,000 koku (1601); then to 20,000 koku (1623); and finally to 30,000 koku (1705). Initially this appropriation went to support the entire imperial family, but in 1630 separate lands were set aside for the maintenance of abdicated sovereigns. In later years the senior abdicated sovereign had goryō of 7000 to 10,000 koku, and the others of from 5,000 to 7,000 koku. Imperial consorts

[127] *Shugakuin gokō-shi,* in *Koji ruien,* vol. 12, p. 747.
[128] Teishitsu Rinya-kyoku (comp.), *Go-ryōchi shikō,* pp. 248–59. Tanaka, *Tennō no kenkyū,* pp. 46–56.

and former consorts received 3,000 koku each, and other imperial women 2,000 each. The Crown Prince received a stipend of 2,000 hyō (roughly the same as a goryō of 2,000 koku). Collaterals of the imperial family and kuge received additional "fiefs" (chigyō), as did the naishi and other palace functionaries during their terms of office. The apportionments to various independent establishments varied considerably. However, the trend throughout the period was toward an increase in the total funds set aside for the support of the court. The following is a tabulation of the various allotments for the Manji period (1658–61).[129]

Kinri goryō (the Palace Lands, i.e., the central fisc)	19,658 koku
Sentō goryō (lands of the abdicated Emperor Go-Mizunoo)	10,172
Collaterals (three families)	5,013
Fiefs of 93 kuge families	33,056
Monzeki priests	16,048
Monzeki nuns	3,201
Fiefs of naishi and other palace ladies	9,576
Fiefs of other palace officials and functionaries	2,481
Total (rounded)	99,000 koku

By the Kyōhō period (1716–36) the total had gone up to 118,000 koku. In 1867 it was about 130,000 koku.[130]

The entire court establishment had basic revenues that would have placed it in the upper middle rank of daimyo domains. The wealth or poverty of the court is not to be determined by

---

[129] Ishin shi, vol. 1, pp. 13–14.

[130] Ibid., pp. 14–15. The lands comprising the goryō were located in a number of discontinuous segments in the provinces of Yamashiro and Tamba. These lands are sometimes described as though they were the emperor's "domain," i.e., under a similar kind of political subservience, either to him or to his court, as with the domains of the shogun or the daimyos. In fact, the governance of the goryō was entrusted to a shogunal official known as the Kinri daikan, who in the latter part of the Tokugawa period was always a member of the Kobori family. See Tanaka, Tennō no kenkyū, p. 59; Okuno, Kōshitsu go-keizai-shi no kenkyū, pp. 44–45.

absolute standards. They were poor in the sense that they felt
the need of additional revenues, which they sought from various
quarters. On special occasions, such as enthronements and imperial marriages, the court received gifts from the shogunate,
rich daimyos, or Buddhist temples.[131] Sometimes the shogunate
simply absorbed on its own some of the expenses of the court.
It might do this by making up yearly deficits in court accounts
(a more or less regular procedure from the 1720s on), or it
might undertake to meet some especially onerous expense such
as the repair or rebuilding of palace buildings after a fire or
earthquake.[132]

Budgetary figures from a normal year, 1777, will illustrate the
court's dependence on regular supplements to the basic revenues.[133] The Kinri goryō was figured at 30,260 koku. Over half
of this, 18,678 koku, was the tax base for the emperor's rice
revenue of 8,031 koku. The remaining 11,581 koku of the
goryō was the tax base for revenues paid to the court in the
form of silver, 302.48 kan (1 kan = 3.75 kilograms). To this the
shogunate added 442.52 kan of silver as a direct supplement to
meet the year's deficit. In addition the shogunate added 800
gold ryō (equivalent in value to about 48 kan of silver) for the
support of the imperial women, plus 515 kan of silver for supplementary expenses of the abdicated sovereign. All of this was
in addition to the very considerable expenses of the shogunate's
establishment in Kyoto, the Nijō Castle and the offices of the
shoshidai and the Kyōto machi bugyō.

Let us now review the most important characteristics of the
imperial court in the Tokugawa period. The persons of the
court were arranged as in a series of concentric circles having
as their center the reigning emperor. Access to the emperor was

[131] See for example the lists of gifts received on the occasion of various
enthronements in *Koji ruien*, vol. 12, pp. 434 *et seq.*: from *Gyokuro-sō*.
Tokugawa jikki. Go-shōdan-ki, etc.
[132] *Ishin shi*, vol. 1, pp. 16–18.   [133] *Ibid.*

greatest in the innermost circles and diminished progressively as one approached the periphery. Social prestige also increased with proximity to the center, and in general so did wealth. The innermost circle of court society consisted of the members of the emperor's immediate family—the abdicated sovereign or sovereigns, the empress, and the young imperial children. Collateral members of the imperial family formed the next ring. Heads of the five highest ranking kuge families were next, followed by the various inferior grades of the kuge caste. This concentric social arrangement was reflected to a certain degree in the physical disposition of the court's residences. The emperor's quarters were in the center of the Kindairi; his immediate family also lived in its enclosure. Imperial collaterals and the senior kuge tended to have residences immediately outside the walls of the Kindairi, and other kuge occupied the surrounding portions of the Gyoen enclosure.

Otherwise the physical setting of the life of the court was most conspicuously marked by its isolation and its confinement. Courtiers had relatively little contact with the world outside the Gyoen, and the emperor none at all. His life, in fact, was confined to an area about the size of the deck of a large modern aircraft carrier.

The physical isolation of the emperor and the court worked both to veil their activities from those outside and to limit their opportunity of obtaining direct experience of life in other classes of society. One result of this was to prevent the emperor and kuge from having the slightest influence over public affairs. Another was to increase the mystery and awe with which contemporary society invested the persons of the court and their works.

In this confined, austere setting, almost entirely hidden from public view, the court performed acts which were regarded as having profound public significance. Most of these were recurring ceremonial or ritual performances, almost of the nature of an endless folk drama symbolizing the most awesome processes of nature, of human life and regeneration, and of the ordering of society. The specific symbolic denotation of many of the rites had long ago been forgotten, but all of them were studied and practiced with great devotion in order to preserve them in as ancient a form as possible.

The effective government of the country, that of the Tokugawa shoguns, protected the court and provided for its material support. Such contacts as the government permitted between members of the court and the outside world were through the intermediation of high shogunal officials stationed in the imperial capital. The governing aristocracy of the country were deeply solicitous of the welfare of the court at the same time that they sought to curb possibly disruptive manifestations of freedom or power in its members. The material wealth which the shogunate permitted the court to enjoy was not as great as that of the shogun or of numerous other members of military society, but it was sufficient to allow the life and the work of the court to be carried out with dignity.

In return for the protection and income which the court received from the shogunate, it performed certain services of inestimable value. Principally, these took the form of patents of appointment to members of the shogun's government, which allowed them to speak of themselves as the functionaries of the emperor's government and therefore as the rightful rulers of Japan.

Such were what we may call the objective characteristics of the imperial institution in the Tokugawa period. They would not of themselves account for the uniquely important role which the institution is considered to have played in the political and social history of modern Japan. A few hundred effete individuals, utterly unfit by training and experience to deal with the problems of nation or society, could not be expected to become the agents of large historical movements. Their essential role in the history of their time was of the utmost importance, but it was passive. They were important not for what they did but for what their contemporaries outside the walls of the Gyoen thought of them. It is to this aspect of the institution that we turn in the following chapter.

III

IMPERIAL LOYALISM

✻ THE TRADITION of thought and writing that concerned itself with the imperial institution is known in Japanese as *kinnō*. The literal meaning is "loyal service to the emperor"; as the name of a school it may be translated "loyalism," and those who belonged to the school were "loyalists." For purposes of rough identification the loyalists may be defined as those scholars and writers who emphasized the central position of the emperor in the Japanese nation and society.

In a certain sense all thinkers, all men, of the period were loyalists. That is, no one denied the emperor's lofty position, and everyone agreed that the throne should be revered. The very word kinnō referred to a moral obligation no less taken for granted than, say, filial piety or respect for law and order. The loyalist writers were a group characterized not by their beliefs but by the area of their concern. In other words they were not a faction battling some other that had an "anti-loyalist" or "disloyal" attitude toward the throne. While other writers concentrated on practical questions of political morality or on the efficient exercise of power, the loyalists examined the imperial throne, which they treated as the source, the token, or the justification of power. To translate the field of their specialization into Western terms, they were men who speculated about political legitimacy and whose ideas other men in the main accepted, or moralists about ultimate social values, whose moral code made explicit what the rest of society felt and respected.

To say that the emperor was an object of reverence for all indicates that loyalism was, among other things, the manifestation in the articulate sectors of society of a mass national religion. While it is hoped to show that that popular cult was only part of Tokugawa loyalism—that the peculiar nature and role of loyalism came about in fact as the result of a complex interplay among religious and secular, intellectual and popular elements—it may be fruitful to focus for a moment on the emperor's role in sub-articulate folk religion.[1]

Emperor worship among the people was part of folk Shinto. In fact it is difficult to draw a line between worship of the imperial institution and religious practices directed more diffusely among the Shinto pantheon. The Kyoto establishment of emperor and court does not seem to have been a *place* of popular worship, at least until the closing days of the shogunate. The cult centers that one may connect firmly or loosely to the emperor were the great Shinto shrines dedicated to his ancestors, and the principal of these were the shrine to Amaterasu in Ise and the Iwashimizu Shrine between Kyoto and Osaka.

The two ancient shrines at Yamada in the province of Ise have numerous associations with the Imperial family. The object of worship at the *Naikū* (Inner Shrine), the more important of the two, is Amaterasu, the imperial ancestress. The original of the sacred mirror, one of the imperial regalia, is housed there. Until the dynastic schism of the fourteenth century, the chief ministrant in the shrine was an imperial princess, the *Saigū*, whose presence helped spread imperial influence beyond the capital. Even in the Tokugawa period there were a number of kuge houses that monopolized certain priestly offices of the Ise

[1] The subject is not well treated in Japanese secondary studies of the imperial institution, which typically limit their discussion of religious practices in reverence of the emperor to those performed by shogunate or domain rulers. Tanaka Sōgorō is an exception, and I am indebted to his *Tennō no kenkyū*, pp. 79–86, for its having guided me to the information herein.

shrines. Finally, from the Kamakura period on Ise was the location of an influential school of Shinto study, known as Ise Shinto, which was one of the chief transmitters of articulate imperial loyalism outside the imperial capital.

Ise Shinto has relevance to Tokugawa period loyalism primarily because of its influence on the syncretic Shinto-Confucian philosophy of Yamazaki Ansai (Suika Shinto). The popular cult took the form of a vogue for religious pilgrimages to Ise, lasting throughout the Tokugawa period and erupting sporadically into movements of hysterical fervor and mass dimensions. There are reported to have been six such eruptions, in 1650–51, 1705–06, 1771, 1830–31, 1855, and 1867.

The first of these is associated with a period of considerable mass unrest, the most important manifestation of which was the *rōnin* rebellion under Yui Shōsetsu, occasioned by the accession of the minor Shogun Ietsuna.[2] The last three occasions were clearly reflections of the growing nationalism of the early and middle nineteenth century.

In the 1771 affair the number of pilgrims to Ise was reported in contemporary sources to have exceeded four million, and in a three month period in 1830 about five million people were said to have visited the shrines. Even though the figures are probably highly inflated (for it seems unlikely that some one-fifth or one-sixth of the population of Japan had the freedom or leisure for such trips at that time), other details leave no doubt about the intensity of the vogue. An observer describing the 1771 pilgrimages reported the highways clogged with men and women of all ages from provinces as far away as Echigo and Bizen, hoisting paper banners and walking along as though possessed. Many of the pilgrims had no money, but begged for food and lodging or slept on bridges or under eaves. Residences by the wayside accommodated travelers, sometimes as many as 150 or 200 in a single dwelling, and often with little or no compen-

[2] See Sansom, A *History of Japan, 1615–1867*, pp. 54–57.

sation to the householders. Acts of grace such as these gave to this whole series of mass enthusiasms the name *o-kage mairi*, meaning something like "charity pilgrimages." In some instances the charity was said to come from a supernatural source. The 1771 observer mentioned above reported hearing that souvenir paper whisks and "hailstones" of silver fell upon the pilgrims from the sky. In 1867 a shogunal official named Tsutsumi reported seeing lumps of gold which, he was told, had fallen from the sky for the benefit of Ise-bound travelers.

Another phenomenon associated with Ise worship was the *nuke mairi*, "pilgrimage by stealth." Commoners kept their travel plans secret from their fathers, employers or the local authorities on account of the standing proscription against unnecessary travel. It is said that on their return they were not punished, but rather congratulated for their piety and resourcefulness.

Pilgrimages to Ise are susceptible to several interpretations. Most simply, they afforded one of the few opportunities for commoners to travel for pleasure. The authorities, whose attitude toward frivolous behavior was at best one of suspicion, officially made it a crime to leave one's place of employment without approved cause (although there is ample evidence that the restriction was not effectively enforced). Perhaps more to the point, a generally straitened economy and a serious, even puritanical, strain in the national character combined to prevent most people from traveling on vacations unless they could justify them by a purpose that seemed more important.

Of course the o-kage mairi cannot be explained away as mere pleasure trips. They were undeniably products of a certain mass hysteria, for which it is difficult to discern a single social or political cause. Several of the outbreaks occurred in times of national crisis, and more particularly times when there was widespread disaffection with the shogunal government. One obvious possibility is that the o-kage mairi were a mass turning-away toward the consolations of religion in a society that felt hostile to the temporal order. There is no doubt that the emperor, who headed a pseudo-government and who symbolized perfection in the temporal order, was the country's most natural recipient of religious veneration in such times as those.

Despite the circumstantial evidence that some degree of latent hostility to the Tokugawa government and yearning for an alternative to it were present in the religious enthusiasms that centered about the Ise shrines, one should not overstate this aspect of the matter. The hostility remained latent, not overt, until virtually the end of the period, and the alternative for which the enthusiasts yearned was not political, but religious. That is, the emperor himself was not a contestant in the realm of temporal power but rather one who beckoned the disaffected to another realm altogether. The government did not regard Ise pilgrimages as a threat to its security, and it seems to have done little or nothing to prevent, or even to control, them. After all, they were useful indexes of popular sentiments and afforded a safety valve lest mass resentment lead to insurrection.

There is evidence in another quarter that the shogunal authorities actually fostered a species of emperor worship in order to instill feelings of reverence and awe toward their own government. This evidence is the deliberate encouragement of popular worship at the Iwashimizu Shrine, the principal religious institution in Japan that was sacred to both the imperial and shogunal institutions. Iwashimizu was officially a branch of the Hachiman-gū at Usa in northern Kyushu, sacred to Hachiman, the god of war. In fact the branch shrine became more important than its parent, because it was accessible to courtiers of the imperial capital and to the main population centers in general. Hachiman himself was venerated as the deified spirit of the fifteenth emperor, Ōjin, a legendary warrior hero who more than any other figure of Japanese myth symbolizes the linkage between the imperial throne and the military power of the state.

The shoguns, of the Tokugawa as well as earlier houses, stressed Hachiman worship for two reasons. The shogunal office was in theory the military arm of the emperor's government. Furthermore, the Minamoto clan, from which all shoguns claimed descent, sprang from the imperial house and hence had as good a claim to be descended from Ōjin as did the emperors themselves. In the entire Shinto pantheon only Tōshō-gū, the deified Ieyasu, received similar reverence from the Tokugawa. To foster a popular cult of the Iwashimizu Shrine was to cultivate a feeling among the people that the government had foundations in divinity and tradition. Here, as in the more articulate manifestations of loyalism, there can be seen a purposeful association of the imperial and shogunal houses, by and for the benefit of the latter, though it must be understood that the shoguns were only taking advantage of deeply engrained national attitudes that had existed earlier.

· 2 ·

The popular cult of the emperor exhibited sincere enthusiasm on the part of its adherents, deliberately channelized to the purposes of a conservative state and society. Articulate sentiment—the kinnō movement properly speaking—showed these features still more clearly and allows one to draw firmer inferences concerning their meaning.

The tradition of loyalist writing may be broken down in various ways. The history of its development falls into discrete or overlapping periods; its members were of several sects or schools; some loyalists were active in politics and some were not. However, none of the distinctions which one may make for purposes of analysis should blind one to the very large area of agreement among men who wrote about the imperial institution, as though to echo the enthusiastic concord of the less articulate members of that society. But if one is therefore justi-

fied in speaking of a consensus toward the throne in the Tokugawa period, it was nevertheless a consensus comprised of many
diverse elements, even embracing fundamental ambiguities too
deep-seated to be analyzed or resolved by those who held them.

The loyalists began with the already stated belief that the
emperor was at the heart of the life of the nation, and they
posited that belief on their understanding of ethics, religion,
and history. They adduced an ideal moral order, which all agreed
the emperor symbolized and which some asserted might be
realized by reverence to him. But aside from their assumption
that morality urged a higher standard of behavior than humanity usually displayed, there was in the loyalists a certain general
optimism, a satisfaction with things as they were. This is seen
most clearly in their attitude toward the structure of Tokugawa
society and the constitution of the Tokugawa government. In
both regards the loyalists with few exceptions shared the conservatism of most of their contemporaries, and when pressed,
even rushed enthusiastically to the defense of the institutions
under which they lived.

So far as the imperial institution was concerned, this meant
that loyalists did not in any practical way urge a restitution of
its ancient political powers. What seems to contradict this is the
ideal of "restoration," which figures prominently in their writings. The equivalent Japanese words *fukko* and *chūkō* mean,
respectively, "return to antiquity" and "regeneration [of a
dynasty]." They were words borrowed from the Chinese language representing concepts of Chinese political ethics. Like
most ethical precepts the ideal of restoration exhorted society to
better standards of conduct and even called the attention of
society to specific moral flaws in contemporary behavior that
the loyalists implied should be eradicated. Though this indicates
that restorationism might be used as a moral guideline for the
performance of ordinary political acts, it was not intended as a
call for some extraordinary political settlement.

Loyalists always invoked the imperial name in their call for restoration, most frequently as a token of all the ancient values to which they urged a return. To say that the emperor was the loyalists' main symbol of national values is true enough, but it fails to satisfy the student who would like to know what features of the imperial institution dramatized what particular values, and it does not explain what the emperor and his court were expected to do about it all. Loyalist writings give some answers, but they are frustratingly silent in the main on matters that pertained to the emperor's ideal relationship to the effective powers of government. They permit two different views, or rather one may perceive in them, even within the work of a single writer, a tension between two half-formed but assumed or accepted views that are mutually exclusive. One of them is the idea that the emperor, who had once had secular powers, had delegated them to the shogunate, and hence, by implication, could rightfully redelegate them or reassume them himself. The other was the idea that the emperor's role was essentially religious or moral; that as a symbol of national values, he defined the standards by which the government ought to rule, but could not in any practical sense alter the fact that the government *did* rule. Eventually there was a realization that the two views were incompatible, and then the tension between them called for a resolution. The result, when it came, was the concept of the Meiji Restoration.

Loyalism, in the sense of a creed concerning the significance of the emperor to Japan, existed before the Tokugawa reunification,[3] but in the more limited sense in which the term will be used here, it was a strictly Tokugawa period phenomenon. That is, it was a response to the condition, at once peculiarly secluded and peculiarly sacrosanct, which the Tokugawa rulers created

[3] See Mikami, *Sonnō-ron hattatsu-shi*, pp. 1–15. Tsuda, *"Gukanshō oyobi Jinnō shōtō-ki* ni okeru Shina no shigaku shisō," in *Hompō shigaku-shi ronsō*, vol. 1, pp. 491–524.

for the imperial institution shortly after 1600. The intellectual justification lagged some years behind the political settlement, and its origins can be dated little earlier than the middle of the seventeenth century. From then until the Meiji Restoration one can discern four main periods of development of the loyalist idea. The first, or formative, period saw two or three generations of articulate writers about the emperor, the latest of whom lived into the second quarter of the eighteenth century. A second period of doctrinal conservatism and stagnation followed. If anything it witnessed a decline in concern for the institution and a growing reluctance on the part of the authorities to countenance new modes of thought on that or any other aspect of the social structure. It lasted until about the 1820s, when new foreign pressures on Japan shocked many of the ruling class to a reappraisal of the nature and fate of Japanese society. The third period was characterized on the one hand by a reaffirmation of the basic loyalist message of a century earlier, and on the other by a dawning realization of the practical value which that message might have in an age of crisis. When the crisis mounted to threaten the very existence of Japan (at least in the institutional form in which she was then constituted), a fourth phase appeared, one of dissident loyalism. The patron saint of this final phase was Yoshida Shōin; its apostles included the loyalist rōnin of the 1860s; its work culminated in the revolution of the Meiji Restoration.

This chapter is concerned with the first and third phases of Tokugawa period loyalism, those of formulation and reaffirmation of the consensus; the phase of dissident loyalism is dealt with in the following chapter. The description will necessarily be illustrative rather than exhaustive. It is hoped that the few examples chosen are truly representative of the whole tradition, and important exceptions to the generalizations that one can draw from them will be examined in greater detail.

One generalization, all but without exceptions, is that the

members of the loyalist tradition up to the start of the dissident phase were of the ruling class; that is, they were samurai and can be limited further to those samurai whose training and ability suited them to a more active role than most. Most were teachers, some of them to feudal rulers. A few were in positions of real political power as official advisers on ethical questions.

Loyalists were to be found in several of the competing schools of thought of Tokugawa Japan. All of them may be enumerated under the two heads of the Confucian and National Schools. The Confucian group may be broken down further into Ortho-dox and heterodox schools, and the heterodox movements may be subclassified into two main branches: the Wang Yang-ming School and the School of Ancient Studies.

The Confucian School, though not native to Japan, had long-established roots there. It was introduced even before the im-portation of Buddhism in the sixth century. Confucianism had been of vast importance as a vehicle for the adaptation of Chinese ideas to Japanese society, but from the Heian period on it was no longer a major independent school, having become naturalized as one of many strands of the Japanese intellectual tradition. It is significant that until the Tokugawa unification formal Confucian studies were confined largely to the great Buddhist and Shinto centers of learning, particularly the Tendai headquarters on Mount Hiei, the large temples of Rinzai Zen in Kyoto, and the Ise Shrine, where they were associated with Ise Shinto. The Confucian revival of about 1600 made the school independent once more, and its capacity for stimulating in its adherents new modes of thought on state theory dates from that time.

Several divergent schools of Confucian thought were studied from time to time in Japan, but one of them, which had already become orthodox in China, predominated because of the offi-cial patronage given to it by the shogunate and many of the han governments. In that sense, from the seventeenth century on it may be called orthodox for Japan as well.[4] The principal rival school in China was that of Wang Yang-ming, which had Japanese adherents—some of them in the loyalist tradition—from late in the seventeenth century. In addition, independent Japanese Confucianists of about the same time broke away from the orthodox tradition to found a group of sects which claimed to return to the tenets of ancient Confucianism and are hence known as *Kogaku-ha*, the "Ancient Studies School." More Japanese than the other schools in emphasis (because less hobbled by influences from later Chinese tradition), the Ancient Studies School produced some leaders of the early loyalist movement.

The National School (Kokugaku-ha) is usually considered to date from the closing years of the seventeenth century and to have come to full flower in the years around 1880 with the writings of Motoori Norinaga and Hirata Atsutane. The school claimed to base its teachings on whatever was indigenous (non-Chinese) in the Japanese tradition, but it applied to them the synthesizing techniques that were habits of mind learned from the study of Chinese philosophy. For all that the National School was supposed to be a return to native ideas and ideals, it was deeply influenced by Chinese thought, particularly by that which is associated with the Confucian revival. Chinese influence may be seen clearly in the National School's theory of the state. This is entirely understandable, for that is a subject about which ancient, indigenous Japanese thought had almost nothing to say, and, as will be shown, it is at the heart of the neo-Confucian system. For these reasons, it is appropriate to treat the thought of the National School as a natural outgrowth and modification of the main Confucian theory of the state.

Tokugawa loyalism was part of the state theory that was

[4] See, however, the argument in Bitō, *Nihon hōken shisō-shi kenkyū*, esp. pp. 28–31, that "orthodox" Confucianism held no particular ideological primacy with the shogunate until the anti-heterodox policies of the 1790s, though members of that school had customarily been employed to advise on learned matters since Ieyasu's time.

formulated in the main between 1650 and 1725. We shall here consider six individuals or groups which may be specified as leading contributors to state theory and whose concern at the same time conspicuously involved the imperial institution. These were (1) Hayashi Razan and his family and school, (2) the school of Yamazaki Ansai, (3) Arai Hakuseki, (4) Kumazawa Banzan, (5) Yamaga Sokō, and (6) the early Mito School. Banzan was of the school of Wang Yang-ming; Sokō was one of the founders of the Ancient Studies School; the others were Orthodox.

Hayashi Razan (1583–1657)[5] founded the greatness of his family, who were the hereditary heads of the officially sponsored shogunal academy, and hence in the middle of the seventeenth century he was the leading Japanese member of the Orthodox (Ch'eng-Chu) School of Confucianists. Razan was not the introducer of Ch'eng-Chu Confucianism to Japan as an organized school. That distinction belongs to his teacher Fujiwara Seika (1561–1619), who had served as an academic adviser to Tokugawa Ieyasu. But Razan may truthfully be called the first really orthodox of the Japanese Orthodox Confucianists, for Seika and his contemporaries had been eclectic, admitting other schools and sects to their scholarly program. Razan, however, was intolerant of other schools than his own, or to put it more positively, he found as much freedom as he needed within the confines of the Ch'eng-Chu system. He was a polymath. He is said to have read "every book in Japan,"[6] an exaggeration that no doubt points to the truth, and he wrote essays or books on most learned subjects. Allusions to the imperial institution do not figure especially prominently in his writings, but they are important because of his unique eminence in the scholarly world

---

[5] See Tsunoda et al., *Sources of Japanese Tradition*, pp. 351–61. Langston, "The Seventeenth Century Hayashi, A Translation from the Sentetsu Sōdan," pp. 1–32. Earl, *Emperor and Nation in Japan*, pp. 19–22. Mikami, *Sonnō-ron hattatsu-shi*, pp. 183–87.

[6] *Sentetsu Sōdan*, in Langston, "The Seventeenth Century Hayashi," p. 15.

of his time and because he was a pioneer in the attempt to rationalize Japanese institutions in the light of Chinese theory. Japan's foremost advocate of Chinese philosophy was understandably attracted by Chinese culture. It is perhaps unfortunate that Razan the political thinker is best remembered for having denigrated native Japanese institutions where they clashed with their Chinese analogs. He suggested in an essay on Jimmu, the legendary founder of the Japanese dynasty, that Jimmu was descended from the royal house of Chou China.[7] That opinion had been advanced as early as the fourteenth century and has been repeatedly anathematized by Japanese nationalists ever since.[8] In most respects, however, Razan's work was less controversial. He was a servant of the Tokugawa shogunate and helped to formulate the justification for shogunal government that other loyalists accepted—those of more nationalistic inclinations included.

Yamazaki Ansai (1618–1682)[9] is usually listed in the official Ch'eng-Chu School. He served as adviser to Hoshina Masayuki (a son of the second Tokugawa Shogun, Hidetada), who had been enfeoffed as daimyo of the strategic northern han of Aizu. Ansai built on the foundation of Ch'eng-Chu orthodoxy a peculiarly Japanese system of thought in which teachings of the Shinto religion are included. To Ansai there was no incompatibility between the basic tenets of Chinese and Japanese religions. It must be admitted, however, that he went to extreme lengths to prove similarities between them, often by means of

---

[7] *Jimmu Tennō-ron*, in *Hayashi Razan bunshū*, pp. 280–82. Translated in Tsunoda *et al.*, *Sources*, pp. 358–60.

[8] Notably by Emperor Go-Daigo and Tokugawa Mitsukuni. See Kurita (ed.), *Sui-han shūshi jiryaku*, p. 2. Webb, *The Early Mito School*, pp. 21–22.

[9] On Ansai see Tsunoda *et al.*, *Sources*, pp. 363–71. Abe, "Yamazaki Ansai to sono kyōiku," in *Kinsei Nihon no jugaku*, pp. 335–56. Mikami, *Sonnō-ron hattatsu-shi*, pp. 207–25. Tsuji, *Nihon bunka-shi*, vol. 5, pp. 255–59. Bitō, *Nihon hōken shisō-shi kenkyū*, pp. 40–44. Watsuji, *Sonnō shisō*, pp. 228–37.

far-fetched linguistic coincidences, and that the characteristic rationalism of the Chinese system often emerges in his writings as more akin to the mystic or intuitional tenets of Shinto. The syncretic religion of Ansai became institutionalized as a sect of Shinto and is called Suika-Shinto.

Arai Hakuseki (1657–1725)[10] attained perhaps the greatest purely political eminence of any Tokugawa period scholar, for he was a friend and one of the most trusted advisers of the sixth shogun, Ienobu. The dominating force of his life was rationalism, of a purity such as few other premodern Japanese attained. This comes across to us in his writings (which covered a wide range of subjects, notably history, administration, and autobiography) as an almost twentieth-century matter-of-factness about what his common sense told him and a skepticism of all that it did not. He served the shogunate and worked to justify its existence intellectually, but he did not ignore the emperor. By the definition of "loyalist" given at the head of this chapter, he was a loyalist, but an untypical one in utter antithesis to the mystic, sentimental Yamazaki Ansai.

Kumazawa Banzan (1619–91)[11] was the most famous disciple of Nakae Tōju, who first taught the creed of Wang Yang-ming in Japan. Tōju had shunned public office to devote himself to filial and pedagogic duties, but Banzan, a rōnin (masterless and incomeless samurai), took government employment, first at the han of Okayama, then with the shogunate. He was a sharp-minded thinker on economic and administrative questions, but there was also a poetic, sentimental strain in his character that responded to the beauty of ancient Japanese legend and the emotional attractiveness of the imperial institution.

[10] On Hakuseki see Tsunoda et al., Sources, pp. 470–79. Earl, Emperor and Nation, pp. 27–29. Katsuta, Arai Hakuseki no rekishi-gaku, esp. pp. 4–42; 293–95. Watsuji, Sonnō shisō, pp. 259–67.

[11] On Razan see Tsunoda et al., Sources, pp. 387–92. Earl, Emperor and Nation, pp. 19ff. Mikami, Sonnō-ron hattatsu-shi, pp. 465–76. Tsuji, Nihon bunka-shi, vol. 5, pp. 254–55. Watsuji, Sonnō shisō, pp. 216–21.

Yamaga Sokō (1622–85)[12] left the Ch'eng-Chu fold to found his own Confucian school, the School of Ancient Studies. He was more of a rationalist than Yamazaki Ansai, but like him he was intent to show that the proper focus of attention for Japanese Confucianists should be the Japanese, not the Chinese, state. Sokō applied to Japan the term "Middle Country," (Chūchō and Chūgoku), which to Confucianists had always represented the ideal Chinese realm submissive to a Confucian ruler and to Confucian morality. In addition he devoted himself to the justification in terms of Confucian ethics of the income and privileges of' the samurai, the class to which he belonged.

The Mito School was patronized by the daimyos of Mito, a han in the northeast corner of the Kantō plain whose rulers were of a cadet branch of the Tokugawa family.[13] Shortly after the middle of the seventeenth century Tokugawa Mitsukuni (1628–1701), the second daimyo of his house, organized an academy and center of historical scholarship and employed there a group of Japanese and Chinese historians and thinkers, known collectively as the early Mito School. From the 1650s to approximately 1715 the school was engaged in the writing of a huge history of Japan from the foundation of the dynasty to the late fourteenth century. This is the famous *Dai Nihon shi*, "History of Japan."

The objective of the early Mito School was described by one of its members as "to define the legitimate dynasty and describe the morality of subjects."[14] While their contemporaries mentioned above were loyalists only incidentally or in certain por-

[12] On Sokō see Tsunoda *et al.*, *Sources*, pp. 398–410. Earl, *Emperor and Nation*, pp. 37ff. Tsuji, *Nihon bunka-shi*, vol. 5, pp. 253–54. Watsuji, *Sonnō shisō*, pp. 248–54.

[13] On the early Mito School see Tsunoda, *Sources*, pp. 371–75. Webb, *The Early Mito School*. Mikami, *Sonnō-ron hattatsu-shi*, pp. 292–338. Tsuji, *Nihon bunka-shi*, vol. 5, pp. 247–51.

[14] This formulation appeared as early as 1691 in an inscription which Mitsukuni wrote to be included on his memorial stone. Kurita, *Sui-han shūshi jiryaku*, p. 13.

tions of their work, the Mito scholars made loyalist concerns their whole endeavor. The *Dai Nihon shi* belongs to a Chinese tradition of historiography which aims through subtle devices of organization and style in the composition of a historical work to indicate the writers' points of view. A study of that work reveals a great deal of the Mito School's theory of the state, though in an implied form rather than directly stated. Other writings by certain of the compilers such as Asaka Tampaku (1656–1737)[15] and Miyake Kanran (1673–1718)[16]—books, essays, or notes written while compiling the *Dai Nihon shi*—fill in gaps in the system.

It would be misleading to stop with schools of formal affiliation in one's categorization of the leading early formulators of Tokugawa period loyalism. The sects of Confucianism to which they belonged are of significance in helping to make clear their points of view on metaphysics, ethics, or political theory. Where the meaning of the imperial institution was concerned, however, other points of distinction among them are of greater importance. Here they displayed differing combinations of two strains of thought—rather, two attitudes of mind. One can give various pairs of names to them: rational and intuitional; intellectual and emotional; positivistic and mystic; even (it seems sometimes) prosaic and sentimental. The two attitudes were mutually exclusive only in their extreme forms. The one sought to clarify and define; the other to celebrate. Neither attitude can be associated especially with formal schools, but both could be found in all schools. If the Orthodox Arai Hakuseki represents a relatively pure type of the first attitude, the Orthodox Yamazaki Ansai is an equally pure case of the second, and the Orthodox Mito scholars represent a mixture of the two. Of the remaining early loyalists mentioned, the Hayashi school stands rather to the

---

[15] Principally *Dai Nihon shi sansō*, in *Mito-gaku taikei*, vol. 6, pp. 2–335. *Shiron shiden*, in *ibid.*, pp. 338–426.
[16] *Ronsan bakugo*, in *Mito-gaku taikei*, vol. 7, pp. 163–229.

rationalistic side of things, and Banzan and Sokō closer to the middle position of Mito.

The second, nonrationalistic, strain of belief about the emperor, where definite enough to permit paraphrase, tended to the idea that he possessed supernatural powers to effect change in the world of men. The understanding of what these powers were might vary from one writer to another. Few or none implied that he possessed divine omnipotence, and in Tokugawa Japan there are scarcely any references to the magic powers that might be emphasized in a primitive society, for example, to influence weather or appease other natural forces. Instead the main emphasis seems to have been on the hardly less supernatural ability to perceive moral truth whole and simple, and then to impart it to society without the medium of the voice so that society succumbs to its necessary obligation of harmonizing opposing individual wills.

To Yamazaki Ansai the emperor's role was magical and therefore unfathomable to the intellect. He did not worry about the precise mechanism by which morals descended from god through king to man, nor should we labor to supply the logic which he lacked, for beyond indicating the existence of beliefs such as these there is nothing that one can say about them in a discussion of the significance of the imperial institution.

The rationalistic and positivistic side of the temper of Confucian Japan is a far different matter. The rationalism of an Arai Hakuseki imposed on him the necessity of explaining to his own satisfaction and without recourse to supernaturalism how the emperor fitted into the framework of Japanese society. Even with the less rationalistic, like the Mito School, the systematization of the rest of their ideas on state and society modified their views on magical imperial power. Briefly, the position assigned by loyalists of the rationalistic temper to the emperor was a symbolic one, and in general the denotation of the symbol was twofold: first, as for the emperor's place in reference to the apparatus of government, he symbolized the government's legitimacy, its right to rule; second, as for his place in Japanese society as a whole, he symbolized abstract ethical truth.

Not even the most rationalistic of the seventeenth-century formulators of a loyalist argument framed a completely satisfactory schematization of the emperor's place in the Japanese polity in their own or in any other time. Fragmentary statements as to the significance of this or that feature of the imperial institution may add up to a general picture of the whole, but they are admittedly less informative than would be a single integrated description with all the parts accounted for and all the apparent internal inconsistencies explained. The student must constantly eke out what is stated or clearly implied with what writers and their readers merely assumed to be true, principally with those tenets of Confucian or native Japanese belief common to all educated Japanese of the period who did not categorically deny them. To understand this area of common assumption, one must examine the two main traditions, Confucian Chinese and native Japanese, against the background of which the seventeenth century loyalists advanced their new ideas.

· 3 ·

A little-known but influential figure in introducing orthodox Confucian studies to the Kyoto court was Asayama Irin'an, or Soshin (1589–1664), who had studied under a Korean scholar resident in Japan, Yi Munjang, and who had previously been attached to the households of the Hosokawa family and of Tokugawa Tadanaga of Suruga, a son of the shogun Hidetada.[17] In the middle of the century he was employed by several kuge families, and in 1653 he was tutor to the former sesshō Nijō

---

[17] Tsuji, *Nihon bunka-shi*, vol. 5, pp. 227–28.

Yasumichi. At that time he came to the attention of the young Emperor Go-Kōmyō, who invited Soshin to lecture to him on the Confucian classic, *The Doctrine of the Mean*. Soshin's early career is cited in illustration of the fact that the Sung School of Confucian studies was initially patronized by members of the military aristocracy, including the shogunal family, and was well established there before penetrating the world of the Kyoto court. Nevertheless, once it had been introduced to kuge society, the new learning commenced a tradition parallel to that in the military aristocracy and one that was to have a profound influence on the thought later to be called "loyalist."

Go-Kōmyō is said to have been the first sovereign to have patronized neo-Confucian studies, which he thought a more proper basis for the training of the imperial court than the poems and tales of the classical Japanese tradition, which had been its principal intellectual food in the past. In an illuminating discussion of this emperor's character and career Tsuji Zennosuke[18] quotes a writing of Go-Kōmyō's to the effect that the decline of the Japanese imperial court stemmed from its extreme overevaluation of waka (the classical Japanese verse form) and its addiction to the prose works of the Heian period such as the *Tale of Genji* and the *Tales of Ise*. The Emperor wrote, "Until the middle ages no emperors nor ministers of state who were intent on governing according to rites and music were fond of waka, let alone the indecent *Tale of Genji* and *Tales of Ise*."[19] Tsuji adds that Go-Kōmyō did not enjoy waka at all and that he never read the Heian prose works whose influence he deplored.

Go-Kōmyō's disapprobation of Japanese poetry and fiction contrasts with his admiration for Chinese poetry and philoso-

[18] *Ibid.*, p. 222.
[19] Quoted from *Shōō iji*, in *Shiseki shūran*, vol. 17, pp. 480–84.

phy. Virtually all Japanese sovereigns since ancient times had written verse both in the Japanese and the Chinese languages. Understandably the former far outweighed the latter in the works of most of them. Go-Kōmyō, on the other hand, reversed the proportion, for he wrote comparatively few waka and a great many Chinese poems.[20] From an inspection of some specimens of his Chinese verse it is easy to see what it was in that literary tradition that appealed to him. Chinese poetics permitted the treatment of political and moral matters, but those of Japan did not. Even the best waka would appear trivial to a man of uncompromising seriousness, as Go-Kōmyō is reputed to have been. Writers of waka aimed at skilled evocations of fleeting emotions, usually by means of terse nature descriptions, but there are practically no waka concerned with social relations or moral values. Go-Kōmyō's Chinese verses revolve around such subjects as the inspiration derived from the achievements of former rulers, the salutary moral effects on society of having a virtuous ruler, and lament for the faded glory of ancient institutions.[21]

The same qualities of Go-Kōmyō's character attracted him to the neo-Confucian theory of the state. Just as his espousal of Chinese poetry was partly in reaction to native Japanese literature, his espousal of the new Chinese philosophy was a reaction to the older higher learning of Japan, which was Buddhist. Here again what he deplored was the lack of concern for practical affairs, particularly those that would be of use to rulers. To quote from another of his writings:

While Buddhist studies are interesting and full of substantial truth (tai), there is nothing in them that can be applied. The sovereign and the feudal lords are different from ordinary men and are their rulers. They should study what is practical. Even among Confucian

[20] Wada, Kōshitsu gosei no kenkyū, p. 391.
[21] Hōtei-shū, in Zoku-zoku gunsho ruijū, vol. 13, pp. 5–17.

commentaries the older ones from Han and T'ang times are thought to be not especially penetrating. Henceforth the lectures [to the emperor] should be in accordance with the new interpretations of the Ch'eng-Chu School.[22]

What was the nature of this Ch'eng-Chu School that it should suddenly have made a new appeal to military and court society in the early years of the Tokugawa regime? Like most new sects of old faiths it claimed to be a reaffirmation of the teachings of the founders. Many of its essential qualities are to be explained in terms of the tenets of classical Confucianism.

The school of Confucius is first and last a philosophy of man in society. A man's life becomes meaningful, it proclaims, through his relations with other men. The Confucian ethical system makes a place for all the small-scale human relations— bonds of friendship, family attachments, and even sexual attraction—but what gives it its universality is its vision of an all-embracing world society in which every human being should be free to assume his proper position in harmony with every other. The social mechanism for realizing universal harmony is conceived of as a universal state, organized according to Confucian principles. Thus, in the area of its broadest application Confucianism is a political philosophy, as Buddhism, Taoism, and Shinto are not. For the ultimate concern of those other schools is man's place in the world beyond man.

The deficiency of early Confucianism from the point of view of more sophisticated thinkers of the later T'ang and Sung dynasties was precisely that it failed to support its humanistic and social ethical system with as rationalistic and integrated a conception of nonhuman nature. Confucianists no doubt envied the Buddhists and Taoists their possession of advanced metaphysical systems at the same time that they rejected certain elements of them and deplored their rejection or neglect of this-worldly concerns. The supreme achievement of the neo-

[22] Tsuji, *Nihon bunka-shi*, vol. 5, p. 226.

Confucian movement of the T'ang and Sung was to provide the metaphysical underpinnings for the early Confucian ethic—to integrate man and nature into a single composite world-picture.[23]

That branch of the neo-Confucian movement which was to become the orthodox state cult in China is known by various names: the Orthodox School; the Chu Hsi School (from its final and greatest formulator); the Ch'eng Chu School (from two eleventh-century precursors of the Ch'eng family and Chu Hsi); and the School of Reason (or School of Principle, "Li Hsüeh"). The last name indicates something of the philosophical content of the school, its assumption that the universe contains a pervasive order or principle, of which every orderly thing is a reflection. This order is susceptible to the ratiocinative faculties of man's mind. Human reason thereby becomes the means for harmonizing society and incorporating mankind into the order of the universe. The proper use of reason is indispensable for the ethical life.

Education, in the view of Orthodox neo-Confucianists, is the training of the individual in the proper use of his reason. The basis for its curriculum is of course the classics of ancient Confucian teaching, but always accompanied by commentaries or interpretations by Chu Hsi or other masters of the Ch'eng-Chu School. Hardly less important in a Confucian program of study are works of history, for history is the record of the meaningful experiences of society. It is hence the concrete exposition of human morals, much as the classical literature might be called the exposition of morals in the abstract.

The man whose reason has been developed through an educational program of the kind indicated has the potentiality of becoming a moral man, but more than that, he almost inevi-

[23] English language descriptions of Chu Hsi orthodoxy may be found in Fung, *A History of Chinese Philosophy*, vol. 2, pp. 455–493. Bruce, *Chu Hsi and His Masters*. de Bary, Chan, and Watson (comp.), *Sources of Chinese Tradition*, pp. 411–557.

tably *is* a moral man, for his natural inclination *as a man* is to make use of his reason to conduct himself in harmony with natural order as he comprehends it. Such a man may be expected to live harmoniously with all those with whom he comes into intimate contact—relatives, friends, and members of his community. But he will have another moral obligation as well. His moral understanding will equip him to assume political office, and through it to help all other men to live ethically.

Fujiwara Seika's first application of neo-Confucian ethics in Japan was in the world of international trade, an unlikely quarter, for Confucianists customarily regard commercial activity as unproductive, and thus immoral. As an adviser on matters of international etiquette to the traders employed by the great Suminokura family, Seika commended them to the only system of moral values which he thought would be effective in other areas of eastern Asia.[24] In other words, he conceived of the system as a moral code which transcended the confines of any one political state. Later Japanese Confucianists, from Hayashi Razan on, perceived that the system could be applied with equal value to internal affairs.

Japanese neo-Confucianists started with the understanding, then the modification, of Confucian theory of dynastic legitimacy, for that subject was central to the justification of government itself and was prior to the judgment of particular institutions and acts.

Legitimacy, to define it informally, is like legality, but stands a plane removed. It is the standard for judging, not the behavior of individuals in society, but laws themselves and the legal and administrative framework of society. To call a government "legitimate" or "illegitimate" is not the same as to say that its laws and deeds are individually "good" or "bad," for legitimacy pertains to the whole of a society's political establishment, which may embrace inconsistencies and inequities

[24] See Tsunoda *et al.*, *Sources*, pp. 347–50.

in its parts. A theorist of legitimacy simply asks of the state which he is examining, "Has it the right to govern?" This "right" is normally described in terms of some single principle which is assumed to be permanently applicable and which has usually been associated with the religious or philosophical premises of the society that conceives it.

The principle of legitimacy, to Chinese and Japanese, was monarchic. That is, those peoples assumed that at any instant in their history all rightful political authority derived ultimately from a single individual, the ruler, and that the legitimate succession passed on his death or abdication to some other single individual. Furthermore, the principle of legitimacy was dynastic, for it stipulated that the succession was normally hereditary. However, Confucian theory of legitimacy included an all-important qualification to the dynastic principle, for it posited as the ultimate test of legitimacy in a ruler, not membership in a certain family but conformity to the will of Heaven.

Confucians and other Chinese thinkers described the universe as comprising three orders, Heaven, earth, and man. Heaven, the source of morals, is a realm of perfect order, and earth, man's physical environment, is always in harmony with Heaven. Man, the third term, sometimes is but sometimes is not in harmony with the other two. The good society can be brought into being only when man pays heed to Heaven's ordinances. The will of Heaven is made known to man in several ways: weather phenomena tell him how to order agricultural affairs; celestial phenomena enable him to keep an accurate calendar and, through the interpretations of astrologers, they portend future fortunes; finally, the happiness or hardship of the people indicates whether the ruler is governing well or badly by Heaven's exacting standards. Conformity to Heaven's will is the criterion for legitimacy. If the signs indicate that a ruler has lost Heaven's favor, he may properly be deposed.

If a whole dynasty so defaults, a new dynasty may justifiably take its place.

This reservation aside, the traditional Chinese theory of legitimacy was dynastic. That is, it was assumed that Heaven's will favored successive members of the same family until that family was actually dispossessed because of its failure to govern well.

From early times Chinese theorists recognized the possibility that a man or a dynasty might "rule" the country and still not be legitimate. This point is made with special clarity in the works of Mencius, who frequently wrote of the distinction between the true king, *wang*, and the man whose authority was contingent on his exercise of physical force, the overlord, *pa*. Some quotations will help to make clear the nature of the distinction. "He who uses his strength to simulate benevolence is an overlord; an overlord must possess a large country. He who uses his virtue to practice benevolence is a king; kingliness does not depend on size."[25] Furthermore, "Yao and Shun had benevolence and righteousness by nature; Yü and Wu achieved them; the overlords feigned them."[26] Still, government by the overlords was not wholly bad, for Mencius tells us: "Under the overlords the people were happy; under the kings the people were deeply content."[27] And one of Mencius's disciples suggested to Mencius that if the latter imparted his knowledge to one of the local princes whom he served, he might cause the prince to rule the land; "if [he were taught] for a short time, as an overlord; if extensively, as a king."[28]

There is a clear implication in the works of Mencius that in his time no true king existed. Good government, on however small a scale, was to be encouraged because it approached the state of affairs under the rule of the sage-kings of antiquity. If virtue in a ruler were sufficiently magnified, he would indeed become a true king.

25 Mencius, II, 1, iii, 1.   26 *Ibid.*, VII, 1, xxx, 1.
27 *Ibid.*, VII, 1, xiii, 1.   28 *Ibid.*, III, 2, i, 1.

Mencius's statement that the true king governs by moral suasion and that the overlord rules by force seemed to justify turning the actual work of the government over to the ministers. Legalist and Taoist thought in the third and second centuries B.C. was still more definite on the point that the emperor need take no active role in governmental affairs beyond the appointment of high officials and the bestowal of his approval on transactions already carried out by the ministers. Two statements from the works of the third century B.C. Legalist Han Fei Tzu will illustrate this idea:

The sceptre should never be shown. For its inner nature is non-assertion. The state affairs may be scattered to the four directions but the key to their administration is in the centre. The sage holding this key in his hand, people from the four directions come to render him meritorious services. He remains empty and waits for their services and they will exert their abilities by themselves.[29]

When everything exercises its special qualification, the ruler will not have to do anything. If the ruler has to exert any special skill of his own, it means that affairs are not going right.[30]

And the tersest of all statements of the desirability of "non-assertion" in the ruler is the deceptively Jeffersonian-looking line from the most highly respected text of the Taoist cult, the *Tao Tê Ching*: "That government is best of which only the existence is known."[31]

The question as to whether or not imperial government ever actually approached the condition here described is of no great consequence to the present discussion. The *ideal* of non-assertion remained influential, enabling historians to praise, for example, Emperor Wen of the Han (r. 180–157 B.C.) for exercising his benign influence through the intermediation of ministers and to blame Emperor Wu (r. 141–89 B.C.) for his personal, even despotic, rule.[32]

[29] Liao (trans.), *The Complete Works of Han Fei Tzu*, vol. 1, p. 52.
[30] *Ibid.*, p. 53.　　[31] *Tao Tê Ching*, XVII.
[32] See Dubs (trans.), *The History of the Former Han Dynasty*, vol. 2, pp. 8–10.

Despite the Legalist or Taoist influence on the Chinese conception of monarchy, it must be stressed that the Confucians' insistence on a ruler's moral responsibility for his government prevented the Chinese monarch from becoming completely dissociated from the actual administration. The government's mistakes were regarded as his mistakes, and the inexorable operation of Heaven's mandate made it impossible that a dynasty which had fallen into evil ways could perpetually escape retribution.

Between the Han and the Sung dynasties, the frequent changes of ruling houses and the alternation of periods of unity and disunity provided a large body of historical data to which theorists of legitimacy could apply their ideas. A number of great historians of the Sung dynasty described the operation of Heaven's mandate by pointing out the particular rulers and dynasties in Chinese history who had held it.

Sung theorists posited that there had been many changes of legitimate dynasty in the past. The Hsia, Shang, and Western Chou dynasties, all agreed, had successively enjoyed the mandate. The legitimacy of some later dynasties, however, was in question. The first Sung historian who used rationalistic principles to settle the problem as to where the legitimate line lay was Ou-yang Hsiu (1007–72), author of the *New History of the Five Dynasties,* titular editor of the *New History of the T'ang Dynasty,* master prose stylist, bureaucrat, and lexicographer. The work in which he summarized his ideas on legitimacy is called *Cheng-t'ung lun ch'i-shou* ("Seven Essays on the Theory of Legitimacy").[33] The cogency of Ou-yang Hsiu's reasoning, the brevity and directness of his presentation, and, above all, the absence of tendentiousness from his argument make this a cardinal document in the history of Chinese governmental thought.

In working out his own theory of dynastic succession, Ou-

[33] In *Ou-yang Wen-chung-Kung chi.*

yang Hsiu with patient logic refuted the fallacies in previous theories. One theory, held by many Confucianists from the Han to the Sung, ascribed to each dynasty the character of one of the five elements, which were believed to follow one another in a natural order of precedence. The exact order varied from one theorist to another, as did the elements assigned to the particular dynasties, but all theorists agreed that the Ch'in dynasty, to which the Han had succeeded, had come out of turn and that the Han was the rightful successor to the Chou. Ou-yang Hsiu called those who held this theory ignorant men and concluded that it was impossible to tell from it with certainty what dynasties had been legitimate.[34]

A second fallacy in previous legitimacy theories, he said, was their tendentiousness. The theorists employed by a certain court during a period of disunion invariably found plausible arguments for their own court's legitimacy, ignoring the claims of all their rival courts' apologists. Clearly the conflicting claims of rival dynasties would have to be examined in the light of some impartial test.

Ou-yang Hsiu's theory defines legitimacy as "rectification" and "unification." "Rectification" implied taking over the orderly and proper elements of the preceding dynasty and at the same time setting aright the misrule which had caused it to lose the country. A dynasty which both rectified and unified was clearly legitimate. Such a dynasty maintained Heaven's mandate until it was actually overthrown, even though it might long since have fallen into grievous mistakes that cried aloud for rectification. Thus, the Ch'in dynasty under the First Emperor (r. 247–207 B.C.) was legitimate, because (1) it unified China and (2) under earlier rulers (but not under the First Emperor himself) it had rectified the mistakes that had caused the Chou to crumble.

Ou-yang next conceded a certain sort of legitimacy to some

34 *Ibid.*, *kan* 59, p. 7a.

other dynasties in Chinese history: those who had inherited the orderly elements of a former legitimate dynasty but which failed to unify the country (for example, the Five Dynasties, 906–60); and those such as the Sui who came to power by upsetting the traditions of the preceding period but who unified the country and transmitted it to another, "rectifying" dynasty.

Many past theorists had gone on the assumption that Chinese history showed a single continuous line of legitimate dynasties, and that even in periods of complete disorder some one state could be called legitimate. Ou-yang Hsiu denied this, saying that in periods when no state satisfied the conditions for legitimacy, no rightful sovereign existed.

Ssu-ma Kuang (1019–86) included in his general history of China, the *Tzu-chih t'ung-chien* ("Comprehensive Mirror for Aid in Government"), a paragraph explaining his own theory of legitimacy.[35] The rightful sovereign, he implied, must unify the country, rule virtuously, and transmit the throne to his descendants. States that failed to meet these qualifications were not legitimate. All that one can say of periods of disunion is that rival states displayed varying degrees of good and bad government. One cannot call any of them legitimate.

The *T'ung-chien kang-mu*, Chu Hsi's abridgment of the *Tzu-chih t'ung-chien*, reflected in its organization and nomenclature Chu Hsi's ideas on legitimacy. These ideas are described in the book's preface (*fan li*).[36] Chu classifies all Chinese states and reigns under eight heads: (1) legitimate dynasties; (2) states enfeoffed under legitimate dynasties (for example, the feudal states under the early Chou dynasty); (3) usurping rulers who interrupted legitimate dynasties, for example, the Empress Lü (r. 187–180 B.C.) and Wang Mang (r. A.D. 9–23)

---

[35] *Tzu-chih t'ung-chien, chuan* 69, p. 8b. Translated in Fang, *The Chronicle of the Three Kingdoms (220–265)*, vol. 1, pp. 45–48.

[36] The *fan li* is prefaced to standard editions of the *T'ung-chien kang-mu*.

during the Han, and the Empress Wu (r. 684–705) during the T'ang; (4) rulers who established new states by means of their own kingly qualities, as with certain of the "warring states" before the Ch'in unification; (5) states in rebellion against a legitimate dynasty, for example, the Wei and Wu states in the "Three Kingdoms" period; (6) periods of anarchy, such as the 24 years that preceded the Ch'in unification and the four years preceding the Han unification; (7) rulers who inherited legitimate authority but lacked the ability to rule, for example Liu Hsüan; (8) small independent states remote from the central authority.

Ou-yang Hsiu, Ssu-ma Kuang, and Chu Hsi all agreed that a legitimate ruler ought to govern the whole country, or at least the major part of it, and they also agreed that some other factor of an ethical nature was essential if a dynasty could truly be said to possess the Mandate of Heaven. Of key importance to all three theories was the fact that in Chinese history there had been several legitimate dynasties, as well as several periods during which no state could be said to be legitimate.

· 4 ·

The earliest known Japanese conception of the imperial office may be described in very simple terms. The emperor was the intermediary between the gods and the people. The gods betokened nature, including both its benign and its malignant forces. On balance, however, they were conceived of as conferring an unearned blessing on the people, a blessing that took the forms of a habitable land to live in, plentiful food, and protection from natural hazards. These were the benefits that later Japanese comprehended under the general term *on*, the limitless and unrequitable divine gift that is the starting point for human ethical transactions. Morality required a reciprocal gift from the people to the gods. In its essence the repayment was an attitude compounded of gratitude and awe. Later Japanese used a Chinese derivative, *kei*, to describe this attitude, and its associations for them were close to those of the English word "reverence." The emperor was regarded as the central term in the transaction. He received *on* from the gods and repaid it with reverence; he conferred *on* on the people and in return was the object of their reverence.

The attempt by the Japanese to transform their country into a participant in Chinese civilization occurred between the sixth and eighth centuries of the Christian era. Governmental forms in this period came to be patterned after those of contemporary T'ang China, and it is only natural that Confucian ideas of monarchy were also assiduously studied in Japan. The far-reaching consequences to the political role of the emperor have been described in an earlier chapter. Where the religious foundations of the emperor's position in Japanese society were concerned, Japan in the main merely superimposed Confucian terminology on the earlier native beliefs. The subsequent history of thought on the emperor is largely one of adjustment of the terms of Chinese doctrine to native institutions.

Japanese rejected the claim of the Chinese monarchy to universal dominion. In so doing, they unconsciously rejected the idea that a perfect Confucian society implied a single world-state. The ideal domain of the Chinese monarch was called in Chinese *t'ien-hsia*, "all under Heaven." Even in China the word often meant the existing Chinese realm. As a loan-word in Japanese (tenka), it normally signified "the country" (Japan) and nothing more.

"Heaven" too, as the source of the sovereign's mandate, acquired a somewhat different sense in Japan from that of the Chinese word. As in the case of China, native Japanese theory assumed that a supernatural commission or mandate had established the monarchy and continued to guard it. However, the agency of the commission, as conceived of in Japan, was the anthropomorphic Sun Goddess, head of the Shinto pantheon. One can well imagine that the Japanese who first learned of the Heaven of the Chinese could not resist identifying it with the Sun Goddess's home. The relation of the Japanese emperor to the source of his authority had been regarded as a personal one, inasmuch as his main functions were ministrations to the deity and communication between her and the people. The concept of the mandate, which to Chinese meant the sovereign's attunement to universal order, was taken by the primitive Japanese to mean magic communion between king and god. More sophisticated Japanese of later times continued to confound the distinction between the two concepts by using the same terminology for both.

On one important point Chinese and Japanese theory agreed. The primary function of the sovereign was conceived of in both countries as something essentially different from the mere supervision of governmental administration. Hence it was possible for theorists of both countries to justify the sovereign's turning over the work of governing to his ministers and confining his own activities to those demanded by the symbolic or ritual nature of his role.

The problem of how to judge the transfer of sovereignty from one dynasty to another, which had given rise to so much of the Chinese legitimacy theory described above, did not arise in early Japan. A single dynasty of Japanese emperors had reigned from time immemorial, and it continued to do so after the adoption of Chinese institutions. Until the ninth century the Japanese dynasty could be said to have "governed" Japan. Even after the assumption of political power by successive Fujiwara ministers there was no question of dynastic revolution. The Fujiwara were in a pragmatic sense a new "dynasty" of rulers, yet they differed categorically from supplanting Chinese dynasties in that they made no claim to the magic and ritual functions of the imperial dynasty nor to the titles that belonged to it. The Minamoto, Hōjō, and later military families who ruled Japan continued to call themselves the emperor's subordinates or deputies, and the theoretical bases of the emperor's office did not change.

Nevertheless, the waning of imperial power led to the first native Japanese formulation of a theory of political legitimacy. This appeared soon after the rise to power of the first Hōjō regent. The Gukanshō,[37] written in 1221 by the Buddhist priest and aristocrat Jien (1155–1225), related national history to current political circumstances; Jien believed in the desirability of cooperation among the three vessels of power of his time, the imperial house, the shogunate, and the Hōjō regency. The Gukanshō was a book of conservative doctrine, tending to support the political status quo. Jien was motivated by a pressing occasion in writing it: he knew of the retired Emperor Go-Toba's hopes of overthrowing the military powers in Kamakura by force and feared the upset in polity that would result from such an attempt.

The last chapter of Gukanshō contains a discussion of Jien's ideas on the nature of the Japanese state. Jien addressed himself particularly to a defense of the Japanese custom by which the emperor reigned but did not rule. He said:

Though one might think that anyone with kingly qualities might be considered a king, since the age of the gods it has been the rule in Japan not to make emperor anyone who is not of the imperial family. It is also natural, however, that the country should desire a good ruler from among the members of the imperial family. Since it would be difficult for the sovereign to govern successfully by himself, he employs subjects as advisers and appoints them to great offices of state, directing that they manage the affairs of the country while paying reverence to him.[38]

In another paragraph Jien defends the custom of allowing minors to succeed to the throne:

[37] Gukanshō (in Kokushi taikei, vol. 19). Cf. Rahder, "Miscellany of Personal Views of an Ignorant Fool," pp. 173–230.
[38] Gukanshō, p. 212. Cf. Rahder, "Miscellany," p. 186.

From ancient times to the present, none but legitimate heirs have succeeded to the throne. If there were objections to the succession of a minor, the imperial line might die out, so such an objection would be unreasonable.[39]

It is plain from this that Jien's ideas on legitimacy differ in two major ways from those of the great Sung historians discussed above. Of the two criteria for the right to rule, heredity and ethical qualifications, Jien thought heredity was of greater importance, a reversal of the Chinese emphasis. By the same token, Jien apparently believed that, since legitimacy in Japan was defined in terms of the dynasty, the continuance of the dynasty from the foundation of the state meant that the nation had never been without a rightful ruler. Jien's justification for the delegation of governmental power to an emperor's ministers resembled the Legalists' and Taoists' ideal of a "non-assertive" sovereign. Jien's argument, however, was different. Whereas the Chinese would have argued that non-assertion was a positive good in a sovereign, Jien merely said that delegation of functions was sometimes necessary if the country was to live under an effective, as well as legitimate, government. Both the Chinese and Jien would have agreed, however, that the custom of delegating imperial powers to others was a reflection of the fact that a sovereign's first function was something other than the administration of the government.

The enunciation of a theory of legitimacy to bolster dynastic claims occurred quite naturally to men of the middle fourteenth century, when the allegiance of the nation was split between two branches of the imperial family. The *Jinnō shōtōki* ("Record of the Legitimate Line of the Sacred Dynasty"),[40] written in 1339, is spiritually the direct ancestor of loyalist works of the Tokugawa period. Its author, Kitabatake Chikafusa (1293–1354), was a leading minister in the court of the Yoshino (Southern)

---

[39] *Gukanshō*, p. 212. Cf. Rahder, "Miscellany," pp. 186–87.
[40] *Jinnō shōtō-ki*, (in *Yūhō-dō bunko*). Translated by Bohner as *Jinnō shōtō-ki, Buch von der Wahren Gott-kaiser-herrschafts-linie*.

Emperors Go-Daigo and Go-Murakami (r. 1339–68). Under siege while fighting Kyoto (Northern) forces, he wrote a history of the imperial dynasty, the background of the dynastic dispute, and the struggle to which he had been an eyewitness. The work includes many of Kitabatake's personal views of government, ethics, and the Shinto religion. He took special care to relate the history of Japan to that of the rest of the world as he knew it.

In the preface to the work he attempted a reconciliation of Indian, Chinese, and Shinto beliefs about the origin of the world and the destiny of mankind.[41] Surveying the history of Japan, he saw its dynastic stability as evidence that superhuman agencies guided its fate. He accepted the ancient account of the origin of the Japanese monarchy as he found it in the earliest chronicles, the *Kojiki* and *Nihon shoki*. He attributed the long continuance of the dynasty to the magic power of the three imperial regalia, mirror, jade ornament, and sword, given by the Sun Goddess to her grandson and thence to his descendants, the emperors of Japan. Yet Kitabatake failed to find in the chronicles an adequate explanation of what the regalia represented or why they had such unique force. Chinese philosophy, both Confucian and Buddhist, supplied the ethical terminology which he needed to account for the workings of the regalia in the world of men. In a triumph of applied syncretic mythology he explained what possession of the regalia implied: not just some inexplicable magic potency but also, at the same time, moral qualities of palpable earthly efficacy. The mirror, he said, has no permanent qualities of its own but reflects what is placed before it. Its virtue is "responsiveness," which is the source of honesty. The virtue of jade is its soft and yielding quality, the source of compassion. The sword is hard and sharp; its virtue is decisiveness, the source

---

[41] *Jinnō shōtō-ki*, pp. 1–22. Translated in Tsunoda, *et al.*, *Sources*, pp. 237–82.

of knowledge.[42] Kitabatake firmly believed in the supernatural character of the regalia, just as many Japanese who have written about them in more recent times have done, and past a certain point the theory of legitimacy which takes them as its basis can be understood only in terms of magic. Still, it is clear that the theory had already advanced a significant step beyond pure primitive magic when the elements in the myth had come to be explained in terms of ethical concepts wholly borrowed from outside the mythology.

Kitabatake went further than any of his predecessors in associating the emperor with ethical universals. There is an implication in his work, but nothing more definite than that, that the ethical values which he said existed as the essence of the imperial institution should also be attributes of the polity and of society. Nevertheless, it would be an enormous misreading of his work to assume that his political ethics were what sociologists call universalistic. The only practical issue of an ethical nature of concern to him was which of the two rival courts was legitimate. In his answer he did not say, for example, that the true emperor could be recognized by the test of his greater honesty, compassion, and knowledge. Nor did he say that the allegiance of subjects to the true sovereign was essentially determined by their prior devotion to those abstract ethical values. In the last analysis his formulation of the whole ethical duty of subjects was that they should first find the true regalia and then pay their loyalty and obedience to the emperor and government who possessed them.

We may sum up the lasting contribution of pre-Tokugawa thought on the imperial institution as follows. The emperor was taken to be the intermediate term in the principal religious transaction between the gods and men, a transaction by which infinite bounty was exchanged for infinite gratitude and awe. The emperor was also taken to be the token by which the right-

[42] *Jinnō shōtō-ki*, p. 21. Tsunoda *et al.*, *Sources*, p. 281.

ful government could be recognized. With Kitabatake Chikafusa a true theory of political morality centering in the imperial
institution began to emerge, but it went no further in his work
than merely to rationalize a particularistic ethic of obedience as
it applied to the emperor's subjects.

• 5 •

It was the unique achievement of certain Japanese Confucianists of the seventeenth and early eighteenth centuries that they
produced a theory of the Japanese state which embraced the
fundamental Confucian concepts of political ethics but at the
same time adapted them to the institutional peculiarities of
Japan. Similar in some obvious ways to the work of Kitabatake
Chikafusa, the neo-Confucian theory of the Japanese state proceeded from a different—almost an opposite—direction. Kitabatake's ethical presuppositions and values were of Japanese origin,
or at least he claimed that they were. He merely borrowed elements of Confucian or Buddhist doctrine to bolster or systema-
tize his beliefs. The seventeenth century thinkers, on the other
hand, were nurtured first of all in the foreign teaching, which
of course they did not regard as alien, but as universal. They
displayed genuine concern about the seeming incompatibilities
between Confucian and native Japanese values, and they did
what they could to explain them away.

In the time of the first Shogun, Hayashi Razan likened the
new Tokugawa state to a "supplanting" Chinese dynasty. In
fact he compared Ieyasu to those prototypes for virtuous over-
throwers of corrupt houses, T'ang and Wu, who founded the
Shang and Chou states.[43] The obvious implication is that for
Razan the philosophic place of the Chinese emperor was the
same as that of the Japanese head-of-effective-government, in

[43] *Hayashi Razan bunshū*, pp. 342–43. Cf. Earl, *Emperor and Nation*,
pp. 45–48. See also the discussion in Maruyama, *Nihon seiji shisō-shi
kenkyū*, pp. 12–13.

this case the shogun. Razan's terminology even allows us to assert that his entire understanding of Confucian ethical values was similar to the classic Chinese formulation that made the sovereign's ethical fitness to rule prior to his hereditary claim in determining his legitimacy.

"The will of all the people makes one a sovereign; without it, one is only a commoner."[44]

The sentiment here expressed is utterly incompatible with any earlier Japanese doctrine about the imperial institution, but of course he did not apply it to the imperial institution. It is quite fitting that it should have been spoken by a Confucian moralist to the shogun about the institution of the shogunate.

The firm ground which Razan establishes when he equates the Chinese emperor with the Japanese shogun crumbles at his treatment of the Japanese imperial institution. It is tempting to say that he considered that the emperor occupied the place of Heaven in the Chinese system, but there is nothing specific to confirm this conclusion. Many of Razan's references to emperors appear in historical contexts, in which imperial power or the absence of it in past reigns is described as a matter of fact; he even describes early emperors as "possessing" rather than bestowing the Mandate.[45] In contemporary contexts he usually associated the emperor in one way or another with Shinto institutions and tenets.[46] He frequently asserted the essential compatibility of Shinto and Confucianism. One may interpret this to mean that Shinto provided for him the mythic conception of a source for abstract ethics, much as he could find expressed in a more rationalistic way in the metaphysics of the Ch'eng-

[44] *Hayashi Razan bunshū*, pp. 342–43.
[45] Cf. *Jimmu Tennō-ron*, in *Hayashi Razan bunshū*, p. 280, in which Razan clearly considers the "hundred generations" of Jimmu's descendants institutionally analagous to the sovereigns of ancient China.
[46] "Our country is the birthplace and dwelling of the gods. Therefore it is called the land of the gods. Its regalia are called the implements of the gods. He who guards them is called the god-emperor." *Jingi hōten jo*, in *Hayashi Razan bunshū*, p. 558.

Chu School. He likened the three Japanese regalia to the three abstract virtues of wisdom, benevolence, and courage, which according to the Confucian classics were the specific moral tests of a sovereign's legitimacy.[47] His was of course a metaphorical rather than a literal way of speaking. It merely hints at the formulation which a latter-day rationalist might make that the emperor, for Razan, *symbolized* the moral order that was the arbiter of legitimacy in an effective government.

Two things, in short, deserve emphasis concerning Razan's beliefs about political legitimacy. The first is that here, where Chinese neo-Confucian thought on the subject first entered Japan, the ethical values which pertained to the imperial echelon of the Chinese state were applied squarely to the shogunal level of the Japanese. The second is that the name of the Japanese emperor hovers over Razan's political system as the metaphorical term of a poet rather than the hard, denotative word of a political philosopher.

Two generations later Arai Hakuseki stood precisely where Razan had stood in his judgment of shogunal legitimacy. The shogunal dynasty was legitimate, he said, if the tests of Confucian morality showed it to govern well.[48] There was little poetry in Hakuseki's soul, and it is hard to say that the emperor had even a metaphorical meaning in his state system. As with everything else he wrote about, the emperor was a palpable fact of life to him which had to be explained in the same terms as the rest of society's institutions. According to him the emperor was a man, superior in rank to the shogun (as having more ancient family pedigree), and he was not quite a figurehead, since he governed his own court and issued the patent of office that made the real ruler a "shogun."[49] The history of the institution explained for Hakuseki why things were done in this way in his

---

[47] *Jimmu Tennō-ron,* in *Hayashi Razan bunshū,* p. 286.

[48] See the discussion in Katsuta, *Arai Hakuseki no rekishi-gaku,* pp. 274–85.

[49] See Kurita, *Arai Hakuseki no bunji seiji,* pp. 571–90.

time, and he did not labor the point as to whether there was more to it—symbolic, magic, or moral—than that.[50]

Kumazawa Banzan and Yamaga Sokō were loyalists who stressed the magical or supernatural nature of the emperor's function in society, and who then went on to link it to processes of effective government in a manner that the intellect can apprehend. Banzan's formulation of governmental legitimacy cannot be called fundamentally different from that of Razan and Hakuseki, for he implied throughout his works that shogunal rule was fully justified so long as it was in accordance with the abstract principles of the Confucian school. However, to these ethical principles he added another, loyalty (or reverence) to the imperial throne. Banzan was one of the first to state explicitly a relationship which later loyalists, particularly the later Mito School, made much of. The feudal lords, he said, would serve the shogun in emulation of the loyalty which he in turn paid to the emperor:

Japan is praised even more than China as a land of superior men. This is because except for China there is no other country in the world where the Way of Rites and Music is practiced with such purity and refinement. And *this* is because of the Imperial Court. Since Taira Kiyomori and Minamoto Yoritomo warriors have been the rulers, bringing the country under control by means of martial courage. In their military skill they resembled uncivilized men. Yet despite the fact that they were soldiers, when they had ruled for a certain length of time they became effeminate and luxurious living made them soft. Though they might remain martial at heart, the effectiveness of their military skill declined. Most of them became lax in spirit. With their decline other uncivilized men appeared to conquer the country. Therefore, though they are called rulers of the country, they were not much different from peasants. If it had not been for the imperial court these frequent changes would within two or three hundred years have made us as barbarian as the Indians or Europeans. Because the imperial court exists the

[50] See the discussion of Hakuseki's *Tokushi yoron* in Katsuta, *Arai Hakuseki no rekishi-gaku*, pp. 138–81.

country was pacified. Since then the shoguns have unfailingly paid their obeisance, and when the daimyos assemble to witness the court ceremonials conducted with proper costumes and implements they know for the first time who is the proper exemplar for their own acts. Only when they hear the music of the court do they come to desire peace. When they ask of themselves what they are, they know that they are truly barbarians and that it is difficult to govern the land if one lacks the way. In order for a man born without civilization to govern the land he must respect the ancient rites, cherish the ancient music, hold the imperial court in reverence, and teach the duty of sovereign and subject to the land. The people of the land will see this, and seeing that a man without might or strength is taken to be the head and sinew of Japan they will offer their reverence in the same way.[51]

This is an application of an idea from ancient Confucianism that a ruler, by his own virtuous behavior, stimulates virtue in his subjects. Note that the "ruler" throughout his passage is the shogun, not the emperor. It is scarcely necessary to point out the essential parallelism of terms here: the emperor, civilization, and peace are ranged on one side of a balance whose other side is effective rule, warfare, and barbarism. The dualism of bun and bu have never been more forcibly expressed, nor has the infinitely greater desirability of the one over the other. The ruler's submission to a realm of peace will make his own domain a realm of peace.

Banzan implies that the emperor's very lack of effective power will aid him in performing his harmonizing function, for it will serve to convince the shogun's underlings that their obligation to obey is not based on fear but on universal ethical truth. Therefore, the emperor need not and should not be a temporal ruler.

It is said that Heaven destroys those who have ruled the country for many generations. However, the king[52] is a descendant of gods,

[51] *Shūgi Washo, kan* 8, in Inoue (ed.), *Nihon rinri ihen, Ō Yōmei-gaku no bu,* vol. 1, pp. 400–1.
[52] Banzan uses the word *ō,* usually translated "king," in analogy to the Sage-kings of Chinese antiquity. Of course he is referring to the Japanese emperor, whom other writers would most frequently call *kō* or *tennō.*

not an earth-born man at all. As the Japanese king is of especially broad virtue, he dispenses with power and resides gently above. This is the reason that he will always be the sovereign of Japan. It would be difficult for a military ruler to make himself a king, even if Heaven permitted it. But it is easy for him to take charge of the country if he does so with the spirit of a subject ruling in place of another. . . . Even if the shogunate were to return power to the emperor the state of affairs would not last. Even in the time of the Emperor Go-Daigo the court became estranged from the hearts of the Japanese people, and when this came about it lost the country. . . . For a military ruler to rise to the imperial position and for the king to take charge of the land would be little different from each other.[53]

Banzan stops short of identifying the emperor with the "Heaven" of the Chinese system, but he would appear to have gone one step nearer the identification than, say, Hayashi Razan, for he posited his beliefs as to the effectiveness of the emperor's moral force on his understanding of the supernatural condition and powers of the imperial dynasty. However he might have described his conception of what the emperor "did" in earthly society, he believed that he did something. In other words, the emperor for him was not a mere literary device to stand for the source of legitimacy, as one suspects he was for Razan, but the active agent which caused the government to act in accordance with correct ethical principles.

Yamaga Sokō's understanding of the throne's legitimating role appears to have been similar to that of Kumazawa Banzan. He too ascribed divine or magic power to the dynasty, and he also directed the preponderance of his attention to the level of effective government, which he implied was the actual possessor of the legitimacy (right to rule) the emperor bestowed.[54] Confusion arises from Sokō's treatment of the Chinese terminology, for he explicitly equated the emperor's place in Japanese society with that of the emperor in Chinese society. That is, the em-

---

[53] *Shūgi Washo*, pp. 402–3.
[54] See Mikami, *Sonnō-ron hattatsu-shi*, p. 389.

peror, not the shogun, possesses the Mandate, and the ultimate obligation of political obedience is to Kyoto rather than Edo.[55] The ambiguity resulting from this treatment of terms is not easily resolved. Sokō himself did not explain satisfactorily what it meant, but some of his contemporaries did, at least to a degree. For the moment, let us say simply that Sokō apparently regarded the shogun as a deputy of the emperor (as of course the earliest holders of the title had been considered from the start), but one whose deputized powers were total.

> The throne descends—fearful to say—from the Sun Goddess. Its lineage is eternal. Though the shogun wields power and governs the country, in truth he is only rectifying things for the imperial court. The shogun's greatest obligation as a subject to his sovereign is to carry out the affairs of the imperial court tirelessly in every detail.[56]

The terminology used of emperors varied among these different writers, as did some of the particular content of their political thought. What links all of them is the unstated assumption that it was shogunal government that was to be judged or justified in terms of Confucian theory of the state. All of them treated the imperial institution as in some sense superior to the shogunate, and as a result the emperor was a term in the systems of all of them that somehow stood apart from the classic Confucian formulation of political ethics as they understood it.

· 6 ·

When Yamaga Sokō asserted that Japan and not China was the "middle country," he offered as evidence the historical fact that China had had many imperial dynasties and Japan just one. He was not talking about dynasties of effective rulers, and in fact he does not seem to have been much concerned with the location

---

[55] See, for example, *Chūchō jijitsu*, in *Kogaku sōsho*, vol. 12, pp. 117–19.
[56] *Buke jiki*, quoted in Mikami, *Sonnō-ron hattatsu-shi*, p. 389.

of political power in his theory of legitimacy. He offered as one example of virtuous subjects the Fujiwara regents, whose deputized power lasted, he said, because "they were not as deficient in duty and morals as the rebels and bandits of China."[57] Sokō's contemporary Yamazaki Ansai was even more definite about rejecting the doctrine of justifiable revolution. According to him the founders of the Shang and Chou dynasties were not virtuous men at all, but usurpers who broke the ultimate moral commandment of loyalty to their sovereigns. In fact, the only figure in all of Chinese history who justifiably seized the throne by force was Emperor Kuang-Wu (r. 25–55), the founder of the Latter Han dynasty. He was a true restorationist, who brought back the legitimate Han dynasty after the interruption by the usurper Wang Mang.[58]

Ansai's ethical system would appear to have been a hierarchy of particularistic loyalties, with loyalty to the national polity as embodied in the emperor as the highest of all. The exact substance of the loyalty varied with the character of the collectivity to which it was directed.

> Between parent and child there is intimacy.
> Between lord and minister there is duty.
> Between husband and wife there is differentiation.
> Between elder and junior there is precedence.
> Between friend and friend there is fidelity.[59]

This particularism is of the classic Confucian kind, and Ansai made no changes in it. A more original contribution was to apply the Chinese concept of kei, "reverence," as the generalized term for every kind of obligation. Kei did not specify what acts one performed to discharge each obligation. It described the single attitude of mind that was the proper accompaniment of

---

[57] *Haisho zampitsu*, in *Yamaga Sokō shū*, p. 422.
[58] *Kō Yūsō shi-batsu*, in Mikami, *Sonnō-ron hattatsu-shi*, p. 212.
[59] *Hakka-dō gakki*, in *Zoku Yamazaki Ansai-shū*, vol. 3, p. 2. Translated in Tsunoda, *et al.*, *Sources*, p. 365.

every loyal act. Kei was conceived of as repayment for blessings received, or rather was the individual's inward recognition that the blessings had been received and ought to be repaid. Kei to the emperor was the acknowledgment of the total blessing that Heaven and earth provided for mankind. In Yamazaki Ansai's thought kei was increasingly identified with all those acts of Shinto worship by which one signifies one's gratitude for the bounty of nature and one's awe before its mystery.[60]

The loftier reaches of Ansai's thought are too abstract to be of much use in describing his attitude toward the institutions under which he lived. If he had written a history of Japan, he might have included in it some clues about the relevance of imperial loyalism to the processes of effective government. He did start a history, called the *Wakan*, "Mirror of Japan," but none of it is extant except the table of contents.[61] The most one can tell from this is that Ansai seems to have forecast certain of the Mito School's ideas as to the exact location of imperial sovereignty throughout Japanese history. In this and in numerous other ways Ansai was an important precursor of the early Mito School.[62]

The early Mito School devoted more attention to the question of political legitimacy than did any of their contemporaries. Their work is very valuable to us, because it gives us more definite answers where answers exist to the questions which loyalists then considered. Even where the contemporary beliefs about the emperor's place in a Confucian state system were too ill-formed to permit resolution, it is the Mito School whose writings reveal the ambiguities best.

Like Yamaga Sokō and Yamazaki Ansai, the Mito scholars treated the emperor in Japan as analogous to the emperor in China. They differed in that when they asked the question,

[60] See Tsunoda, *ibid.*, pp. 366–67.
[61] In *Yamazaki Ansai zenshū*, vol. 2, pp. 686–88.
[62] Mikami, *Sonnō-ron hattatsu-shi*, p. 210.

"Has the state the right to rule?" they directed their attention to the imperial rather than to the shogunal level of the state which they knew. In other words, their first question was not "By what test can one recognize the true government?" but "By what test can one recognize the true emperor?" On closer inspection it will be clear that the Mito School did not ignore the former question. In fact their work makes its possible for us to be more definite in answering it than one can from the imperial loyalism of a Yamazaki Ansai, a Hayashi Razan, or an Arai Hakuseki.

Let us therefore start where the Mito scholars started, with an examination of the general criteria upheld by them for legitimacy in a sovereign. Legitimacy, in Chinese and in earlier Japanese theory, had contained two ingredients: heredity and ethical fitness to rule. Chinese thinkers tended to believe that the latter was more important than the former, for they recognized that egregious misgovernment by ruling families had many times in the past justified dynastic revolutions. Jien ranked heredity over ethical qualities as a criterion for the legitimacy of sovereign. Kitabatake Chikafusa held that the criterion for legitimacy was possession of the imperial regalia, but that amounted to a criterion of blood inheritance, since he asserted that only the family to which they had originally been given could ever be said to "possess" them. However, Kitabatake included ethical considerations as well in his definition of legitimacy by asserting that the regalia necessarily carried with them certain ethical qualities.

The Mito School believed with Jien that heredity was the first principle of Japanese legitimacy, and with Kitabatake that legitimacy was also related in some fashion to the ethical criteria for good government. Mito scholars accepted Kitabatake's idea of the supernatural link between the regalia and imperial virtue, but they reinforced the relationship with an appeal to the neo-Confucian concept of the "Mandate of Heaven." "Heaven" to them meant not only the supernatural source of the imperial regalia but was also conceived of in Confucian terms as the natural order of the universe to which society should correspond. The School started from the assumption that at any particular time there is an earthly sovereign (of Japan) who bears the observable signs of legitimacy. They then sought to define these signs and to point out the individuals throughout history who possessed them.

The main criteria which the Mito School accepted are the easiest parts of their system to explain. They were (1) membership in the imperial family, and (2) possession of the regalia. The School accepted the accounts in the *Kojiki* and *Nihon shoki* of the transmission of the regalia by the Sun Goddess to the founder of the Japanese dynasty. They reasoned from later histories that the regalia had been handed down to successive members in the direct line of the imperial family. A reigning emperor had normally chosen his own successor by naming one of his relatives (son, brother, nephew, or cousin) Crown Prince. Still, the absolute test of legitimacy was possession of the regalia.

The efficacy of the regalia was interpreted partly as pure animistic magic, as in Kitabatake and Yamazaki Ansai, and Mito scholars also followed the examples of earlier writers in assigning symbolic values to the regalia in terms of Confucian ethics. One level of interpretation is similar to that in the *Jinnō shōtō-ki*: the regalia are linked with specific triads of values, such as honesty, compassion, and strength; or knowledge, benevolence, and courage. In other contexts or passages the possessor of the regalia is spoken of as the personal embodiment of all of the values which the natural order implies. It is impossible to say for certain what all of this means. One can be quite definite on one point: the Mito scholars were not asserting that the emperors of Japan *ought* to be virtuous, but they were in some way identifying them with virtue. Their work was not conceived for the edification of emperors, and they gave no particular attention to how the ordinary canons of Confucian ethical judgment should be applied to them. The conclusion that one can draw from this is that the symbolic ascriptions of the regalia were ethical values that should be translated into action by the emperor's subjects. It is *we* who should be virtuous, the Mito School says, and we may be helped to become so by the example of the emperor.

Yet it must be reasserted here that the Mito School accorded absolutely no practical value to a man's ethical fitness to rule as a guide in determining his legitimacy. The School believed that Go-Daigo was the legitimate sovereign and that his rivals in the Northern court were not. Nevertheless, Asaka Tampaku, a leading scholar of the early Mito School, in effect criticized Go-Daigo as a bad administrator and said that that was why the Kemmu Restoration failed. "His powers of discrimination were not equal to the task of distinguishing loyal subjects from those who only seemed to be loyal."[63] The *Dai Nihon shi* records countless instances of emperors deficient in virtue, whether cowardly, stupid, or fiendishly cruel. The text of the history does not especially linger over such descriptions of moral flaws, but it describes them unequivocally for what they were. Other writings by the School were sometimes openly critical of the acts of emperors. A striking instance of this is the School's execration of Emperor Temmu, whom they believed to have usurped the throne from his nephew Prince Ōtomo in 672, and then to have reigned as the legitimate ruler after Ōtomo's death in the same year. This is Asaka Tampaku's judgment of Temmu:

When a man has acted villainously in order to gain his own private ends, and then for an excuse has pointed to the examples of T'ang and Wu, it sometimes happens that later generations consider such behavior entirely normal and see nothing strange in it. Alas, taking

[63] *Dai Nihon shi sansō*, p. 80. Translated in Webb, *The Early Mito School*, p. 262.

possession of what one wants in this way is heinous from the start; how much the more so when one's own flesh and blood are the victims. . . . Though Temmu defended what he had seized with rites and music, he nevertheless used sword and spear to seize it.[64]

Aside from imperial blood and possession of the regalia the Mito School applied some other tests to determine whether a man had been emperor or not.

(1) If the court and the people of a certain time recognized that an otherwise qualified claimant was the sovereign, this was usually a sufficient indication to later historians that the claimant was legitimate. To the Mito School this test presupposed that the people of the time were of a certain level of sophistication. It was not applicable, for instance, in the case of the Empress Jingū (traditional reign dates, 200–69). The ancient chronicles indicate that she was regarded as the sovereign in her time, but the Mito School disqualified her on other grounds of which her primitive contemporaries would have been unaware. As a negative test, however, public recognition was of some usefulness. That is, a man whom none of his contemporaries regarded as legitimate could scarcely be considered so by later historians. A somewhat equivocal statement of Asaka Tampaku has it that "the importance of the regalia hinges on the loyalty or defection of people's hearts. If people's hearts are loyal, the regalia are important; if the people are alienated, the regalia are unimportant."[65]

(2) The legitimate sovereign at any given time had usually been designated as heir during the predecessor's reign. On the death or abdication of the sovereign, the heir automatically succeeded. The ceremonies of accession and enthronement were usually a sufficient indication to later historians that the court and country recognized the new reign and hence that the acces-

---

[64] *Dai Nihon shi sansō*, pp. 25–26. Translated in Webb, *The Early Mito School*, p. 196.

[65] *Dai Nihon shi sansō*, p. 84. Translated in Webb, *The Early Mito School*, p. 263.

sion had been legitimate. Negatively, the test might be used to disqualify a claimant. Empress Jingū was not designated as heir by her husband Emperor Chūai, and she did not undergo a regular accession ceremony.

(3) There could be no transfer of sovereignty without the death or voluntary abdication of a sovereign. Hence, Go-Daigo, who refused to abdicate, remained sovereign until his death.

What is the practical effect on government of legitimacy in rulers? The Mito School implies throughout its works that without a legitimate sovereign no good government is possible. Under a legitimate sovereign, good government is possible but still not automatically assured. The explanation seems to lie in a doctrine of "moral exemplification," the idea that if the ruler is virtuous the people will imitate him. Yet in this case we have moral exemplification of a complex kind. When the Mito historians wished to uphold a virtuous example for ordinary men to follow, they usually described a virtuous minister who demonstrated loyalty to his sovereign. For example, Lord Takeuchi was a devoted minister of several early rulers, including Empress Jingū. Asaka Tampaku says of him: "His devoted service to her was an example for the other ministers. The ministers in their turn all knew that they should be loyal to the legitimate line."[66] Mito writings about Go-Daigo's loyal minister Kusunoki Masashige state or imply that his loyalty stimulated loyalty in those less closely associated with the throne.[67] This is reminiscent of Kumazawa Banzan, who applied the concept of the moral exemplar to the ministerial, rather than to the imperial, level of the state.

Nevertheless, the emperor was also spoken of as a virtuous example, and the loyalty and other virtues of his ministers were in some sense in emulation of imperial virtue. Inasmuch as the

---

[66] *Shiron shiden*, in *Mito-gaku taikei*, vol. 6, p. 365. Translated in Webb, *The Early Mito School*, p. 169.
[67] See for example *Dai Nihon shi sansō*, pp. 218–19.

emperor need not have any of the qualities of moral excellence that the School described for ordinary men, the statement is susceptible to only one interpretation. The emperor was a symbol of virtue. He was a physical reminder to the ministers and the other subjects that society is founded on universal principles of order and morality. There are therefore three terms to be described in the Mito School's doctrine of moral exemplification. These are the people, the ministers, and the emperor. The morality of the people is in imitation of the ministers' virtuous acts, but the ministers behave virtuously in emulation of the ideal of virtue of which the emperor is the personification.

There are thus two requisites for good government. One of them is the perpetual existence in concrete form of a political ideal. The other is virtue in ministers, or to apply the same terms as before it is the existence of officials who look to the natural order and morality exemplified in the sovereign and apply them to the management of the country's affairs.

Men of excellent wisdom have established an imperishable thing in the imperial dynasty, and their superior knowledge and great discrimination have distinguished them far above the average of men. Yet, unless they are unwavering in discharging their public duty, their wisdom will not suffice to bring the hearts of men to submission and destroy the misconceptions of the people.[68]

There is a strong implication throughout works of the seventeenth century legitimist tradition that in the realm of political behavior the acts of a reigning legitimate sovereign must not be judged by any of his subjects. In this sense the attitude that was required of subjects was that the sovereign can do no wrong, and that his only shortcoming is his physical inability to discharge all of the affairs of the state and society. But this shortcoming would be of no consequence if the officials to whom the sovereign delegates his authority always exercised their power wisely.

[68] *Ibid.*, p. 350. Translated in Webb, *The Early Mito School*, p. 200.

Hence, there was no necessity for legitimists to deny the human merits of men of power who were not legitimate sovereigns, for imperial legitimacy to them was different in kind from ordinary virtues in subjects, and men of authority were living up to their ethical responsibilities as long as they paid heed to what the legitimate sovereign symbolized. For example, the *Dai Nihon shi* shows an attitude of general approval toward the Empress Jingū, whose martial vigor and patriotic ambition seemed to compensate for the fact that she was outside the rightful succession.

But if direct imperial rule was not a mark of good government, then what was? It is difficult to answer the question directly, but Mito works, especially the *Dai Nihon shi*, describe by implication an ideal state and society, which enables one to abstract from it the principal ingredients of good government.

Foremost among the desirable qualities of government was that the entire nation be under one strong central authority. A phrase recurs in Mito writings that illustrates this ideal: "As Heaven has not two suns, so earth has not two masters."[69] Post-Restoration writers could easily take the existence of military government separate from the imperial court to be a species of government by "two masters," but the phrase is equally explainable as an argument that there should be only one national government. Sixteenth-century disunity in Japan sufficed to convince seventeenth-century thinkers of the value of unified rule. The *Dai Nihon shi* deplores disunion and division as nothing else. These are precisely the practical consequences of disloyalty to the sovereign. In illustration, take the revolt of 672. The rebellion by the future Emperor Temmu against the legitimate government of his nephew Ōtomo created two courts with plausible claims to legitimacy. The country was rent and did not

---

[69] The phrase is from the *Li Chi*, the Confucian Classic of Rites. Legge (trans.), *The Li Ki*, in Müller (ed.), *Sacred Books of the East*, vol. 27, p. 323; vol. 28, p. 285; p. 467.

know which government to obey. However, after Ōtomo's suicide, legitimacy plainly resided with the victorious Temmu, who thenceforth reigned undisputed monarch over an undivided country.

The case of the first Ashikaga shogun, Takauji, was an instance of the reverse order. As leader of the anti-Hōjō armies, he helped suppress the disunity that previously existed between the Kyoto and Kamakura courts. When he turned against Go-Daigo to support a rival claimant to the throne, however, he was a sower of discord and as such was to be condemned.

In both these cases the *Dai Nihon shi* reacts sharply to the change in role of the men involved. Temmu as rebel is execrated; as unifier he is lauded. Takauji as suppressor of disunity is praised; as bringer of schism he is damned.

A second qualification of good government is peace, or stability. Strong, unified rule goes part way toward ensuring this ideal, for it implies the absence of civil disputes among local rulers, such as had characterized the period before the reunification of Japan. Still, good government must guard in addition against two other kinds of disturbances. It must defend the national frontiers against "barbarian" (including overseas) invasions, and it must protect society against revolts by subjects.

Throughout most of the period covered by the *Dai Nihon shi* Japan was plagued by the constant threat of depredation by non-Japanese natives in the Japanese archipelago. The portions of the work dealing with the period up to the ninth or tenth century give much space to the military exploits designed to expand the frontiers of Japanese settlement. As barbarians in southwest Japan were subdued, the government turned to the northern aborigines, the Emishi or Ainu. The detailed attention given to all of these campaigns in the *Dai Nihon shi* and the hero-worshipping biographies of generals and soldiers who fought in them attest to the importance given to national security. Likewise, the *Dai Nihon shi* accords especially detailed treatment to two attempted invasions in the thirteenth century by the Mongols under Kublai Khan and to their repulsion by a fortuitous typhoon, which to the Japanese meant supernatural aid attributable in some fashion to imperial virtue.

There are also countless references in the part of the *Dai Nihon shi* dealing with late Heian and Kamakura times to civil disturbances of a kind that the compilers thought to be wholly deplorable. These were invasions of the capital by armed Buddhist monks out to settle grudges against the government or against rival monastic groups. The age-old standing war between the rival Tendai monasteries on Mt. Hiei and at Ōtsu (the Enryaku-ji and the Onjō-ji) continued into the fourteenth century. The *Dai Nihon shi* significantly omits all mention of the causes or issues of these affairs, for the only matter of concern to the compilers was the deleterious effect which they had on orderly civil government.

A third desirable quality in the ideal state is a certain level of economic security and general well-being among the common people. The *Dai Nihon shi* mentions all major famines and other calamities known to the writers, though they give less attention to such matters than would be usual in a Chinese work of the same scale. The apparent explanation is that famines in Japan had never been occasions of anti-imperial rebellions, as had many in China. Still, economic distress was regarded as an evidence of misgovernment and worthy of prominent mention.

Another mark of a good administration was an aggressive or evangelizing spirit measured in successful attempts to bring overseas nations under Japanese rule. Until the sixteenth century, Japanese military adventures overseas were limited to sporadic attempts to conquer or dominate parts of Korea (third to seventh centuries) and forays along the China coast by Japanese pirates, some of whom were backed by local rulers in Japan (thirteenth to sixteenth centuries). The Empress Jingū's invasion of Korea is the only foreign conquest to be fully described in the *Dai Nihon shi*. The account is a classic instance of a successful battle story: the magic portents of success, the hesitance of pusilanimous advisers, the effortless conquest, the magnanimity shown toward the defeated enemy, and finally the ceremonies of exultation and gratitude by the victorious army—all contribute to the epic character of the narrative. To the outside observer the conquest may well appear to have been pure aggression, but there is not a hint in the *Dai Nihon shi* that the campaign was anything but a master stroke for bringing the benighted Koreans under enlightened Japanese rule.

The fifth and last of the major ingredients of good government, as revealed in the *Dai Nihon shi*, is adherence to the ceremonies and forms of the ideal state. One feature of the work that strikes the modern reader is the excessively detailed attention given in the Annals to appointments, resignations, and deaths of figurehead officials. Equally striking is the amount of space devoted to imperial rituals. But the detail did not seem excessive to the compilers. Many of the ritual practices were prerogatives of the emperor. When a man performed them, he signified that he claimed to be a legitimate sovereign. When the court and the people participated in the rites performed by such a claimant, they indicated their acceptance of his reign. On this level the rites were a concrete symbol of the compact between a sovereign and his subjects. Furthermore, some of the rites performed by the emperor were thought to have magic potency. Most important, the whole system of offices, ceremonies, and usages symbolized adherence to natural morality and order, on which a good society must be founded. Each rite and office of the ideal state was a term in an elaborate mythology of nature, man, and society. Even after the ritsu-ryo system became a mere formality, it remained a concrete reminder to the country of the natural principles without which society would disintegrate. The Mito writers were not so naive as to suppose that so long as the official and ritual systems remained intact, all would be well in the state. But they quite reasonably believed that departure from the forms signified disregard for the most essential principles of social morality.

The *Dai Nihon shi*, being a history in the Chinese tradition, existed for the sake of moral instruction; it is a record of adherence to or departure from the requirements for good government. The existence and recognition of a legitimate sovereign supply one indispensable requisite for a well-governed society, but ultimately good government depends on the morality of ministers who put into practice the precepts which the sovereign symbolizes.

All that has been said so far about the necessity of there being a legitimate sovereign if society is to function properly would seem to indicate that the emperor himself, as a person, need take no part at all in most of the practical affairs of state. While this was true, the Japanese emperors were expected by the Mito scholars to perform certain functions which were regarded as of some importance to the administration.

The sovereign's functions in the actual government followed naturally from the legitimating function of the imperial institution. Any principle of legitimacy in government serves two ends: to ensure *acceptance* of government by those governed, and to provide for orderly *continuation* of government and social organization.

The first of these ends, acceptance by the governed, is not the same thing as "consent of the governed," as conceived of in democratic theory. Indeed, no such idea ever occurred to members of the Mito School, or to other premodern Japanese political thinkers. Chinese political thought makes a place for consent of the governed in its doctrine that when the people revolt and overthrow a government, it is shown to have lost its legitimacy. Even so, popular satisfaction in Chinese theory is nothing more than an index of the real criterion for legitimacy, which is the Mandate of Heaven, that is, correspondence of the human state to the natural order. Japanese theory has still less to say about popular will. By the terms of its doctrine of legitimacy, the legitimate dynasty cannot be dispossessed. Yet with all these qualifications, there is still a relationship in Japanese theory between legitimacy and popular acceptance of government. To a Japanese theorist the relation could be expressed as follows: If the people know the identity of the legitimate sovereign, they will willingly submit to him and as a consequence they will be happy and at peace.

The same relationship can also be described in other terms. Force alone cannot achieve orderly, efficient government, but once the entire society has understood that even an autocratic government is preferable to sheer chaos, and once the people as a whole begin to pay taxes and obey the laws out of the perception, however dim, that it is a social necessity to do so, then the state can rest on firm foundations. Any universally accepted theory of legitimacy in government serves to make people believe that life in an orderly society is preferable to the existence of animals in the fields. The first function of the Japanese sovereign, then, was a natural consequence of this aspect of his legitimacy. It was simply to "be there," to give his sanction to the government, so long as it was in accordance with broad principles of order and morality, to perform the magic rites of his office in the full view of the ministers, and by doing all these things to demonstrate to the people that there was a single, authoritative government in the country to which they ought to submit.

The second end which a principle of legitimacy serves is the perpetuation of government in an orderly fashion from generation to generation or through times of upheaval. The emperor had a personal responsibility in ensuring the continuance of the Japanese state. It consisted of his producing offspring, then providing unequivocally for a successor upon his abdication or death, and refusing to yield his position without first knowing that his successor would be universally recognized as sovereign. The *Dai Nihon shi* and its commentaries by members of the compiling staff contain many explicit or indirect statements about what these responsibilities meant in practice. It is said, for example, that the Empress Jingū's ultimate service to the nation lay in the fact that she bridged the interregnum between the death of her husband and the birth of his posthumous son. When her biography in the *Dai Nihon shi* says that she "personally arranged for the succession," it means that she fulfilled the duty of the imperial office that her husband had failed to do.[70] The compilers deplored the fact that Emperor Tenji left the matter unclear at his death as to whether his successor should be his brother Temmu or his son Ōtomo; he thereby was the indirect cause of the revolt that followed.[71] Most conspicuously of all, the history lauds the exemplary way in which its supreme hero Go-Daigo lived up to his responsibilities by refusing to yield the regalia to a successor whom he regarded as a mere puppet of Ashikaga Takauji.[72]

The Mito School categorically denied that there was any right of dynastic revolution, because such a right seemed to them to destroy the very order and continuity that the imperial institution existed to preserve. Chinese political theorists sought to justify dynastic changes because Chinese history showed the continuance of a single tradition of political institutions under many different dynasties. Superficially, there has been no need for such justification in Japanese theory, because a single imperial dynasty has reigned from the beginning of Japanese history until the present. Yet the ideas that a government is responsible for

[70] *Dai Nihon shi*, vol. 4, p. 14. Translated in Webb, *The Early Mito School*, p. 145.
[71] *Dai Nihon shi*, vol. 1, pp. 128–40. Translated in Webb, *The Early Mito School*, pp. 172–93.
[72] *Dai Nihon shi*, vol. 3, pp. 299–333. Translated in Webb, *The Early Mito School*, pp. 211–60.

its acts and that it risks losing Heaven's approbation if it mis-
governs for long were so central to Confucian political theory
that the Mito scholars could scarcely have called themselves
Confucian if they had not incorporated similar ideas into their
own theory.

Seventeenth-century Japanese scholars knew too much about
the history of their country to believe that divine protection of
the dynasty automatically ensured good government. They
realized that Japan had often been misgoverned and that from
time to time the incompetence of men of authority had led to
political upheavals of a sort that in China would have meant
actual changes of dynasty. In explaining and justifying those
upheavals the Mito School was applying the Confucian theory
of revolutions to Japanese history.

The Mito School believed with Chinese Confucianists in the
triad of Heaven, earth, and man and agreed that man was the
variable factor. They conceived of the good society in much the
same terms as did Chinese Confucianists and accepted the role
of portents, astrology, and popular well-being as signs of good or
bad government. They even accepted the idea that if the government was irredeemably bad, it might be overthrown. Witness
their approval of Ashikaga Takauji's overthrow of the Hōjō
regency. The one significant part of the Chinese system that
they did not accept was the idea that the dynasty itself might
be overthrown and that a new, legitimate dynasty might take its
place.

Mencius's distinction between the king, who governs by
moral suasion, and the overlord, who governs by force, is not
strictly appropriate to the Mito theory. In the world Mencius
knew, no true king could be found, but any local ruler might
hope to attain kingliness if his fitness to govern were sufficiently
manifest to the whole country. In the system described in Mito
works, a legitimate sovereign could be determined from the

founding of the empire until the time of the work's termination, and indeed the legitimate line could even be projected forward until the end of human history. To the Mito scholars it was impossible that a ruler who was not of the imperial dynasty should attain or even approach legitimacy merely by being virtuous. "We have legitimate sovereigns," they seem to say, "and they *are* virtuous." Still, the Mito scholars recognized that there were imperfections in society. Since they could not ascribe them to imperfections in the sovereign, as Chinese thinkers might have done, they could only blame them on the failure of responsible ministers to reflect properly the virtuous example of the emperor.

The emperors of feudal Japan had something in common with the "non-assertive" rulers commended by Legalist and Taoist theory in China. In Japan, however, the sovereign maintained a separate court geographically far removed from the center of the administration. The Mito School took advantage of this fact in its governmental theory, but by doing so it made a change of great importance in Chinese Confucian theory of the state. Mito scholars removed the sovereign entirely from his place at the head of responsible earthly government and made him part of the Heavenly order which is the pattern for earthly society. The emperor, to them, was as far beyond criticism and responsibility for the administration as the stars themselves.

The place which the sovereign occupied in Chinese theory was taken in Mito thought by the responsible human agencies of government: prime ministers, regents, shoguns, or regents for shoguns. These were the men who risked losing the approbation of Heaven (that is, of the sovereign) if they governed badly. If they governed well, they normally passed their authority on to their descendants. Thus dynasties of responsible officials ruled Japan for longer or shorter periods of time, much as dynasties of emperors had ruled in China, but here, as in

Chinese Confucian theory, the ancestry of a ruler was ultimately of less importance as a test of his right to govern than his conformity to Heaven's will.

· 7 ·

Having accepted the idea that reverence for the sovereign by the responsible agents of government was equivalent to respect for Heaven's will, the Mito School could go on to appraise the affairs of the Japanese state on the basis of an orthodox Confucian standard of public morality. Hence the importance to the system of their second avowed aim in compiling the *Dai Nihon shi*, "to establish the morality of subjects."

The writings of the early Mito School imply a theory of personal ethics which is an indivisible part of their theory of the state and of imperial legitimacy. Yet it is a theory which is never explicitly stated. No single concept from the vast body of Confucian ethical works appears in their writings with sufficient frequency or prominence to enable the student to hold it up to view as the kernel of their system. Modern scholars tend to describe the political and personal ethics of Tokugawa Mitsukuni and his Confucian retainers in terms of certain words and phrases which, while not prominent in seventeenth-century Mito writings, are strongly emphasized in those of their nineteenth-century successors (the later Mito School). The words most frequently used to describe the ethical content of the *Dai Nihon shi* have been *taigi* and *meibun*.

The expression "taigi-meibun" is used almost as though it were a single indivisible thing. In fact the two words were originally quite separate concepts. Taigi is ultimate, or supreme, duty, or righteousness. Translation is difficult because the Chinese concept *i* (Japanese, *gi*) is elusive. To all Confucians it meant the proper performance of specific duties that were called for by the particular time and circumstances. As a social ethic it meant behaving toward whomever one saw in accordance with the specific obligations that existed between the two persons. In classical literature the term taigi seems to have meant merely an extremity of righteousness. The locus classicus is in the *Tso Chuan*, where a loyal minister is praised as having shown the highest sense of duty by having his own son executed as a rebel against the sovereign.[73] Obligation in that case demanded that the minister sacrifice his mere human affections. Japanese always use the term taigi in a political sense, as a subject's duty to ultimate political authority. More particularly, it refers to a person's obligations to the national polity, as opposed, say, to narrower feudal loyalties. The Mito School demanded that the recipient of a subject's taigi be the emperor rather than the shogun. In other words they personified the national polity in the imperial symbol. They were not unique in doing this, for Yamazaki Ansai and Yamaga Sokō said substantially the same thing in different words. In none of these writers is there the slightest indication that duty to the sovereign implies disloyalty to the shogun. Indeed, all of their work shows that they respected the institutional framework of the shogunate and regarded it as the contemporary embodiment of the national polity. To say that taigi is directed toward the emperor rather than the shogun was a means of generalizing the obligation of patriotism as it had existed in diverse ages. The emperor served equally well as a token for the national polity in the age of Shōtoku Taishi, the time of the Fujiwara Regents, the Kemmu Restoration, and the seventeenth century.

Meibun means "name and portion." The "name" referred to here is that of an individual's official position or social class, to which his "portion" (his lot in life, and also his behavior) should correspond. Meibun is therefore like taigi in that it calls for a proper matching of ethical behavior with social status.

[73] *Tso Chuan*, in Legge (trans.), *The Chinese Classics*, vol. 5, part 1, p. 15.

Furthermore, the particular social distinction to which Mito scholars invariably referred when they used the word meibun is that between sovereigns and subjects. As an ethical ideal meibun means that a subject should recognize that he is a subject and should not aspire to the treatment of a sovereign. He should moreover know the identity of the sovereign and tender him the treatment which is his due.

The Confucian doctrine which underlies the concept of meibun is that of "rectification." This doctrine stems from a play on words in the Analects: "To govern (cheng) is to rectify (cheng)."[74] All political phenomena, the doctrine says, are in a process of unceasing change. If bad tendencies are not checked at the start, they will lead to ever greater evil. Rectification consists in studying the tendencies of phenomena and distinguishing the good from the bad. Part of this process is the "rectification of names," by which is meant giving rightful names to things so that people can distinguish between the good and the bad. The Analects provides the classic statement of the importance of this:

What is necessary is to rectify names. . . . If names be not correct, language will not be in accordance with the truth of things. If language be not in accordance with the truth of things, business cannot be carried on with success, proprieties and music will not flourish. When proprieties and music do not flourish, justice and law will disappear. When justice and law disappear, people will suffer from anarchism and warfare.[75]

Rectification of names was one of the functions of the historian. History was conceived of as a collection of good and bad examples for men to imitate and shun. Only exact nomenclature could ensure that a history was properly instructive. The Dai Nihon shi exemplified rectification of names first of all by distinguishing clearly among legitimate rulers, men whose au-

[74] Analects, XII, xvii.
[75] Analects, XIII, iii, 2–6.

thority was derived from emperors, and the governed. The rectification of names in this narrow sense was what the Mito School spoke of as meibun.

It may be seen that taigi and meibun were applied to two different levels of the polity. As they were applied to the governed, they meant necessary subordination to the polity. As they were applied to a nonimperial administrator of the government, they meant subordination to the emperor. Not only must the people obey the authorities, but the authorities, whether they are called prime ministers, regents, or shoguns, should recognize their own status as subjects of the emperor. The proper attitude of a head of government to the sovereign was not so much obedience as reverence. Of course, reverence implied that there should be no flouting of the emperor's will, but it also implied that the secular authorities should act with constant attention to what the emperor symbolized, namely the moral principles and natural forces that held society together.

Another of the Mito School's favorite epigrams for describing their ethical point of view was *Chūkō itchi*, which means "Patriotism and filial piety are the same thing." The word *chū* is usually translated "loyalty." It has a more inclusive meaning than the English word "patriotism," for it may be applied to the bond between an individual and any of his political superiors, including, for example, his local feudal lord. However, as the Mito School almost always applied the term to the individual's proper submission to the national polity, "patriotism" seems to have connotations more appropriate to the present case than does the broader word.

Robert Bellah has described Japanese social values with great succinctness by saying that "the family is the polity writ small."[76] In other words, pyramidal organization and the emphasis on upward-directed obligations are characteristics of both kinds of social unit. That is one meaning implicit in the Mito

[76] Bellah, *Tokugawa Religion, the Values of Pre-Industrial Japan*, p. 18.

School's epigram. It meant that a man's natural sentiments of love and respect for his parents and his obedience to them should be transferred in his political life to the emperor and through him to the polity and to society as a whole.

However, as we have noticed with taigi-meibun, there are two hierarchical levels to which Mito ethical thought was directed, and as a consequence there were two very different levels of interpretation of their ethical maxims. As they pertained to the relations between ordinary people and the government, Mito ethics emphasized submission, loyalty, and obedience to superior persons. As they pertained to the relations between the authorities of the government and the emperor, they emphasized dedication to universal values. Filial piety, as Chinese and Japanese treated it, is the most conservative of all ethical ideals. It demanded not only that there be a hierarchy among the living members of one's family, but also that reverence must be shown to all one's forebears, to whom one owes infinite obligation in exchange for the infinite gift of life that one has received from them. In manifestation of this reverence one must preserve the family and protect it from shame. The maxim that patriotism and filial piety are the same, when directed toward the shogun himself, likened his charge to an ancestral legacy, which must be preserved in moral health out of reverence for the benevolent dead from whom he had received it.

A third slogan is used to describe the convictions of the Mito School on political morality. This is *Bumbu fugi,* "the civil and military orders are not divided." Herein the entire ethical system of the Mito School is summarized. The order to which the Tokugawa family of Mito belonged was the military order, not only in the sense that the founder of the family had been a soldier, but also in the sense that the government that the family maintained was based on force. In Western terms the effective basis of Tokugawa period feudal government was the police power of the shogunate and the han.

One main purpose of the Mito scholars, as of all other loyalists of the seventeenth century, was to devise a system of
political absolutes that could be shown to be independent of
the vicissitudes of military power. The theory which they devised was in no way incompatible with the existence of feudal
government. On the contrary, it was a way of bolstering the
authority of the shogun and the han, for it gave to them an
essential place under the emperor in their ideal state.

On the practical level, the maxim that "the civil order [that
is, the ideal system over which the emperor presided] and the
military order are one" meant that the feudal lords' obedience
to the shogun and the people's obedience to the feudal lords
were sufficient manifestations on the part of these underlings
of reverence for the throne. Emperor, shogun, feudal lords, and
commoners were thereby brought together under a single consistent theory of the state.

On the ideal level the maxim meant that those values of law
and morality that were implicit in the term *bunji seiji* ought to
govern the secular state. As the emperor and the administration
might be described as the head and torso of the political body,
so might the means of law and force be described as its left and
right hands. Force instilled fear in men and thereby compelled
their obedience to an authority external to themselves. Law
filled them with reverence and thereby caused them to understand within themselves how to live in harmony with other
men. Both force and law were necessary. For ordinary men they
were complementary, force being required to subdue a man who
did not understand law. For rulers they were complementary
in a different sense. No force was imposed on them from outside, but the force which they wielded ought to be governed by
a higher law. That law, as the early Mito School and other
seventeenth-century loyalists implied in all their works, was
universal moral truth, though the name which they gave to it
was imperial will.

· 8 ·

Institutional conservatism marked the words and deeds of the formulators of Tokugawa period loyalism. Yet they created a concept that appeared to be as subversive as possible of the status quo. This was the ideal of Restoration, the return of the country to the happy condition in which it had once been but from which it had long ago departed.

The ideal of Restorationism must be explained in terms of a view of history that was essentially Confucian but that may have been foreshadowed for the Japanese by certain ideas of Buddhism. There is an idea that is especially associated with Japanese Buddhism of the late Heian and Kamakura periods that the tendencies of history are in the main degenerative. The idea took its most characteristic form in the doctrine of *Mappō*, the "Latter Days of the Law." According to this, in the age of the historical Buddha his teachings were expressed in all their perfect wholeness and complexity, and those who heard them were blessed with the capacity to understand them; the teaching, the "Law," remained, but with time men's understanding declined, and they could no longer perceive the Law clearly or practice it correctly; a millennium and a half after the death of the Buddha—about the middle of the Heian period in Japan— the world was supposed to have come upon its maximum degeneration, wherein men's own powers failed them utterly, leaving them dependent on external grace to save them from perfect depravity.[77]

The Confucian counterpart of the idea of Mappō is to be seen most clearly in the fundamental presupposition of the Ancient Studies School of Japanese Confucianism: early China had been ruled by sages whose virtue made their subjects virtuous, but after the Duke of Chou sages no longer occupied the

[77] See Eliot, *Japanese Buddhism*, pp. 184; 424–25.

throne; Confucius and Mencius lived in an age of institutional decline, but they had complete understanding of moral truth; after their time even moral understanding failed, and the new developments which Confucianism underwent in the Han and in the Sung were perversions that led ever further from the Way of the Sages.[78]

The Orthodox and Wang Yang-ming Schools denied the part of this argument that pertained to their own teachings, but they agreed that the institutions and usages of the Sage-kings of Chinese antiquity furnished an ideal that no society since their time had ever lived up to completely. We have here a view of man's nature that seems scarcely less pessimistic than that of the Buddhists, saying that there is something about mankind that causes him to corrupt the good institutions and pervert the correct moral teachings that have been bequeathed to him.

Counterbalancing this pessimism there is another view shared by Confucianists of all persuasions that man can through his moral understanding combat these degenerative tendencies. We have seen that Confucius regarded government as "rectification," a process of continuous moral awareness in which every small deviation from the Way was seen instantly for what it was and immediately checked. Though moral excellence of an ordinary kind might succeed in keeping things from degenerating further than they had already, it required virtue of a quite extraordinary kind to erase the past marks of decay and restore the happy condition of antiquity. Chinese historians from Ssu-ma Ch'ien onward tended to take the view that that degree of virtue had most frequently been found in founders of dynasties, men whom Heaven commanded to set aright with a sudden decisive effort the corruption into which the former reigning house had fallen.[79] The prototypes for those who restored the

[78] Based on the Preface to Itō, *Kokon gakuhen*, in Inoue (ed.), *Nihon rinri ihen, Kogaku-ha no bu*, vol. 2, p. 216. Translated in Tsunoda *et al.*, *Sources*, pp. 412–13.
[79] See Watson, *Ssu-ma Ch'ien, Grand Historian of China*, pp. 5–6.

old by setting themselves anew on the throne were King T'ang of the Shang dynasty and King Wen of the Chou dynasty. Implications of both oldness and newness are indivisible in the concept of restoration. A poem about King Wen in the *Book of Odes* provided the classic statement of this: "Though the Chou state was old, as for the Mandate, *this* was new."[80] The characters for "*This* was new" became a synonym for restoration, especially in Japan, where they were pronounced *ishin*.

Chinese historians believed that there had also been occasions when restoration had been effected without a change of dynasty. These came about when a man of truly kingly virtue succeeded to an office which his ancestors had allowed to become degenerate. Ssu-ma Ch'ien described several of these "regenerations" (chung-hsing; Japanese, chūkō), in the Shang, the Chou, and the Han dynasties. They were regarded as renewals of the Mandate, in the sense that Heaven bestowed its command for the second time on a house whose misrule had begun to make it lose Heaven's favor.[81]

Japanese Confucian historians of the Tokugawa period accepted the Chinese concepts concerning restoration and frequently applied them to the events of Japanese history. The treatment which they accorded to the foundation of the Tokugawa shogunate is a clear instance of this. Hayashi Razan likened Tokugawa Ieyasu to T'ang and Wen; the concrete manifestation of his virtue was the restoration of peace and firm government after centuries of turbulence and anarchy. A number of historians implicitly ascribed to the Tokugawa a position in Japanese history similar to what the imperial reunifiers of the Ch'in and Han dynasties had occupied in Chinese history. At least as early as the time of Arai Hakuseki the period from the Ōnin war to the reestablishment of an effective

[80] *Shih Ching*, III, 1, i, 1. (Legge, *The Chinese Classics*, vol. 4, part 2, p. 427.)
[81] Watson, *Ssu-ma Ch'ien*, pp. 5–6.

central government was referred to as the "Warring States" (sengoku) period. This was an obvious allusion to the name which Chinese historians gave to the turbulent, disunified condition of China in the fifth, fourth, and third centuries before Christ. Other historians emphasized the meritorious role that the Tokugawa had played as restorers of the ancient rituals of state, meaning of course the rituals that were associated with the imperial court. As we have seen, this was one of the main points made by Kumazawa Banzan in his discussion of the imperial institution. Members of the early Mito School characteristically treated the Tokugawa achievement as a kind of "restoration," stressing not only the reimposition of peace and order but also the marked improvement in treatment which the governing authorities gave to the imperial court and the imperial house. With them too the restoration of ancient court ritual was a cardinal factor in Tokugawa success. Ieyasu had rebuilt the imperial palace and greatly increased the court's income; *thereby* he enabled the rituals to be performed properly; *thereby* peace and order returned to society.[82]

The deeds of the Tokugawa seemed to most loyalists to merit quite different treatment from that accorded to T'ang and Wen. It would never have occurred to any loyalist to have applied the word ishin to the Tokugawa conquest. So far as terminology was concerned, the "Mandate" was something that belonged to the emperor, and it was neither conferred on a new family nor newly confirmed in the posession of an old one by means of the achievement of the first Tokugawa shogun. There is an ambiguity in all Tokugawa political thought, including this, as to which level of the state, the imperial or the effective, corresponded to the kingly, responsible, and governing institution

---

[82] Based on Asaka, "Tō Shissei ni itasu no sho," in *Mito-gaku taikei*, vol. 6, pp. 413–14. Translated in Webb, "The Development of an Orthodox Attitude Toward the Imperial Institution in the Nineteenth Century," in Jansen, ed., *Changing Japanese Attitudes Toward Modernization*, pp. 174–75.

described in Confucian state theory. The terminology which they used most of the time suggests that the corresponding term in Japan was the emperor, but the practical application by them of Confucian ethics invariably suggests that it was the effective ruler.

When the Japanese used the word chūkō they meant the sudden appearance of a new sovereign of such great personal merit that he instantly reinvigorates his enfeebled family. The archtype of such a restorer, in the works of Japanese history produced by Tokugawa Confucianists, was the Emperor Go-Daigo. If we examine typical loyalist attitudes toward Go-Daigo's career, we may perhaps see more clearly what the loyalists meant by restoration and what ethical judgments they made about it.

To men of the Tokugawa period Go-Daigo seemed a heroic figure. However, he was a tragic hero, for his noble aspirations came to nothing on account of a fatal personal flaw. Everyone agreed that his destruction of the Hōjō regency had been an act of just vengeance against a family which had humiliated his ancestors. The act was also regarded as having rid the country of a regime that had sunk into corruption and become unfit to rule. The institutional system under the Kemmu Restoration resembled that of the Engi period, which in turn was the same as the symmetrical structure of a Chinese-style state that had flourished in the Nara period. The emperor ruled as well as reigned. Of course he did not rule alone, for he had to rely on ministers to carry out his intentions. It was the choice of his ministers that revealed Go-Daigo's tragic failing and brought about his ruin. He trusted Ashikaga Takauji, who turned out to be his betrayer. Not only that, but in one famous instance he allowed Takauji to poison his mind against one of his sons, who was also one of his most loyal supporters. The son was Prince Morinaga (1308–35), who had earlier led a military force against the Hōjō on behalf of the Emperor. After Go-Daigo's restoration he was a prominent member of the government.

Ashikaga Takauji was jealous of his position and falsely accused him of harboring rebellious thoughts against the Emperor. The Emperor then had Morinaga arrested and sent to Kamakura in the custody of Takauji's brother and cohort, Ashikaga Tadayoshi. Tadayoshi had Morinaga killed in 1335, while the latter was in prison.[83] Misjudgments of character such as this caused the Emperor's government to fall. Nevertheless, the net judgment of historians was that Go-Daigo had been a righteous and noble ruler and that his character was therefore worthy of emulation by later generations.

Even here Tokugawa writers showed some ambivalence, for they left it unclear how far contemporary society should go in imitating Go-Daigo's example. Kumazawa Banzan used the case of Go-Daigo to show why power should *not* be returned to the emperor. The Mito School, with its characteristic ambiguity about the problem of imperial rule, merely asserted that the task of an imperial restoration is fraught with dangers and that its success or failure is unpredictable. As Asaka Tampaku put it:

[Go-Daigo] tried to restore the government of the Engi period, but in the end he could not. Since ancient times everyone has agreed that the task of founding a country is difficult and the task of maintaining it is even more difficult. With hard work one can build a nation, but if one is negligent one is likely to forget that one also has a duty to perpetuate it.[84]

Another Mito scholar, Kuriyama Sempō (1671–1706), went further in linking Go-Daigo's experience to contemporary society. He did so in his most influential work, *Hōken taiki* ("Illustrious record from Hōan to Kemmu [1123–1336]"), more particularly in the portion of that work in which Kuriyama discusses the causes of Go-Daigo's failure. Kuriyama agreed with his fellow-schoolmen that Go-Daigo possessed some of the

---

[83] *Dai jimmei jiten, sub* Morinaga Shinnō.
[84] *Dai Nihon shi sansō*, in *Mito-gaku taikei*, vol. 6, pp. 80–81. Translated in Webb, *The Early Mito School*, p. 262.

personal qualities necessary for restoration but was deficient in others. To use Kuriyama's own metaphor, Go-Daigo caused the branches to luxuriate, but he was insufficiently attentive to the root. Kuriyama then added:

If the sovereign were assiduously to discipline himself and cultivate virtue, he would not have to make further provision, but the hearts of the people of the country would submit to him of their own accord; he would not have to instill fear in them, but they would fear him spontaneously. Heaven's Mandate follows naturally what people's hearts obey and fear. Nothing can obstruct that which has the Mandate of Heaven. The sovereign should devote his attention to this.[85]

It is not entirely clear from Kuriyama's words whether he intended this passage as a generalized statement of the preconditions for a restoration, or whether he was simply stating the conditions that would have been required for Go-Daigo's restoration to have succeeded. The English translation is in accord with the interpretation of modern Japanese scholars, who take the passage to be a prescription for Kuriyama's own time.[86] If this interpretation is correct, the passage is unusual, for loyalists of the time rarely even hinted at the existence of moral deficiencies in living emperors and practically always directed their ethical injunctions to emperors' subjects rather than to emperors. It should be noted that whatever ambiguities there may be in the passage, it is unequivocal in defining the basis of restoration as moral regeneration rather than some more specific institutional or social reform.

With this evidence before us, we may make several deductions about the concept of a restoration in the work of seventeenth-century loyalists. A real restoration was unequivocally desirable, if it succeeded; the motives that prompted a man to attempt a restoration were praiseworthy even if the attempt

[85] *Hōken taiki*, in *Mito-gaku taikei*, vol. 7, pp. 64–65.
[86] See Tsuji, *Nihon bunka-shi*, vol. 5, pp. 268–70. Mikami, *Sonnō-ron hattatsu-shi*, p. 299.

failed. There was no ambiguity and no particular danger in those principles so long as they were used only for passing judgments on past historical events. The ambiguity and the potential danger arose when the principles came to be seen as practical precepts for action. Until the advent of dissident loyalism late in the Tokugawa period the ideal of restoration was so tame as to have had virtually no effect on larger historical movements, but the ideal was nevertheless an important part of loyalist thought on the imperial institution, and its implications must therefore be examined.

In the first place, restorationism may be explained in part as a kind of racial nostalgia, the historical counterpart of that habit of the individual's memory to veil whatever is unpleasant in his past experience and retain only what is pleasant. It has been explained in an earlier chapter that the historical nostalgia of the Japanese has tended to be focused simultaneously on two contrary parts of the nation's experience. One part was the Native Way, in other words, whatever was non-Chinese about Japanese civilization. The other part was the Nara period, when at least upper-class Japanese had imitated Chinese ways most successfully. The two ideals were mutually incompatible, but ever since the Nara period itself there had been attempts to rationalize the contradiction. The rationalization took the form of an assertion that in the legendary dawn of Japanese nationhood the forms and usages of the state, particularly those that related to the emperor, had been somewhat similar to those that existed in the imperial reigns from Temmu to Kammu. Jimmu ruled as well as reigned, but his rule was by "rites and music." He was an evangelizing nationalist, for he extended the frontiers of Japanese rule from Kyushu to the Yamato plain. He was solicitous of the well-being of his people. He maintained peace and presided over a national government, all of whose provincial units were loyal to him. In short, all of the virtues that classically educated scholars of the Tokugawa period had

learned from Chinese studies to associate with the ideal state
they believed to have belonged to Emperor Jimmu. The source
for this view of the earliest state of the Japanese monarchy was
the *Nihon shoki,* and few Tokugawa Japanese doubted its ac-
curacy.

The particular temporal focus of the nostalgia of a Tokugawa
period restorationist could equally easily be the Kemmu Restoration, the Engi period, the Nara period, or the age of Jimmu.
Yet the details that figured the ideal for which restorationists
longed were always those of a civilized and sophisticated age
utterly different from primitive Japan as historians now know
it to have been.

There was more to restorationism than hopeless yearning for
the real or imagined glories of the dead past. The ideal of a
restoration was the characteristic mode of Japanese utopian
thought. The premise that the reign of Jimmu had been a
golden age seemed to imply the conclusion that any characteristic which one believed to be a property of an ideal state had
existed in the reign of Jimmu. Only a very naive person would
have accepted the full implications of this argument. It would
have been absurd to say, for example, that because castellated
fortifications and firearms were features of the best defense systems, they must have existed in Jimmu's time. The recent introduction from Europe of those technical devices would have been
ample refutation of that idea. However, if there was no definite
evidence to the contrary, almost any institution or practice that
one thought desirable could be said to have originated in the
time of Jimmu. A man who advocated an original solution to
some political or social problem might not literally believe that
there were any precedents for his proposal, but he would most
likely describe the proposal in the form of a legendary or fictitious account of enlightened antiquity.

The result is utopianism of a kind, but one should refer to it
as "inverted utopianism" to distinguish it from the classic

modes of utopian thought in the West. Some classic utopian thinkers of the West, like Plato and Thomas More, described an ideal state as something that might perhaps be achieved in the future if one were not too hobbled by existing institutions. Some writers, like George Orwell, have created ironic "pseudo-utopias," describing the horrors toward which existing institutions seemed to be headed. Common to both types is the projection into an unknown future of a society that might rise out of existing institutions but that will be very different from any society known in history.

Quotations can be found in the works of virtually every Confucian writer of the Tokugawa period that illustrate the inverted utopian mode of their thought. Here is one from Muro Kyūsō: "Under the Three Dynasties the rulers regarded the people as Heaven. Therefore they lightened taxes and aided the people in times of distress, so that the people were not reduced to fleeing elsewhere and wandering about the country."[87] Kumazawa Banzan said: "On the whole, a noble and lasting social order can only be built on a farmer-samurai basis. Now is the time to restore the farmer-soldier of olden times."[88] Here we have Yamazaki Ansai exhorting his disciples to steadfastness of mind, which he equated with the "element" metal: "The Sun Goddess was female, but when the Storm God got out of hand, she put on warlike attire and took up a sword. Even Izanagi and Izanami ruled the land by use of the spade and sword. From very earliest times Japan has been under the rule of the metal power."[89]

Japanese thinkers rarely wrote whole literary works of the class of the many "utopias" of Western literature. Utopian thought must be sought in sentences and paragraphs, usually in the context of discussions of Chinese and Japanese history.

[87] From *Shundai zatsuwa*, translated in Tsunoda *et al.*, *Sources*, p. 440.
[88] From *Daigaku wakumon*, translated in Tsunoda *et al.*, *Sources*, p. 392.
[89] Translated in *ibid.*, p. 369.

As often as not, writers left unstated the obvious implication that what they described as good in some golden age of the past should be taken as a model for future action. When they wished to be explicit about it, they needed only to make the single exhortation: "Restore antiquity!" To their contemporaries those words were infinitely more inspiriting than some rough equivalent in prose such as "Work to create an ideal society."

Historical nostalgia and the utopian character of restorationism both account for why the emperor was associated with restoration. The imperial institution preserved the traces of the distant past better than any other institution. It was indigenous, but its externals were as they had been in the heyday of Chinese civilization in Japan. Even the impotence of imperial society increased its value to nostalgic men. The defencelessness of the court made it all the more in need of being cherished by loyal subjects. The sadness of the court's state mirrored perfectly the sad decline of society from its earlier splendor.

Sophisticated men found another way of putting the imperial institution to use in their calls for restoration. The ideal toward which "utopian" restorationism tended may be summed up as "government by rites and music." That classic Confucian phrase has just the right combination of definiteness and vagueness for our purposes. The ideal was definite enough on two points, that it demanded the performance of magic or symbolic rituals and that it called for a society responsive to understood moral principles rather than force. For the rest, the phrase "rites and music" is rather ambiguous. It might involve farm work for a samurai, as Kumazawa Banzan seemed to believe, or again it might mean a strict demarcation between the military and peasant classes, as the Tokugawa authorities demanded.

The qualities of imperial "government," the behavior of the court in Kyoto, made it a perfect concrete image of government by rites and music. It wielded no force, and its work consisted wholly of ritual. Beyond that almost nothing was known of it.

Ethical ascriptions were made of it, but they were curiously empty of specific qualities. Men of the Tokugawa period knew no more about the particular virtues of their sovereign than they did about, say, the tax structure of Jimmu's government. That ethical emptiness about the imperial institution made it just the right token for the restorationist ideal, for even men of opposite beliefs about specific moral issues could all employ the imperial symbolism when they discussed what they thought to be the properties of the ideal state.

It may be argued that nothing was accomplished by this, that the loyalists could have described their ideas on political ethics equally easily without reference to empty tokens of abstract morals. Man has always clothed his most cherished social and moral beliefs in aesthetic dress. There can be no doubt that Plato's and Thomas More's descriptions of the ideal state gain force from being presented in the form of beautiful works of art. The Japanese are an art-loving and an art-making people, and it would be strange if they had produced no aesthetic representations of their vision of the perfect society. Yet there have been no Platos or Thomas Mores among them. The artistic representation must be looked for elsewhere than in literature, though there are countless literary allusions to it. The Kyoto court performed an endlessly recurring drama which was a symbolic representation of the behavior of society when institutions had been new and morality had reigned.

• 9 •

The changes in loyalist thought from the early eighteenth century until the first half of the nineteenth century were more matters of application to specific problems and occasions than they were fundamental alterations of belief. There was a growing apprehension of serious national problems, particularly problems that faced the shogunal administration, and as before the thinkers who suggested new solutions to them frequently described the solutions in terms of the imperial institution and loyalty to the emperor. As before the denotation of the imperial symbol was not any one principle of political ethics that might be applied to a given problem; it was the entire moral substratum beneath all of society, by which all of the works of society could be justified.

In some quarters loyalism slipped loose from its old Confucian moorings. The National scholars (Kokugaku-sha), who were an extreme case of the nostalgia for the indigenous, reaffirmed substantially the same conception of the emperor in the state and society that their Confucian predecessors had framed, but their expression of it was characteristically Japanese. Even the expression was not completely new, for Yamazaki Ansai, Yamaga Sokō, and the early Mito School had anticipated the most important elements of it. Those scholars had emphasized the essential harmony between Japanese and Chinese conceptions of the good society. The National scholars, with greater or less firmness, rejected the Chinese conception, at least in the terms in which Confucians had framed it. There are many Confucian influences on National thought, but they are covert.

The main contributions of National scholarship lay in the fields of literary criticism, philology, and religion, rather than political thought. Kamo Mabuchi (1697–1769) urged the constant study of the *Man'yōshū*, the great anthology of Japanese poetry of the Nara and earlier periods, as the best way of understanding the "feelings and expressions" of antiquity.[90] He did not think of this as mere entertainment, but conceived of it as having a profound moral purpose. The study of that remote age was a way to become like the people who lived in it, who he thought were the proper exemplars for present men. The

[90] Quoted from Muraoka, *Studies in Shinto Thought*, p. 119. This paragraph and the following are based largely on information in the Muraoka article here cited ("Kamo Mabuchi and Motoori Norinaga"), though I differ from Muraoka in some points of interpretation.

moral superiority of the past was a matter of its "valor and directness," untouched by the effeminacy and sophistication that came with Chinese ways. There was some of the usual kind of ambiguity about the focus of Mabuchi's restorationist nostalgia. That was in part because all written records in Japan reflect a degree of Chinese influence. The *Man'yōshū* was a Nara period compilation, and many poems in it actually dated from that time. Mabuchi's first ideal of a perfect age was the scarcely less sinicized period of the Fujiwara court (694–710), immediately before the establishment of the Nara capital. Late in his life he found a contrary ideal in pre-Taika Japan, and then the ambiguity was dispelled. Mabuchi exalted values that for all one can tell probably did exist in the earliest period of Japanese culture.

. . . The minds of the Japanese were smoothly flowing with no sharp edges, and direct by nature. Therefore the Japanese had no pompous doctrines like those of Benevolence, Right-doing, Propriety, Wisdom, and Good Faith. There was not even any writing. Nor was marriage between brothers and sisters of the half blood necessarily avoided. There was no splendor of roofs, earthen walls, and clothes of bark cloth and hemp. . . . Since the Emperors from the Imperial ancestral Kami on down ruled above in accord with the spirit of Heaven and earth, the ministers served with faithful hearts below.[91]

If, as Professor Muraoka asserts, Mabuchi's concern in the same late phase of his career was moving in the direction of a practical prescription for political action, the features of the dream were exceedingly vague: "If there should emerge a man on high who loves antiquity and who hopes to put the world right, the world will be entirely put right within ten or twenty years. . . . Through the thought and feeling of one man on high, the world can certainly be changed."[92] There is nothing here that a Confucian restorationist—say, of the Mito School—would have disagreed with.

[91] *Ibid.*, p. 122.   [92] *Ibid.*, pp. 126–27.

Motoori Norinaga (1730–1801) pioneered in unraveling the philological mysteries of the *Kojiki*, which he took to be a better account of early Japan than the *Nihon shoki*, because it was less influenced by Chinese prejudices. The *Kojiki* confirmed the other book's legend of divine national origins, but it painted a somewhat less Chinese-looking picture of the condition of Japan in the legendary age. Nevertheless that age had the same associations for him that it had had for Confucian loyalists: bland, peaceful, and otherwise ethically featureless.

Norinaga described the emperor mostly as a chief priest of the national religion who had oracular powers. In the nearest Norinaga comes to a political statement concerning the emperor, he describes him as possessing the country, because he received it as a legacy from the Sun Goddess. Both the land and the people were his, but the shogun was a kind of lessee. The relationship between the two demanded some sort of repayment; for Norinaga the proper repayment took the form of reverence. Ieyasu exemplified that attitude by restoring the fortunes of the court. The imperial institution in Norinaga's time was surely better off, he said, than it had been in the period of the "Warring States," and it could be said to be in a state of decline only if one compared it with what it had been in the period of its greatest power. There is so little here that is new that there would be no point in mentioning it at all if the idea were not widespread that National scholarship created a radically different vision of the essential features of Japanese society from any that had gone before.[93] Hirata Atsutane (1776–1843), who was the most famous National scholar of the nineteenth century, was radical in his exaltation of everything Japanese at the expense of everything foreign, but his thought on the emperor was in no important way different from Norinaga's.[94]

[93] *Tama Kushige*, quoted in Mikami, *Sonnō-ron hattatsu-shi*, pp. 355–56.

[94] See Tsuji, *Nihon bunka-shi*, vol. 5, pp. 357–58.

· 10 ·

The creative thought of the early nineteenth century that involved the emperor continued as before to be Confucian. The seedbed once again was the official academic establishment maintained by the Mito domain. The later Mito School took shape shortly after 1800; its earliest member to attain national prominence was Fujita Yūkoku (1774–1826). Yūkoku's loyalism, a beautifully expressed, but unoriginal, restatement of earlier loyalist ideas, need not detain us here. Respect for the Tokugawa family and for the shogunal institution are as prominent in his writings as are his love of and reverence for the imperial institution.[95]

We reluctantly pass over his son Fujita Tōko (1806–55), a leading Confucian adviser to the daimyo Tokugawa Nariaki (1800–60), for although he was an unusually skillful manipulator of words in the loyalist cause, he had little that was really original to contribute to it.[96] We also pass over, temporarily, Nariaki himself, for he was a figure of state, important not so much for what he said about the imperial institution as for the direct influence he had on its fortunes.

The greatest of the later Mito scholars from the point of view of his contribution to thought on the emperor was Aizawa Seishisai (1782–1863). He too was a Confucian adviser in Nariaki's retinue. He was less eminent as a scholar than as a persuasive rhetorician who applied powerful moral arguments to the consideration of urgent national problems. The main problem with which he was concerned was national defense against European and American aggression. His most important book, the Shinron (1825),[97] was written nearly a generation before

[95] See the passage from Fujita, Seimei-ron, translated and discussed in Webb, "Development of an Orthodox Attitude," p. 177.

[96] See Tsuji, Nihon bunka-shi, vol. 5, pp. 352–55.

[97] Shinron, in Mito-gaku taikei, vol. 2, pp. 2–189. See discussion and translated excerpts in Tsunoda et al., Sources, pp. 592–603.

the forced opening of the country, but Seishisai wrote with an insider's knowledge that aggressive Western pressures against Japan could not be far in the future. He was in close touch with policy-making officials of the Mito domain, and through them with officials of the shogunal government who were already well aware that Western activity in Eastern waters had increased markedly in the past few years. The Mito domain lay on a stretch of Pacific coast that was contiguous to the main shipping route from America to Asia. A large share of the ships sighted off shore, the casual landings on Japanese soil by Western seamen, and the arrival on shore of Western castaways during those years occurred in Mito territory.

The message of the *Shinron* is simple: Defensive installations must be greatly increased, and it is the shogunate's duty to increase them. The message was reiterated in countless ways through nearly 200 pages of Seishisai's passionate rhetoric, but the single rhetorical phrase that summed up Seishisai's work for later generations was "Repel the barbarians!" (jōi). Seishisai chose moreover to place his argument in the framework of imperial loyalism. The reason that the shogun had the duty of maintaining national defense was that the emperor had commanded him to do so. The specific commission that the secular ruler enjoyed from the emperor made him *sei-i tai-shōgun*, "great general for barbarian chastisement." Only by repelling the barbarians could the shogun exemplify his reverence for the emperor. That proper attitude of the shogun to the throne had many names in Seishisai's work, but the name that lived to typify the loyalism of the later Mito School was *sonnō*, "revere the emperor." Sonnō and jōi, inextricably bound together into a single catch-phrase, were the twin concepts at the heart of the *Shinron*.

The use of the emperor's name to lend moral universality to a specific policy was an old loyalist habit, but the application of that technique to this particular issue was new because the issue itself was newly perceived. Sonnō and jōi had a fascinating history in the 45 years following the writing of the *Shinron*. They meant different things to different people and in different periods, as catchphrases are likely to do. It would be wise to consider some of the implications which these ideas had in this earliest stage of their currency.

First, the imperative "Repel the barbarians" was addressed to the shogun, or more aptly perhaps, the policy makers of the shogunate. The whole burden of Seishisai's argument was that *they* had the responsibility of doing something about the foreign threat. In other words, it was not the daimyos, not the samurai as a whole, and certainly not anyone in the lower orders of society to whom Seishisai made his exhortation. Every line of the *Shinron* shows it to be a policy proposal to policy makers, rather than a general call for mass action. Reverence to the emperor, so Seishisai implies, is everybody's duty, but only in the case of the shogun does that duty imply the responsibility for national defense.

A second point to notice about the argument of the *Shinron* is that what Seishisai called for was *national* defense, that is, the defense of all the Japanese islands, not only the portion of the country that was under direct shogunal rule. The shogun's authority varied in different areas. It was most far-reaching in the tenryō, or shogunal domain, and least so in the territories that were ruled by the tozama daimyos. The *Shinron* made the point that so far as national defense was concerned shogunal responsibilities extended equally throughout the tenryō and all of the han. Far from wishing to limit the power of the shogun, either in respect to the emperor or in respect to the feudatories, Seishisai intended the exact opposite. He wished to cause the shogunate to shoulder new burdens and to exercise its national authority in an unprecedented degree.

The national character of the *Shinron's* charge to the shogunate helps to explain further the importance of the imperial symbol to the argument. The nexus of feudal relationships among shogun, daimyos of various classes, direct shogunal vassals of less than daimyo rank, and the direct and rear vassals of daimyos made for bewildering complexity in the mechanism by which shogunal commands were translated into individual action. Specific individual duties, even the duty to obey the law, accorded with specific bonds between persons. The bond that elicited instant obedience from a shogunal elder simply did not exist between the shogun and, let us say, a Chōshū rear vassal. A shogunal order might eventually be enforced for the Chōshū vassal, but not until it had been transmitted through several nodes of the feudal hierarchy. Defense was a national problem and required national cooperation, but that was not easy to achieve in the particularistic loyalty structure that existed.

The emperor was the only man in Japan who stood in exactly the same relation to one feudal person as he did to every other. One way of putting it would be to say that the emperor bore absolutely no relation within the feudal system to any other person, either in terms of bonds of fealty upward or downward, or in terms of obligations to repay temporal services rendered. Aizawa Seishisai's way of putting it was different, for he regarded the benefits which everyone received from the emperor as infinite and therefore regarded the repayment to be received from every man individually as infinite. "The reason that the feudal lords all give respectful heed to the rule and the ordinances of the shogunate is that they all stand subordinate to the emperor's rule in service to the divine ancestors. This is the place where the government of the shogunate and the government of the feudal lords become united."[98]

The Japanese emperor, as the Constitution of 1947 puts it, is the symbol of state and of the unity of the people. And so he has been for centuries, but there is a difference between the unity symbolism in, say, the "Warring States" period and in

[98] *Shinron*, pp. 181–82.

1825. In the earlier period the emperor meant unification, the creation of a national state where there was none. In 1825 a national state did exist, and the emperor betokened the uniformity of its authority and responsibility in every region and toward every subject.

One more loyalist of the first half of the century must be mentioned. This is the historian Rai San'yō (1780–1832), author of the *Nihon gaishi*.[99] His work is a bridge to the final and dissident phase of loyalism in the Tokugawa period. The attitude that defines San'yō's loyalism is a regret that the political power that had once belonged to the emperor had passed into the hands of the military families. The feeling, which was not new to loyalism, seems to have been more active and intense in San'yō's case than, say, with the early Mito School, but one cannot be sure. Whatever attitude San'yō may have held toward the Tokugawa government, it is not very satisfactorily described in his writings. Prewar Japanese scholars claimed to detect hostility there and a desire to see the shogunate overthrown and power restored to the emperor. The evidence, however it may be interpreted, begins to appear on the first page of the *Nihon gaishi*:

When our country was first established, government forms were simple, the civil and military ways were united, and everyone performed military service for the country with the emperor as the supreme commander and the great chieftain and great deity chieftain as lieutenants. No one was specially appointed to be a general. Still less were there such things as military families or military lords. Therefore if there were no untoward affairs in the country, military affairs ceased. If an occasion warranted, the emperor always personally performed the chastisement of the rebels. Or if he did not, an imperial prince or the empress did the work for him. Never would he delegate the work to a subject.[100]

This is surely "inverted utopianism," but is it restorationism in any more active sense than that? It seems rather to be derived

[99] *Nihon gaishi,* (in *Yūhō-dō bunko*).   [100] *Ibid.,* vol. 1, pp. 1–2.

from a nostalgic, faintly pessimistic vision of the processes of Japanese history. Things were once done properly, but they are no longer. The *Nihon gaishi* describes in detail the deviations from the Ancient Way under family after family of military rulers from the twelfth to the seventeenth century. San'yō was a private person, not an official of the government. Unlike Seishisai he did not write to urge that a specific policy be adopted. If he conceived of any practical prescription for reform or restoration, he did not express it in his writings.

· 11 ·

If one were to sum up in a single statement the main quality of loyalism in its first three phases, one would say that loyalists used the figure of the emperor rather to justify than to undermine the institutions under which they lived. The emperor symbolized the legitimacy of the state, and hence national unity, continuity, and stability. Furthermore, he symbolized the morality of subjects, without regard for the specifics of an individual's moral duty. More and more he came to connote the moral duties that transcended particularistic bonds of obligation between persons. When the loyalist message was addressed to ordinary people, the result was to affirm the primacy of that highest particularism, the loyalty of a man to his country. Bellah speaks of loyalty to a figurehead emperor or shogun as a "generalized particularism which was a functional substitute for universalism in the extension and rationalization of power."[101] Elsewhere he speaks of imperial loyalism as "pseudo-universalism."[102] I should like to suggest that the loyalist ethic was that and more. In the hands of its articulate framers of a Confucian persuasion and as addressed by them to rulers it was a true universalism—an ethic that stressed values that were conceived to be independent of time, place, or social status—but one that

[101] Bellah, *Tokugawa Religion*, p. 14.   [102] *Ibid.*

appeared to be particularistic, for it seemed to pivot the ruler's duties on the variable will of a superior person in the authority structure. Furthermore, the generalized duty asserted for the ruler himself seemed to be similar to that obligation of obedience to an external human authority that was at the heart of the political ethics of the Tokugawa period. In this sense, loyalism may be called "pseudo-particularism."

The Japanese are a people whose ethical thought has in general stressed the virtue of obedience at some expense to the claims of the private conscience. Consider the stereotyped characterization, made by virtually every Western writer about the Japanese from sixteenth-century missionaries and traders to the present, that they are law-abiding in the extreme. But it is not necessary to examine the actual behavior of the Japanese to find that the moralists among them exalt the virtue of obedience to rare heights. The most casual inventory of the vast literature from Tokugawa times concerned with moral instruction for the young or the common people reveals an oppressive harping on the monotonous themes of filial piety, wifely submission to husbands, loyalty to feudal superiors, and obedience to the law.

If a distinction is to be made between such moralistic literature and true ethical philosophy, it can be said that, while the business of the former is merely to enjoin correct precepts for action, the latter exists to harmonize conflicting moral values. Even here one finds that Japanese moral philosophers have devoted a preponderance of their writing to the resolution of actual or potential conflicts between competing external authorities. One of the purposes of governmental theory is to define chains of authority that will answer for every individual in society the questions of who is his ruler and what is his law. A rigidly stratified and centralized society like that of Japan in the Edo period affords fewer occasions for conflicts between external authorities than one more open or less tightly organized. That Japan had the kind of society she did is attributable to the government's strict rule and also to the skill with which society as a whole rationalized the competing claims to authority of family, community, feudal unit, and shogunate.

The harmonization in this case involved the erection of a hierarchy of external authorities and the assertion that the individual's ultimate obligation of obedience was to the higher, more centrally placed terms of the hierarchy: feudal lord over father, and central governmental authority over feudal lord. The Mito School's doctrine of meibun, on one of the two levels of its interpretation (that is, as it applies to relationships among subjects of the emperor), is a generalized assertion of the hierarchical arrangement of external sources of authority.

The maxim that "filial piety and patriotism are one" must have struck everyone who has ever seen it as literally nonsense. If one is to reduce it to sense, what could it possibly mean except that in case of conflict between the two values patriotism should win out; that one can clear one's conscience about disobeying one's father for the sake of the country, since if the father really understood his own best interest, he would perceive that it was identical with that of the country.

So far there is nothing here that even hints at the existence of a possible source for moral injunctions other than some vested family or political authority. It may be that this is a basic defect in the generally accepted value system of Tokugawa Japan. Surely there is something deficient in any code of ethics which leaves the filial son of a worthless father and the loyal minister of a wicked ruler no recourse but to kill themselves in protest. I am not satisfied that this is in fact the sum and substance of what the ethics of filial piety and patriotism meant to moral men of the Tokugawa period, but it is at least an interpretation of them to which the moralistic literature and the folklore of the time give some credence.

However, on one level of discussion there is indeed more to Japanese moral philosophy than that. No Confucianist in Japan

or any other place has ever believed that morality began and
ended with obedience to human superiors. The entire ethical
system of the Confucian school proceeds from the assumption
of a moral law superior to any earthly institution, whose dictates the moral man must obey. Moral law is admittedly difficult to understand, too difficult perhaps for sons or subjects to
grasp save as they receive it externally from their fathers or
rulers. But for the latter there is no such easy way out. If *they*
are to act morally, there is no alternative for them but to search
out the matter, "the heaven for height and the earth for depth,"
and to follow the dictates of their own conscience.

The Confucian moral philosophy of the Tokugawa period on
this highest level was written for the education of princes, not
for the people whom they governed. Its main burden is the
delineation of correct principles of government which, if translated into laws, would enable obedient men to act morally. And
what distinguished the imperial loyalists from other writers on
political ethics was not that they denied the abstract moral
law, nor still less that they somehow failed to perceive that
there was such a thing, but quite simply that they found a
poetic, emotionally satisfying name for it. They personified it in
a man whose gentle and blameless mode of life as far transcended the corruptions of competitive society as did their ideal
the imperfections of earthly law.

The loyalist symbol was a thing of perfect fitness and symmetry. By means of it, it was possible to describe Japanese
society as a single political structure in which every individual
was responsive to the commands of the next human being in
the hierarchy superior to him. While the rationalized institutions
of the Tokugawa state achieved this harmony for the governed,
the loyalists added the necessary human figure at the top of the
hierarchy who could be seen as the ruler's own external recipient
of the virtue of obedience. Meibun, as a maxim directed to the
shogun himself, meant that his subordination to abstract moral

law should be as absolute as his subjects' obedience to him. The maxim expresses its meaning metaphorically, describing the abstract moral law as merely one more external authority.

The loyalist mythology also conceives of Japanese society as a large family. As one's own household has at its head the father, so Japanese family units are clustered into clans claiming common descent, a clan having at its head the chōja. In feudal times each han could be likened to a family to whose head, the daimyo, one owed quasi-filial duties. Filial piety was directed not only to parents but also to remote ancestors, all the way back to the founder of the family. Of all the members of a clan the chōja stands in the most direct relationship to the founder, for his is the custody of those rites of obeisance by which the preservation of the clan and the care of its members are ensured. All Japanese are related by blood, common habitat, and common needs. Loyalism conceived of the common progenitor as divine and regarded the emperor as the chōja of the national clan. His subjects revered him for the rites of gratitude which he performed, gratitude for nature's mysterious bounty that they all shared.

IV

THE THRONE
IN POLITICS

❋ FOR NEARLY 250 years the imperial institution remained much as it had been when it had first gone under the protection of the Tokugawa shoguns. It was not an office of state, but one of the state's adornments. The people attached to it—emperors, their families, and their courtiers—were a social class of great eminence, but their prestige was not matched by any commensurate opportunity of affecting society in the large. Of the emperor's throne, "only its existence was known," as Lao Tzu said was true of the best governments. Men outside the court might contemplate it, make judgments about it, and be moved to passion by it, but their knowledge of it was very abstract. As there was little direct contact between the court and society at large, there could be little interaction between them. The changes of technology, economy, and social and political institutions that Japan underwent in the Edo period had little effect on the life of the Kyoto court, and even the changes in the attitudes toward it of those outside had little effect on its operation or its relation to the rest of the world.

In the 1840s, 1850s, and 1860s, the institution at last changed. In brief, it became a political office. Members of the court acquired political influence and some of them became figures of power in the state. The physical barriers between the court and its surroundings began to erode. The kuge community was at last destroyed as the caste merged with a larger aristocracy from the military classes to form a new governing elite. The emperor remained aloof and protected, but he too gained greater physical mobility than before and a new opportunity of association with persons other than his hereditary courtiers. Most important of all, the throne became an *independent* historical agency, independent of those governing institutions of state of whose power it had formerly been one of the chief bulwarks. Gradually the members of the court began to express themselves publicly on matters of national policy, and sometimes their views were at variance with established decisions of the Tokugawa government. Political dissidents appealed to the imperial name in their campaigns against the central authority. Later, with the onset of the fatal clash between the shogunate and its enemies, the imperial throne became the rallying point for all of the anti-shogunal forces, and in 1867 the emperor succeeded the last Tokugawa shogun as head of a new effective government.

The emergence of the imperial throne into national politics was brought about by the interaction of two great issues of public policy. The first was an issue of foreign policy that revolved around the question of how best to maintain national security and independence in the face of aggressive Western pressures. The other was a domestic issue. It came to the fore when an influential segment of the bushi class called into question the competence to deal with the foreign threat of the leadership then in control of the shogunal bureaucracy. This second issue turned on the question of whether the government should continue to be administered through its traditional personnel structure or whether the base of executive power should be broadened to admit the counsel of able outsiders. The foreign issue was prior in time and must be described first.

The general apprehension of foreign aggression that had prompted Aizawa Seishisai to write the *Shinron* in 1825 became

more specific and urgent in 1840, with the outbreak of the
Opium War between China and Great Britain. In 1842 the
British obtained peace terms from the Chinese which included
the cession of Hong Kong as well as the payment of an indem-
nity. In 1844 the shogunate received a letter from the King of
Holland, who used China's recent fate as evidence of Japan's
own precarious position and recommended that the Japanese
government voluntarily end its seclusion policy.[1]

During the same years the shogunate was receiving advice
from its own feudatories that was equally urgently asserted, but
of different intent. Takashima Shūhan (1798–1866) and Sakuma Shōzan (1811–64) were typical of a new generation of
"enlightened samurai" who combined public spiritedness with
technical knowledge of public problems. Both made penetrating
studies of conditions in Western countries and came to the
same conclusion, that only by means of Western technology
could Japan defend herself against Western arms. The end
which both sought was to avoid China's fate in the Opium
War. The means which both advocated was knowledge of the
West. Takashima's reaction when he learned of the outbreak
of the Opium War was to submit a letter of advice to the shogunate recommending better military technology.[2] Sakuma responded to the Chinese defeat by submitting a proposal,
forwarded through his own daimyo the Shogunal Elder (Rōjū)
Sanada Yukitsura, calling for the avoidance of war and the
equally firm avoidance of opening the country.[3]

There was here the beginning of a divisive issue of foreign
policy, but it would be wrong to think of the issue as essentially
whether or not to repel the barbarians. Both the shogunate

[1] Greene, "Correspondence between William II of Holland and the
Shōgun of Japan, A. D. 1844," pp. 99–132.
[2] See Sansom, *The Western World and Japan, A Study in the Interaction of European and Asiatic Cultures*, pp. 248–59. *Takashima Shūhan,
Sakuma Shōzan shū*, (in *Kinsei shakai keizai gakusetsu taikei*), pp. 36–39.
[3] Sansom, *The Western World and Japan*, p. 254. Tsunoda *et al.*,
Sources, pp. 603–16. *Takashima Shūhan, Sakuma Shōzan shū*, pp. 45–66.

and its critics took it for granted that they should be repelled. The issue was rather over methods and speed. Shōzan and Shūhan were members of a growing faction of informed people in and around the shogunate who believed that the foreign threat was more urgent than shogunal policy makers in general realized. Evidence to support their belief came again in 1846, when a United States naval expedition headed by Commodore James Biddle called at Uraga on Edo Bay asking that Japan be opened to American trade. The shogunate refused and Biddle left peacefully, but all the signs indicated that more forceful pressures would be forthcoming.

The dominant figure in the faction known as jōi ("repel the barbarians") was Tokugawa Nariaki (1800–60). Nariaki had been a center of controversy practically since his adolescence. He was associated with the jōi advocates in the Mito domain from the early 1820s, at a time when his elder brother Narinaga was the domain lord. When Narinaga died childless in 1829 Nariaki was the candidate best qualified by family relationship to succeed him. Nevertheless, his succession was opposed by a faction in the domain that regarded with discomfort the fervor of his opinions and the forcefulness of his will. He and his faction won out, and he was Daimyo of Mito from 1829 to 1844. Those were years of vigorous change in Mito. Nariaki was the author of a reform program that was to be a model for several other great domains and, from 1841 to 1844, for the shogunate itself. These were the *Tempō kaikaku*, "reforms of the Tempō Period (1830–44)," which Japanese historians frequently consider the opening chapter in Japan's mid-nineteenth century attempts at economic and social modernization. The reforms in Mito were complex in their specifics, but they may all be described as efficiency and savings measures designed to increase domain capital. With the increase gained Nariaki improved defense installations and armaments manufacture.[4]

[4] See Tōyama, *Meiji Ishin*, pp. 21–39. Sakata, *Meiji Ishin shi*, pp. 37–47.

Membership in the shogunal clan, overlordship of a large territory, intelligence, and firm conviction on major national issues combined to make Nariaki perhaps the most striking single historical personage of the Bakumatsu period. His career furnishes evidence for proponents of the view that great men make history by decisive acts of their will. Even partisans of the opposite view—that historical change obeys impersonal laws with which individuals have no power to interfere—will frequently and of necessity cite Nariaki's acts in concrete illustration of the way in which the impersonal forces are translated into human behavior. In the history of defense policy Nariaki was often the first to adopt measures that caused others to imitate them or to react violently with countermeasures of their own. In the history of ideas he infused the amorphous concepts of sonnō and jōi with such meaning as they possessed up to 1860 by his specific explanations of them and his specific acts in avowed manifestation of them. In the history of the imperial institution the direct or indirect marks of his influence may be seen in every main development from the 1830s through the 1850s.

When one speaks of the shogunate in these years one refers to a bureaucratic structure whose exact constituency, both in terms of administrative organs and of personnel, varied from time to time.[5] The shogun, of course, was the chief titular official, and all decisions were described as coming from him, but the effective power of most of the later Tokugawa shoguns was limited for various reasons. The etiquette of their court made for physical confinement and isolation from all but a few top advisers, in the same way and to almost the same degree as with the emperor in his court. The shoguns consequently lacked

[5] One of the best descriptions in English of shogunate politics in these years is Totman, "The Struggle for Control of the Shogunate (1853–1858)," pp. 52–88.

knowledge and experience of the world outside Edo Castle. In some instances, the later shoguns were literally incompetent, physically or mentally, to administer personally the duties of their office. Decisions tended to be made on a lower level, and then presented to the shogun for ratification. The chief policy-making board in normal times was the rōjū, or "council of elders," which consisted of four or five fudai daimyos of relatively high rank and income. In theory the shogun had absolute power to select and remove members of this body, but in the absence of a strong shogun the body tended to be self-perpetuating and to be rotated among members of the same small number of fudai families generation after generation. There were to be sure certain informal checks that prevented the council from becoming completely irresponsible. Some fudai families, notably the wealthiest one, the Ii, never attained seats in the rōjū. Only a small number of fudai daimyos sat in the council at any particular time. The fudai group as a whole, conferring as shogunal vassals rather than as administrative officers, had indirect influence in the shogunate that might occasionally act to force an unfriendly elder out of office or in other ways to limit the council's power. Nevertheless, the fudai, both those in and those outside the council of elders, were an entrenched clique who held a preponderance of power in the central government in the first half of the nineteenth century.

The great and divisive domestic issue that sprang out of the debate on defense policy was over who should govern the shogunate, the entrenched fudai clique or a more broadly based concert of daimyos of all classes. Those who believed that the base of power within the shogunate should be broadened argued that only in that way could an effective defense policy be constructed. They took this argument from the sentiments, expressed by Aizawa Seishisai and the other members of the later Mito School, that defense was a problem for the whole nation and that it therefore required concerted action by all of the daimyos for its solution. It is not surprising that Tokugawa Nariaki, the leader of the jōi faction, was also the leader of the faction that argued for the participation of a more broadly representative group in the policy-making process within the shogunate. It is also natural that the dominant fudai families should have been opposed to any diminution of their power.

Shogunal politics in the last 30 years of the Tokugawa regime were exceedingly complex and resist description in terms of permanent alliances and oppositions of factions. Nevertheless it is generally true that until 1860 the advocates of jōi—by which one means any attitude toward the foreign powers more urgent or less conciliatory than that held at any particular time by the fudai clique—also advocated an alteration in that clique's monopolistic hold on shogunal power. The converse statement would not be true. Especially in the late 1850s, there were advocates of shogunal administrative reform who favored trade or conciliation with the Western powers. Even they characteristically linked the foreign with the domestic issue, justifying their stand on internal reform on the grounds that the proper future conduct of foreign affairs required firmness and skill which the fudai bureaucracy did not possess.

The strategy of Nariaki and his faction changed as circumstances directed. Until 1853 they endeavored primarily to persuade the Rōjū to bring into the council chambers of the shogunate on a more or less regular basis a group of "able daimyos," that is, daimyos outside the fudai clique who had demonstrated their ability by means of successful policies of han reform.[6] Nariaki himself was a member of that group. Though a high-ranking member of the shogunal family and consequently a person who could always give advice on policy, he was not a member of the fudai group with whom the power of decision

[6] Sakata, *Meiji Ishin shi*, pp. 65–74. Sakata and Hall, "The Motivation of Political Leadership in the Meiji Restoration," pp. 39–41.

lay. From 1841 to 1843 he was consulted frequently by the presiding officer of the Rōjū, Mizuno Tadakuni. Mizuno brought the "Tempō Reform," which had been started at the han level, to the shogunate. Nariaki advised him on various points of the reform program and even induced him to adopt a more vigorous policy of defense implementation. The two men clashed in 1843 owing to the fact that Mizuno would not adopt the other main point advocated by Nariaki, which was to enlist the advice of able daimyos from the tozama ranks. Nariaki was forced into retirement in that year and forbidden to interfere with shogunal policies. In 1844, however, there was an internal reshuffling of top administrative personnel, and Mizuno Tadakuni was out of office. His successor as head of the Rōjū was Abe Masahiro, who was sympathetic both to Nariaki's ideas on defense and to his belief that the crisis of the time required the participation of the able daimyos in shogunal policy making. As a result Nariaki was again called into the service of the Council of Elders, this time as a special adviser on defense. Simultaneously, a number of tozama daimyos, including Shimazu Nariakira of Satsuma, Yamanouchi Toyoshige of Tosa, and Matsudaira Yoshinaga of Echizen, began to be consulted on policy, though in a rather secretive manner. For the next fourteen years Nariaki and the able daimyos were ensconced in the shogunal council chambers, though it must be understood that the tozama daimyos were there on the sufferance of the dominant fudai clique, and that even Nariaki lacked the executive power of, say, the Council of Elders.

In this precarious position partly in and partly outside the national government Nariaki and his faction had need of external support in order to strengthen their influence. At a later day they would surely have appealed to public opinion for help, and it may be argued that the actual source from which they sought it was the closest equivalent to an informed and concerned public which Japan of that day knew. They appealed to the common sense and patriotism of the samurai and daimyo classes, and they based their case on moral values which they knew the members of those classes shared with them. As usual the imperial throne was a natural symbol for commonly shared national values. The appeal to the imperial *name* by the anti-fudai faction at this time accounts indirectly for the fact that imperial *wishes* came to be consulted on specific political issues.

· 2 ·

In the autumn of 1846, three months after the Biddle expedition, the Kyōto Shoshidai forwarded the following letter from the Emperor to the Shogun:

It has been reported to us that in recent years ships of foreign nations have appeared in our waters. We were under the impression that the government was capably led, that military affairs were in good order, and, in particular, that maritime defenses were strong. Nevertheless, there have been numerous foreign encroachments. We are, therefore, filled with anxiety and desire that henceforth our warriors, one and all, so conduct themselves that they may be prepared for more serious challenges. They should, accordingly, perfect military strategy and devote themselves completely to their duty so that the danger to the Land of the Gods will come to an end and, little by little, the Imperial Mind will be put at ease.[7]

Despite its mild wording, this letter was a turning point in shogunate-court relations. It was the first official expression in the Tokugawa period of the court's opinion on a political issue. The nearest recent precedents for such an action were the court's proposal in 1823 that ex-Emperor Kōkaku be allowed to visit the Shugakuin, and the proposal in 1840 that Kōkaku be given a posthumous name of the Chinese style. Though neither case involved a political or national issue, the two together were

---

[7] *Ishin shi*, vol. 2, p. 27. Translated by Lee in *The Political Career of Ii Naosuke*, pp. 25–26.

evidence that the court was beginning to show a new assertive-
ness in its relations with the government.

The 1840 incident provides evidence as to how the 1846 letter
may have come to be sent. The instigator in 1840 seems to have
been Tokugawa Nariaki, who was virtually unique in combin-
ing a high position in the shogunal advisory councils with unusual channels of influence to the Kyoto court. His younger
sister was the wife of Takatsukasa Masamichi (1789–1868),
who was Kampaku from 1823 to 1856, and Nariaki was in close
touch with Masamichi by correspondence. Nariaki's sense of
sonnō had prompted him as early as 1834 to agitate in shogunal
councils for repair of the imperial mausolea. When his direct
influence on the shogunate was unavailing, he conceived of the
stratagem of working indirectly, through the Kampaku. Masamichi hesitated to act on Nariaki's advice for fear of the shogunate's wrath, but immediately after Kōkaku's death Nariaki
renewed his proposals to Masamichi, this time adding the suggestion about the posthumous name. The court then proceeded
to act, as though on its own initiative, to petition the shogunal
authorities. When the petition was received in Edo, Nariaki
used his influence there to have the proposal accepted.[8] Kōkaku's death may have been doubly significant in this episode.
It meant that for the first time since 1817 there was no retired
emperor in the court, a circumstance that could only have
strengthened the hand of the Kampaku in regard to court affairs. This may account as much as anything for the timing of
Nariaki's renewed proposal.

The circumstances in 1846 were similar. This time the reigning emperor, Ninkō, had recently died, and the successor was
the fifteen-year-old boy Kōmei. As regent for a minor sovereign,
Masamichi was in an even more advantageous position to control court affairs than before. It is not known whether the
court's letter to the shogunate of that year was in direct response

[8] *Ishin shi*, vol. 1, pp. 148–49. Inobe, *Ishin zenshi no kenkyū*, p. 434.

to a suggestion by Nariaki, but it is known that secret missives were exchanged between him and Masamichi in the months following Kōmei's accession, and it is supposed that these concerned foreign affairs. The 1846 letter showed a greater sense of urgency over the foreign threat than could as yet be found in many quarters of the national government. This fact is itself suspicious, for the court's sources of information about the outside world were too limited to make it likely that it reached an independent judgment on this grave national issue. Furthermore, the court had never expressed itself in such an unusual fashion on any other national problem. The sentiments of the letter echoed Nariaki's own; in fact they were ideas which for twenty years had been the cornerstone of the Mito domain's public policy, and by the 1840s Nariaki was regarded as the nation's most eminent advocate of them. All of this evidence points to the conclusion that the court's reemergence into politics was occasioned at least indirectly by the influence of Tokugawa Nariaki.

In the next few years there were further incidents of a similar character. In 1847 the court decreed a special ceremonial at the Iwashimizu Hachiman-gū, the great Shinto shrine between Kyoto and Osaka dedicated to the war god Hachiman, at which an imperial rescript praying for pacification of the foreigners was read. In 1850 the emperor called for a seventeen-day period of prayer to be performed at seven great Shinto shrines and seven Buddhist temples. Later in the same year a second imperial letter was sent to Edo largely restating the contents of the first of 1846.[9] These events occasioned surprisingly little outward concern on the part of shogunate officials. Part of the explanation for this may be that the court's acts had so far been confined to matters of ritual, toward which the shogunate's official attitude seems always to have been to encourage more of them rather than fewer, and carefully phrased communica-

[9] *Ishin shi*, vol. 2, pp. 28–30.

tions to the shogunate that were not likely to become matters of public knowledge.

Another explanation of the shogunate's apparent lack of concern is that the court's criticisms were only the faintest echo of a point of view being expressed with growing vehemence inside the deliberative councils of the shogunate. In the last few years before the Perry Expedition the issue over defense policy would better be described as internal to the shogunate itself than as dividing the shogunate from its domestic enemies. Therefore, when the imperial court went on record as supporting a relatively firm stand on defense it could count on the active approval of the jōi faction in the shogunate, while the faction that took a less urgent view of the foreign threat were more inclined to fight the matter out with their fellow bureaucrats at the daimyo or hatamoto level than to become embroiled in an undignified quarrel with the Kyoto court.

Commodore Perry's arrival in Edo Bay in July, 1853, did not lead immediately to further involvement of the court in national politics, though it did effect far-reaching changes in domestic and foreign policies. Abe Masahiro openly admitted his reliance on the able daimyo group. Simultaneously he went still further by soliciting the advice of all of the daimyos as to how the shogunate should respond to the foreign demands. The story of the ensuing debate has been told many times and only its broadest outlines need be retraced here.[10] The daimyos gave the shogunate no clear-cut mandate for action, for they split into several sizeable groups offering contrary advice. Some, including Nariaki, favored maintenance of seclusion even if that meant war. Others recommended peace through temporization, that is, postponement of a response to the demands until defenses had been built up to a point of equality with the West. Still others realized that such a policy would be impossible and

[10] See Beasley, *Select Documents on Japanese Foreign Policy (1853–1868)*, pp. 98–127. Borton, *Japan's Modern Century*, pp. 31–35.

recommended acceptance of some form of trade with America. The Rōjū vacillated, but in the end chose the last course. The Treaty of Kanagawa with the United States, signed in March, 1854, provided for the exchange of diplomatic representatives and the subsequent conclusion of a full-scale trade agreement. Similar agreements with other Western powers followed in 1854 and 1855. The first foreign emissary to reside on Japanese soil was the American Consul-General Townsend Harris, who arrived in 1856. Harris initiated the negotiations for regular trade relations, and in 1858 he persuaded shogunal policy makers to accept his proposed treaty.

With advancing events the substance of jōi changed. The slogan continued to be the property of Nariaki and his supporters, but the character of the supporting group changed significantly. Some influential daimyos, including Shimazu Nariakira and Matsudaira Yoshinaga, shifted to something closer to a *kaikoku* ("open the country") position. In the meantime a growing number of samurai and commoners joined jōi ranks. We may discern three phases in the application of the term jōi up to 1858. Jōi (Phase I) called for improved coastal defense; jōi (Phase II), from 1853, meant resistance to treaty demands. At some time between 1854, when Perry returned to Japan, and 1856, when Harris arrived, jōi (Phase III) came into being. The government had committed the country to a policy of kaikoku, and jōi (Phase III) was a demand that the policy be reversed. Jōi (Phase I) had called for measures to which no one was really opposed, though some questioned their urgent necessity. Jōi (Phase II) had been more controversial, for it called for a program that many believed to be impractical or impossible. Nevertheless, as an ideal it appealed to all conservatives. Jōi (Phase III) was genuinely divisive for it urged the government to reverse decisions which had already been implemented.

We may stop here for the time being. We are not so much

concerned with the shogunate and its problems as with the emperor and the attitudes which people held toward him. For each phase in the development of jōi there was a corresponding phase in the development of sonnō. Sonnō (Phase I) was merely an extension of traditional loyalism; the emperor, who symbolized all political ideals, symbolized the ideal of national security against foreign encroachments. The Emperor's letters to the shogunate of 1846 and 1850 asserted that he, like everyone else, believed in the ideal. Sonnō (Phase II) was different, for it linked loyalty to the emperor to a certain policy in opposition to other policies that were being advocated at the same time. Sonnō (Phase II) should not be interpreted as an assertion that the emperor shared a belief in jōi (Phase II). It cannot be too forcefully stressed that the entire argument of the sonnō-jōi faction following Perry's first arrival was directed to the shogunate and that the faction assumed that the duty of making policy lay solely with the shogunate, not with the emperor. Sonnō (Phase II) did not mean obedience to the emperor, but reverence for him. As a matter of fact, one of the memorializing daimyos of 1853 *did* propose that the emperor be consulted on the Perry issue, but that daimyo was Ii Naosuke.[11] So far from being a member of the sonnō-jōi faction, Naosuke was its archenemy. His recommendation to the shogunate in 1853 was that Japan conciliate the United States. He was not then openly in favor of kaikoku, at least not on the terms demanded by Perry, but in the next few years he moved steadily toward acceptance of full trade and diplomatic relations with the West, and in 1858 he was the official most directly responsible for the conclusion of the Harris Treaty.

Everything about Ii Naosuke made him the natural antagonist of Tokugawa Nariaki. In his institutional position within the shogunal government Ii was the most eminent representative of the great fudai families and therefore was likely to be

[11] See *Bakumatsu gaikoku kankei monjo* (in *Dai Nihon komonjo*), vol. 2, p. 258. Translated in Beasley, *Select Documents*, pp. 117–19.

the staunchest advocate of their retention of a monopoly of shogunal power. The attitudes of the two men on defense and seclusion were incompatible. Even the beliefs and motivations that the two shared were such as to make them enemies rather than allies. Both were strongly attached by family loyalties to the institutions of the shogunate. Both men were fundamentally conservative in respect to national values, but Ii's conservatism led him to fear foreign war as much as Nariaki's led *him* to fear the disruptions that would be occasioned by peaceful acceptance of Western demands. It has not been sufficiently realized that both men shared something of the same attitude toward the imperial throne, but in such a way as to lead to bitter rivalry between them for imperial favor. Ii by his lights was an imperial loyalist, for he recognized the emperor's primacy over the shogun and sought imperial approval for his acts. The motives for which he did so seem to have been similar to Nariaki's in exerting his influence through the Kampaku: in this complex of issues the throne's blessing was likely to be the decisive factor which tipped the balance in favor of one side or the other.

The court was not in fact consulted in 1853, but merely notified of the new developments. A discussion among the kuge about the proper way of dealing with the Americans ensued, but it was no more conclusive than the debate on policy among the daimyos.[12] If there can be said to have been any consensus, it was that the shogunate should be allowed to make the decision. Most of the kuge who expressed opinions felt that the foreign demands should be refused, but not at the cost of war. A surprising opinion came from the Kampaku Masamichi. He advocated acceptance of Perry's terms and opening the country, thereby squarely opposing his friend and brother-in-law Nariaki. He said:

The letter [of the American government] is very courteous and humane, and it should not be despised. In recent times trade with foreign countries has been strictly forbidden, but in former times

[12] *Ishin shi,* vol. 2, pp. 295ff.

there was intercourse with various countries. Therefore there is no reason why we should not have relations [with America]. However, Nagasaki has been fixed as the port for foreign trade, and those who illegally come to other harbors should probably be sent away. The warriors nowadays are lazy and cowardly, and I should imagine it would be difficult for them to fight. Therefore I think that the best policy would be for us to enter into trade relations.[13]

The Kampaku took the initiative in having an imperial letter drafted to Abe Masahiro late in 1853. It is probably as good an index as any of the tenor of the court's opinion at that time.[14] The letter calls the Perry expedition an event of the most serious consequences to the "land of the Gods" and directs the shogunate to act in such a way as not to incur a national humiliation. There was nothing in the letter more specific than that. Sonnō and jōi in Phase II were attitudes held by bushi about the imperial institution, but they were not yet truly representative of the attitude held within the imperial court.

Abe Masahiro was the first shogunal official to solicit the court's official ratification of a policy decision. He did so in 1855, when the shogunate had again succumbed to Western pressure by signing a trade treaty with Russia. Abe's actions in these years were motivated by a desire to conciliate both the jōi and the anti-jōi factions; in this case he hoped to silence the opposition of Nariaki by obtaining from the court an expression of confidence in the Rōjū's conduct of affairs. The court responded as Abe had hoped, thereby temporarily strengthening Abe's and the shogunate's position, but there can be no doubt that the precedent which this action established opened the way for a disastrous confrontation of interests between the shogunal and imperial institutions.[15]

13 Ibid., p. 300. Cf. Sanjō Sanetsumu shuroku, vol. 2, p. 84.
14 Ishin shi, vol. 2, p. 302. Bakumatsu gaikoku kankei monjo, vol. 3, pp. 271–72.
15 Bakumatsu gaikoku kankei monjo, vol. 13, pp. 11–12. Inobe, Bakumatsu-shi gaisetsu, pp. 148–49.

It was during the third phase of the sonnō-jōi movement that the court was finally induced to take an unequivocal stand in favor of jōi. Again the occasion was the shogunate's referral of a treaty to the emperor for ratification. This was the Treaty of Edo of 1858 between Japan and the United States, more commonly referred to as the Harris Treaty. By this time the jōi faction had considerably strengthened its influence over the court, which in the end refused to give the shogunate the sanction which it had requested. When we examine the background of this event we shall see that the court's final emergence as an independent force in national politics came about almost accidentally and as a result of political maneuverings at the daimyo level of the bushi class.

Sonnō (Phase III) implied that the shogunate had already been disloyal to the emperor by surrendering to Western pressure. For the first time loyalty to the emperor was described in such a manner as to be incompatible with the enforcement of a shogunal enactment. Nevertheless, it should not be assumed that sonnō (Phase III) was a call for revolution. The slogan continued as before to be addressed largely to shogunal policy makers, and the specific exhortation into which it may be translated was not that the shogunate should yield its powers, but merely that it should reverse one of its policies. The advocates of sonnō (Phase III) continued to be led by Nariaki, who was just as much attached to the institutions over which his family presided as he had ever been. Until 1858 the appeal implicit in sonnō (Phase III) was to the imperial name rather than to imperial wishes. The court's de facto approval in 1855 of the treaties that had already been concluded indicates that Nariaki's continued opposition to the government's foreign policy was essentially independent of the attitudes held within the court. His convictions here, as with every other matter with which he was concerned in his life, arose as much from his perception of effective means as from his conception of desirable political ends. So far as the ends were concerned—the ends of national independence, defense against foreign encroachments, and the preservation of Japanese institutions—he assumed that the emperor, with every patriotic Japanese, agreed with him. When there was a disagreement on means between him and the emperor's spokesmen within the court, his arguments proceeded from the natural enough assumption that his superior knowledge and experience entitled him to speak with greater authority than they could.

From 1856, when Townsend Harris arrived in Japan, Nariaki's indignation over the government's policies knew no bounds. In that year the conciliatory Abe Masahiro was removed as presiding officer of the Rōjū and replaced by Hotta Masayoshi, an open enemy of Nariaki. Ii Naosuke, the acknowledged leader of the fudai families, was now the other most powerful figure in the shogunate, and his influence was growing continuously. The policies of Hotta, Ii, the Rōjū, and the fudai bureaucracy in general moved steadily toward the acceptance of permanent diplomatic and commercial ties with the Western powers, for it was their conviction that only in this way could peace be maintained. Nariaki's twin concerns over foreign and domestic policy were translated into two new campaigns. He worked for the next two years to thwart conclusion of the commercial agreement with the United States that Harris demanded. Simultaneously, he employed a new strategy to counter his enemies at the helm of the shogunate. This new plan was to ensure that the figurehead Shogun Iesada, whom a childhood disease had left sterile, would be succeeded by a capable ruler and one friendly to Nariaki's cause. The candidate whom Nariaki proposed was his own son, Hitotsubashi Yoshinobu (or Keiki). The fudai clique countered with a candidate of their own, an adolescent nonentity from the cadet house of Kii.[16]

The anti-Ii faction, including Nariaki and the "able daimyos"

[16] *Ibid.*, pp. 160–81. Sakata, *Meiji Ishin shi*, pp. 102–8.

Shimazu Nariakira and Matsudaira Yoshinaga of Echizen, were now united more by their stand on the internal issue than by their sentiments about the Harris treaty. Shimazu was resigned to the necessity of concluding some sort of trade agreement, but he believed that only an able and authoritative shogun, such as Hitotsubashi, could provide the strong national leadership necessary to face up to future challenges from abroad. Matsudaira had come around to the belief that foreign trade was the most efficacious way possible of building up national economic strength for defense purposes, but he too felt that the shogunal leadership, as it was then constituted, was incapable of conducting future foreign relations without further compromises of national independence. Nariaki opposed trade relations of the kind that Harris demanded, but even he had become convinced that some sort of foreign intercourse was inevitable. In 1858 he recommended that this be done through Japanese officials stationed abroad. The common ground of agreement among these three in the summer of 1858 may be described as a belief that the fudai bureaucracy had been weak and irresponsible in its previous handling of foreign affairs, and that therefore its power should be broken by subordinating it to a strong shogun. Shimazu and Matsudaira advocated the internal resettlement of the power structure as a precondition to acceptance of the Harris treaty, while Nariaki thought of it as a means by which Japan might gain the strength to achieve a wholly different modus vivendi with the Western powers.

Matsudaira Yoshinaga appears to have been the first of the able daimyos to suggest that the emperor be called upon to decide the shogunal succession issue. He did so in January, 1858, with the full knowledge that the tenor of opinion among the kuge officials was friendly to the Hitotsubashi cause.[17] That state of affairs was the indirect result of Nariaki's fifteen-year

[17] *Bakumatsu gaikoku kankei monjo*, vol. 18, pp. 444–47. Translated in Beasley, *Select Documents*, pp. 179–85.

cultivation of Takatsukasa Masamichi and the direct result of more recent propaganda efforts by him and other able daimyos upon various kuge. By 1858 not only Masamichi, but other influential kuge as well, were in full agreement with the position of Nariaki in regard to the succession dispute. Furthermore, the disagreements that had existed earlier with Nariaki on foreign relations had diminished when Nariaki moved to a position less likely to eventuate in a foreign war. Early in 1858 Matsudaira dispatched one of his own retainers, Hashimoto Sanai, to Kyoto to do good offices for him in persuading the leading courtiers to have an imperial letter drafted naming Hitotsubashi as the shogun's heir. The highest placed kuge with whom Sanai conferred was Sanjō Sanetsumu, a long-time jōi advocate who was also fully committed to Hitotsubashi's candidacy. Sanai's arguments with him merely confirmed his sentiments on the internal issue. Incidentally, Sanai also attempted to persuade Sanjō of the desirability of Japan's accepting the Harris treaty. He had no success in this, as Sanjō, along with a large faction of leading kuge, had been convinced by the jōi arguments of Nariaki.

In the meantime, the rōjū acted to neutralize the efforts which their opponents were making in Kyoto by sending Hotta Masayoshi there personally. Hotta, acting with the confidence of Ii Naosuke, was to obtain approval for the Harris treaty and also for Kii's candidacy. Hotta went directly to Emperor Kōmei, to whom he presented a draft of the treaty for his approval. The Emperor conferred with his courtiers, who were unable to reach a firm conclusion. Most were in favor of a flat rejection of the treaty. However, one who was not was the Kampaku, Kujō Hisatada, and without his concurrence it was unlikely or impossible that a negative decision would be reached.[18] A common pattern of Japanese group behavior in situations such as

[18] *Ishin shi,* vol. 2, pp. 334–37. *Dai Nihon Ishin shiryō,* vol. 2, part 3, pp. 467–76 *et seq.*

this is to make no decision either way but to temporize, hoping that later developments will suggest a way out. That is what the court did on this occasion. The response to Hotta's request was not an outright rejection of the treaty, but a suggestion that the shogunate again solicit the opinions of the daimyos so that the emperor would have a sounder basis for judgment of the treaty's merits.[19] So far as the court was concerned the matter rested there. Six feverish months of efforts by both bushi factions failed to produce a more forthright response. When the shogunate put the American treaty in effect in July, 1858, the Emperor had not given his assent to it, but neither had he definitely declared it to be unacceptable.

The court's refusal to act caused convulsions in the shogunate. Hotta Masayoshi remained in Kyoto for nearly two months trying to persuade the influential courtiers to switch their position. He was not successful in this, but astonishingly he switched his position in regard to the succession issue. He became a supporter of Hitotsubashi. The explanation was not so much a change of heart on the whole question of domestic policy as it was a realization that the court was completely opposed to Kii and therefore more likely to decide favorably on the treaty issue if the domestic issue were settled in favor of Hitotsubashi. Ii Naosuke, infuriated by what he regarded as Hotta's repudiation of him, went to the Shogun to plot countermeasures. The Shogun was then ill, and in fact dying, and Ii induced him to take several precipitous actions designed to settle matters in Ii's favor.[20]

One of these was to appoint Ii as tairō, "senior councillor," an office to which only the very highest ranking fudai (for example, Ii and Sakai) were customarily appointed. The office was usually left vacant, but when filled was superior to the

[19] *Ishin shi*, vol. 2, pp. 324–27. *Kujō Hisatada monjo*, vol. 1, p. 3. *Dai Nihon Ishin shiryō*, part 3, vol. 2, pp. 480–89.
[20] *Ishin shi*, vol. 2, pp. 408–11.

rōjū and subordinate within the shogunal bureaucracy solely to the shogun himself. Ii took office on June 3, 1858. About July 1 the Shogun decided to name Kii as his heir. On July 3 Hotta and another rōjū were removed from office and other Councillors friendly to Ii were appointed. On July 29 the government accepted the Harris treaty. On August 12 Ii, ostensibly acting under shogunal orders, commenced a series of punitive actions against his enemies, ordering Tokugawa Nariaki, his son the reigning daimyo of Mito Tokugawa Yoshiatsu, and Matsudaira Yoshinaga into house arrest. The two last-named were also deprived of their domains. Hitotsubashi Yoshinobu, whose candidacy for the office of shogun had now apparently aborted for good, was deprived of access to the shogunal castle. The Shogun Iesada died on August 14.[21] Until March, 1860, when he was assassinated by partisans of Nariaki, Ii Naosuke had a virtually unassailable position above the other councils and functionaries of the government and responsible only to a child shogun of no personal abilities whatsoever.

There are two interesting sidelights on Ii's relations with the court in the summer of 1858. The first is that he heeded the advice which the court had given him after they had seen the draft of Harris's treaty by asking yet again for an expression of daimyo opinion. Surprisingly many of the daimyos, a majority in fact, favored acceptance of the treaty, or at least went on record as believing that Japan could not hold out longer against the foreign demands.[22] This would appear to mitigate the charge which historians have usually leveled against Ii that he was disdainful of imperial wishes in his handling of the Harris treaty. Ii had solicited court opinion, despite the fact that none of the precedents of shogunal government would have required him to do so. He followed the court's advice by obtaining a

21 Inobe, *Bakumatsu-shi gaisetsu*, pp. 181–95. Lee, *The Political Career of Ii Naosuke*, pp. 80–104.
22 *Ishin shi*, vol. 2, pp. 463–64. *Bakumatsu gaikoku kankei monjo*, vol. 20, pp. 223 *et seq.*, documents 52, 73, 74, 76, 81, 82, 96, 97, 102, 140.

vote of daimyo confidence. The truthful charge that can be made against him is that having gone that far he did not go one step further by resubmitting the treaty to the Emperor and waiting for imperial approval before taking positive action on it.

The second curious aspect of the affair concerns the final disposition of the succession issue. Appointment to the office of shogun had been the only major act of state that required imperial approval. This was the first occasion in the Tokugawa period on which there was any doubt whatever that the court would follow Edo's wishes in a succession matter. Ii was apprehensive when he notified Kyoto of Iesada's decision to appoint Kii, and his apprehension grew when the court's response appeared to be a long time arriving. On August 2, however, it was announced to the Rōjū that the court had formally approved the settlement in favor of Kii.[23] After Iesada's death the Emperor again obliged the shogunate by issuing the official patent of appointment of Tokugawa (Kii) Iemochi as the shogun.[24] The extreme reluctance of the court to offend the shogunate, to break precedents, and even to shoulder the burden of decision which so many bushi were attempting to thrust upon them are apparent in all of their acts at this time.

The events of 1858 were ultimately fatal to the Tokugawa regime. Their immediate effect on internal politics was to make the imperial court a full-fledged participant in the decision of public policy. It would be a superficial reading of the causes of these developments to say that a pro-imperial (and by implication anti-shogunal) faction had emerged victorious in a long campaign to make the emperor a decision-making officer of the effective government. Rather the new state of affairs came about more or less accidentally because of two developments in shogunate and daimyo politics. One of these was institutional, the

23 Inobe, *Bakumatsu-shi gaisetsu*, p. 194. *Bakumatsu gaikoku kankei monjo*, vol. 20, documents 149, 154, 155, 228.
24 *Kugyō bunin*, vol. 57, p. 512.

substitution of a many-centered, and therefore potentially in-
decisive, executive authority for the older autocracy of the shogun or the Rōjū. The shoguns of the 1840s and 1850s were
personally incapable of decisive action. Mistakes which the
Rōjū was alleged to have made in the past crippled its ability
to command the confidence of the semi-autonomous feudal
lords. Daimyos from the shimpan and tozama ranks attained
advisory power that enabled them to impede actions of the
Rōjū and the fudai clique, but they did not acquire sufficient
power to check them altogether. The second development at
the root of the emperor's reemergence into politics was the
existence among the various components of the executive authority of incompatible policy positions which were so complex
and offered with such conviction that the only hope of resolving them was through the arbitration of an authority outside
the government. It was in this way that the imperial office,
which had earlier symbolized the proper basis on which issues
ought to be resolved, was appealed to as the means for resolving
them.

Not one faction alone, but several competing ones, proposed
overtures to the court between 1853 and 1858. Ii Naosuke in
1853, Abe Masahiro in 1855, Matsudaira Yoshinaga and Hotta
Masayoshi in 1858—all regarded the emperor as a possible last
authority for their respective positions. Subsequent events in
some cases cast great doubt on the serious intent of those who
advocated leaving the decision up to the emperor. The jōi faction continued to rail against the early treaties even after the
emperor had given his approval to them in 1855. In 1858 Ii
Naosuke flouted the imperial will by putting the Harris treaty
into effect and by having Kii Iemochi selected as shogunal heir.
Ten years before the Meiji Restoration the emperor had become a political figure, but there was still much to be accomplished before Japanese political society could regard him
unequivocally as the ultimate power in the effective govern-

ment. In order that that condition should come about it was necessary that the sonnō-jōi movement should move to a broader segment of society and that the slogan should become the battle cry of an essentially dissident group intent upon destroying the Tokugawa power.

• 3 •

Imperial loyalism and political dissidence have had a long conjoint career in modern Japan. The loyalist movement of the last few years of the Tokugawa period was directed specifically against the government of the shoguns. The most frequent and vocal appeals to the name of the emperor in the early Meiji period were those of dissident groups protesting against governmental policies (such as the abolition of samurai privileges and the internal improvements program associated with Ōkubo Toshimichi). The liberal movement of the 1870s and 1880s was propounded in the name of imperial rule and in opposition to political control by an oligarchy which, it was claimed, failed to accord with imperial wishes. The ultra-nationalist movement of the twentieth century made conspicuous reference to the ideal of imperial government, as seen in the frequent use by rightists after the First World War of the clichés "Taishō Restoration," "Shōwa Restoration," and "Imperial Way."

Several features of the imperial institution have made it an attractive rallying point for dissidents during the last century. One of them is its traditional aloofness from practical political concerns, hence its availability as a political symbol to men whose aims run counter to those of the government. More important, the content of traditional imperial loyalism made the emperor an independent symbol of moral authority to which rulers should appeal for justification of their rule. Loyalism had traditionally been addressed *to* rulers, and as a consequence it cannot be said to have been dissident of intent. Loyalists did not by any means wish to give disgruntled commoners moral sanction for disobedience to the authorities. Dissident loyalism arose not because loyalists in general were dissidents, but because dissidents found the loyalist argument attractive. As an active political movement dissident loyalism emerged when the anti-shogunal forces became sufficiently numerous and integrated for them to have a potent and discernable ideology. That was in the period of Ii Naosuke's domination of the government, or at earliest a few years before.

Individual dissident loyalists, to be sure, existed earlier. As we have seen, Rai San'yō may have been one, but one cannot be sure. Two writers and teachers of the middle eighteenth century unequivocally earned the designation, and they had some influence on the dissident movement of the Bakumatsu period. They were Takenouchi Shikibu and Yamagata Daiji. Takenouchi (1712–67) was the more important of the two as an ideologue, but Yamagata (1725–67) had a more disruptive role in the political life of his time.

Takenouchi Shikibu, the son of a Niigata physician, studied Orthodox Confucianism and Shinto, both of them under teachers whose interpretations were derived from the syncretic Suika-Shinto system of Yamazaki Ansai.[25] In the early 1750s Takenouchi opened a school in Kyoto, which both commoner townsmen and kuge attended. The basis of his curriculum was ancient chronicles such as the *Nihon shoki*, but he also drew upon recent loyalist writings, particularly Kuriyama Sempō's *Hōken taiki*. In its initial dress his doctrine appears to have been a more-or-less harmless extension of Kuriyama's restorationism. Takenouchi asserted that the emperor was more worthy of respect and reverence than the shogun and deplored the fact that his contemporaries did not seem to realize this. The reason, he said, was a virtually universal deficiency of talent and under-

25 On Takenouchi see Mikami, *Sonnō-ron hattatsu-shi*, pp. 450–55. Tsuji, *Nihon bunka-shi*, vol. 5, pp. 274–94. *Ishin-shi*, vol. 1, pp. 190–208.

standing among the members of the imperial court. None of the kuge retainers, from the kampaku on down, had any ability, and even the emperors were lacking in proper training for their responsibilities. If all of the members of the court attended to their studies, he said, the country would gladly submit to its rule.

From 1755 to 1758 Takenouchi's teaching was a center of controversy in the court. It had come to the attention of the Kampaku, Ichijō Michiyoshi, that some of the younger kuge were practicing military arts such as archery and fencing, ostensibly with the ultimate aim of opposing the rule of the military order, and that they claimed to have been inspired in this endeavor by Takenouchi Shikibu. In 1755 the Kampaku conducted an investigation, interviewing several of the kuge students at Takenouchi's school. In the meantime, the Shoshidai questioned Takenouchi. The tentative conclusion was that Takenouchi's teachings were not subversive of shogunal rule, but that his doctrines were nevertheless not suitable for impressionable courtiers. The Kampaku took the precaution of forbidding the teaching of Takenouchi's favored textbooks in the court, and Ichijō's successor Konoe Uchisaki repeated the prohibition in the following year.

Indiscipline continued among Takenouchi's students, as a result of which several of them were subjected to punishments of house arrest and loss of office in 1758. Takenouchi was questioned again in the same year, this time in the office of the Kyōto Machi-bugyō. He was asked to explain a statement which he was alleged to have made to his students to the effect that the country was then at a moment of great crisis. Takenouchi explained by reference to a passage in the Confucian *Analects:* "When the country is in possession of the Way, rites, music, and punishments proceed from the sovereign. When the country lacks the Way, they proceed from the feudal lords. When they proceed from the feudal lords, it is rare that these do not lose their power in ten generations."[26] The allusion to the Tokugawa shogunate, then under its ninth hereditary ruler, was not lost on the questioners. The Bugyō then pointed out that in all countries it was impossible for any one man to govern by himself, and that in Japan it was the custom for the shogunal administration to perform the everyday details of government. Takenouchi's response to this shows the essential originality of his thought. He said that the shogunate would not be acting improperly if it conferred with the court and governed in accordance with the court's edicts. Of course it would not be necessary for the shogunate to have the emperor's approval for every single detail of the administration, but the major policies should be made upon consultation among the ministers of the imperial court and the officials of the shogunate. Since that was not the way things were done in Takenouchi's time, he concluded that "rites, music, and punishments" proceeded from the feudal lords and that therefore, on the testimony of Confucius, the time was perilous. On the conclusion of the investigation, the court and shogunal officials stationed in Kyoto thought it best to expel Takenouchi from the city. Ironically, the specific charge for which he was ostensibly punished was that he, a commoner, had attended a drinking party in a Kyoto restaurant with court nobles.

Yamagata Daiji was of a family of farmer-samurai (gōshi) from the province of Kai.[27] When Daiji was a youth one of his brothers killed a neighbor. Daiji helped him to escape and as a consequence he was forced to flee incognito and start a new life. He went to Edo, where he started a school of military arts and Confucian philosophy for members of the military aristocracy. This was at about the same time as Takenouchi Shikibu's activities in Kyoto. Yamagata knew of Takenouchi and was influenced by him.

[26] *Analects*, XVI, 2.
[27] On Yamagata see Mikami, *Sonnō-ron hattatsu-shi*, pp. 455–65. Tsuji, *Nihon bunka-shi*, vol. 5, pp. 294–304. *Ishin-shi*, vol. 1, pp. 208–19.

In 1759, the year following Takenouchi's exile from Kyoto, Yamagata wrote a book which could only have been intended as subversive of shogunal rule. This was the *Ryūshi shinron*.[28] He launched his attack on military government on the first page by asserting that Japan's military rulers from the late Heian period on had confounded the distinction between sovereign and subject. Though they had claimed to rule as generals or ministers of the emperor, their rule was actually an arrogation of the prerogatives of sovereignty. The existence of military government was furthermore a confusion of the "civil" and "military" (bun and bu).

The universal principle of ancient and modern times for achieving good government is that the civil order should defend the country in ordinary circumstances and the military order should attend to occasions of crisis. In the present government there is no discrimination between civil and military affairs. Those who attend to times of crisis also defend the country in ordinary times.[29]

Yamagata was not only an anti-shogunal polemicist, but also an active plotter against the shogun's government. He and his students planned some sort of military uprising, but it was discovered too soon to indicate what it would have amounted to if it had succeeded. One charge against him that appears to have been substantiated was that he had launched an intelligence operation to determine the layout and fortifications of the shogunal castle. Another was that he had made inflammatory statements against the shogunate on the occasion of a peasant uprising in the northern part of the Kantō region. He said that the uprising confirmed an earlier prediction he had made that the shogunate's rule had not far to run. Yamagata was executed for his activities. Takenouchi, who knew of the affair but had not reported it, was exiled to an offshore island,

---

[28] In *Kōgaku sōsho*, vol. 12, pp. 415–41. The title *Ryūshi shinron* means "New Doctrine of the Master Ryū," an allusion to Yamagata's pen name Ryūsō.

[29] *Ibid.*, p. 417.

where he died shortly after. Others involved in the plot were imprisoned.

It is difficult to reach a balanced judgment about the place in history of Takenouchi and Yamagata. Understandably, post-Meiji writers about the background of the Meiji Restoration have tended to see in their careers important signs of the things that were to come a century later. Although they do not appear to have been immediately influential on other people's thought or action, they were certainly interesting as examples of the potential danger that had always been present in the loyalist argument if it was taken literally. There is an obvious similarity between what these eighteenth-century dissidents did and what their successors of the 1860s did, and some of the latter claimed to have been influenced in their ideas by Takenouchi and Yamagata. These facts confirm the judgment of modern Japanese historians that the two men have a genuine place in the history of the Restoration.

On the other hand, it is difficult to accept another judgment implicit in the work of modern historians that their activities reveal an essential and dissident quality in Tokugawa period loyalism as a whole. They differed from other loyalists before the Bakumatsu period not only in that they appealed to force in defense of their arguments, but also in that their ideas were a categorically different conception of the emperor's proper role in society. It is noteworthy that the imperial court was firm in rejecting the teachings of Takenouchi Shikibu, no less firm than the shogunate was in suppressing Yamagata Daiji's activities. Indeed, if a distinction is to be made between the reactions of the two courts, the shogunate responded to a threat of violence, but the imperial court with even greater sensitivity responded to dangerous thoughts.

In the context of their own time Takenouchi and Yamagata seem to have been little more than isolated malcontents, more interesting than most because they had access to highly placed persons and were articulate manipulators of classic Chinese polemic style. They were not spokesmen for their own age, but were prophets of an age to come, when discontent with the very structure of state and society had become endemic.

• 4 •

Yoshida Shōin (1830–59) has a unique place in the history of imperial loyalism.[30] His thought and career illustrate the transition from a loyalism that was respectful of existing institutions to one that was destructive of them, and his writings furnish a clear record of the steps by which he made the transition. Until late in his life his opinions show him to have been a typical "enlightened samurai" of the sonnō-jōi faction. In his last few months, however, he shifted to a position that was so radical that it alienated even his own disciples. It was not until after Yoshida's death that a significant number of others reached the same position. His former students were then in the vanguard of a radically dissident movement, which carried them to triumph over the Tokugawa government and placed them among the chief builders of the modern Japanese state.

Yoshida's social and academic background was similar to those of other nineteenth-century loyalists. He was a samurai of the Chōshū Han, a large and rich tozama territory which had undertaken one of the successful programs of han reform of the Tempō period and which had always been distinguished for traditions of imperial loyalism and independence of interest and action from the Tokugawa shogunate.[31] Yoshida was also a teacher, who had been educated in the classics and exegetical works of Chinese and Japanese Confucianism. His Confucian

[30] The following sources have been used in this account of Yoshida: *Yoshida Shōin zenshū*; Naramoto, *Yoshida Shōin*; Van Straelen, *Yoshida Shōin, Forerunner of the Meiji Restoration*; Earl, *Emperor and Nation in Japan*, pp. 109–210.
[31] See Craig, *Chōshū in the Meiji Restoration*, esp. pp. 9–84.

training had been more eclectic than most. He studied the Orthodox system in the Chōshū official academy, he read the works of Yamaga Sokō as a child, and when a youth he went to Edo to study under various masters, including the Wang Yang-ming teacher Sakuma Shōzan. From his early childhood Yoshida had studied military science. Under Shōzan's tutelage, he came to share the belief that the critical times made it necessary for Japan to learn Western technology as rapidly as possible, while at the same time clinging firmly to the moral values of Eastern civilization.

Desire for self-education about the defense and other conditions of Japan first led him to defy the authorities. In 1851 and 1852 he toured the northeast provinces, stopping at Mito to visit teachers there whom he respected, including Aizawa Sei-shisai and Fujita Tōko. Because his daimyo had not formally permitted him to make the trip he was a lawbreaker, and was punished by seven months of house arrest. A more serious clash with the law occurred in 1854. Yoshida had regarded the Perry expedition as confirmation of his apprehension of Western aggression, but he had also seen it as an opportunity for getting firsthand information about the West. He tried to stow away to America when Perry's ships were leaving Japan for the second time in 1854. The attempt was an open violation of the Japanese seclusion laws, and Yoshida was sentenced to prison for it. The sentence was later lightened to house arrest in Chōshū. In 1856, though still in legal confinement, he had sufficient freedom of action to start a private academy, the Shōka Sonjuku, in which he taught his ideas.

Yoshida's thought and action expressed his perception of three kinds of loyalty and the tensions among them. As a Japanese feudal person, he recognized the political primacy of the shogun in the entire country, and he accorded special importance to the shogun's duties regarding foreign affairs and defense. Loyalty to the Chōshū Han was still stronger in him and he clung to it longer. When the shogunate seemed to him to have failed in its duties, Yoshida's pride in Chōshū led him to believe that the han would be able to right the wrong. When the han failed to heed his advice, he was ashamed and angry. Yoshida reserved his highest loyalty for the emperor. In his case this sentiment was compounded of religious devotion, fidelity to national and universal values that the emperor symbolized, and concern for the personal interests and desires of the man who occupied the throne.

Loyalty to the national government, to the han, and to the emperor seemed to Yoshida to be discrete, but complementary, obligations. He considered the first two to include the duty of giving advice to his shogun and daimyo on how to conduct their affairs. This indicates that he had a high estimation of his private sense of duty. As we have seen, he placed this sense of duty above the law in 1851 and in 1854. However, he was by no means contemptuous of the obligation of obedience laid upon him by external authority. His writings of the middle 1850s are full of references to the shogunate's rightful political authority and to all men's obligation to obey its orders. In 1855 while he was in a shogunal prison, he gave lessons on the Book of Mencius to his fellow-prisoners that became the basis for his longest work, Kōmō yowa.[32] References throughout make it clear that Yoshida saw no great incompatibility among his various political and religious loyalties and that he deplored any turn of events that necessitated a choice of one over another. Such a turn of events occurred in 1858, the year of crisis in Yoshida's life, when the court and the shogunate clashed over the Harris treaty. Yoshida's writings of that year are a poignant record of his reluctant choice of emperor and han over shogun and then of emperor over han and shogun.

Yoshida's attitudes toward public policy up to 1858 had been those of the sonnō-jōi faction in its various phases. He became

[32] Kōmō yowa, in Yoshida Shōin zenshū, vol. 2, pp. 247ff.

reconciled to the inevitability of accepting some sort of trade relations with the West some time before that date, but he shared the view of Matsudaira Yoshinaga, Hashimoto Sanai, and others that the Harris treaty should not be accepted without imperial approval. When members of the sonnō-jōi movement who were higher placed in politics than Yoshida appealed to the imperial court, they tended to emphasize the incompetence of Ii's faction and the desirability of better daimyo representation in shogunal councils. Yoshida, however, did not emphasize practical considerations at all. He knew that the emperor was unfriendly to the treaty, and that single fact seemed to make further discussion useless. He spoke frequently of the imperial will, imperial wishes, and imperial commands. Earlier loyalists had used similar words, but in a metaphorical or symbolic sense, for in earlier times there had been no practical way of ascertaining the emperor's personal opinion on any issue. Yoshida understood imperial will literally, as the expressed desires of the emperor, and he demanded that it not be flouted.

In the spring of 1858 he wrote:

If the imperial command is carried out in all particulars by the shogun and the various han; if the shogun leads the han in obedient service to the imperial court; and if the various han use their influence to mediate between the imperial court and the shogun, so that heaven and earth are associated in tranquillity—then will the Imperial Way not be reborn?[33]

When the treaty issue reached a head, he began to realize that the shogunate might disobey the emperor. Then he wrote: "If by chance the shogun should disobey the imperial command, it would be simple for the country to rise and kill him. However, the shogun will surely not do any such thing."[34] In

[33] Letter to Nakatomi Shōsuke, translated in Earl, *Emperor and Nation*, p. 194.
[34] *Taisaku ichidō*, in *Yoshida Shōin zenshū*, vol. 4, p. 110.

the late summer of 1858, when the shogunate signed the treaty, Yoshida's incredulity gave way to despair. He turned to his daimyo for support, urging him in two petitions to punish the shogunate for its disobedience of the emperor.[35] Yoshida next organized seventeen accomplices into a plot to assassinate the Rōjū Manabe Akikatsu, who was then in Kyoto attempting to obtain belated imperial approval for the treaty. Other samurai who had been invited to join the conspiracy but had refused reported the matter to han authorities, who had Yoshida arrested. In the summer of 1859, he was handed over to shogunal authorities in Edo.

Shortly after he had been repudiated by han authorities, Yoshida also lost the support of his students. A number of them wrote to him in January, 1859, requesting that he moderate his strategy. They argued their position on practical grounds, pointing out that his behavior was likely to stimulate a reaction that might bring great harm to the han.[36] At this date Yoshida was far beyond appeals to practicality, or even appeals to han interest. His devotion to a single abstract ideal had reached such a pitch that one suspects he was no longer entirely sane. He gave up trying to persuade han officials and despaired of further success in influencing his disciples. In prison, he made no attempt to conceal his anti-shogunal acts, but boasted of them. For them he was sentenced to death and executed on November 21, 1859.

In the interval between his arrest and execution he continued to write, and his opinions became even more extreme. He began to speak vaguely of peasant armies that would rise up to take revenge for the misdeeds of the feudal classes.[37] Here, for the first time since Yamagata Daiji, we find loyalism linked to revolt. Yoshida, the lonely dissident of the samurai class, had

<hr/>

[35] *Taigi o gi su,* in *ibid.,* vol. 4, p. 88; *Jigi ryakuron,* in *ibid.,* vol. 4, p. 91.
[36] Naramoto, *Yoshida Shōin,* p. 139.   [37] *Ibid.*

understandably concluded that the hope, if any, for support of the emperor lay among non-samurai. There were times in the early 1860's when it appeared likely that the entire sonnō-jōi movement would take a similar course. Loyalism, from having been an upper-class phenomenon and one that assumed the continuance of basic political and social institutions, passed into the hands of men like Yoshida, without power or even the support of the daimyos or other upper bushi.

The assassination of Ii Naosuke in March, 1860, was an instance of loyalist direct action such as Yoshida had prophesied. The assassins included both samurai and commoners, but the samurai had been repudiated by their han and specifically enjoined from violence. Even Tokugawa Nariaki, supposedly the chief of Ii's victims to be avenged, tried to prevent the plot.[38]

Dissident loyalism between 1858 and 1860 had been directed against Ii's government. In the parlance of the time this was usually described as the shogun's government. However, neither Yoshida Shōin nor Ii's assassins went so far as to suggest that the shogunate as an institution should be done away with. They aimed in one way or another to restore harmony between the imperial throne and the government. Temporarily that aim was actually achieved by the removal of Ii Naosuke from the scene of national politics. Shogunal policies continued to be directed by fudai or shimpan elements in the rōjū and other high organs of state. However, Ii's successors, frightened by the violence that had destroyed him, moderated their treatment of the dissenting daimyos and sought to placate the emperor and his court. Within months they were successful in gaining the support of the leading tozama han and of the imperial court for basic shogunal policies, including the foreign policies that had been initiated with the acceptance of the American and other Western trade treaties.

This "era of good feelings," which lasted among upper-level

[38] Lee, *The Political Career of Ii Naosuke*, p. 168.

bushi and kuge until about 1865, was called *kōbu gattai*, a "unification of the 'civil' and 'military' orders." It might equally well have been called a unification of fudai, shimpan, and tozama. Numerous compromises of position by each group in the new alliance effected a real restoration of concord and control. Chief among the compromises were the following. Hitotsubashi Keiki was named regent and heir to the incompetent shogun Iemochi. The daimyos were permitted to spend a greater proportion of their time in their own domains than they had under the traditional system of "alternate attendance." A marriage was contracted between Iemochi and a sister of Emperor Kōmei. One by one the great tozama han of western Japan—Tosa, Satsuma, Chōshū—lent their support to kōbu gattai and implicitly to the treaty system that had been put into effect. Former opponents of kaikoku ("opening the country") in the imperial court dropped their campaign against the shogunate's foreign policy and reaffirmed their confidence in shogunal rule.

It was in this period that the sonnō-jōi movement, which seemed to have spent itself entirely on the levels of society where it had first been generated, attained its most violent and destructive phase. The denotation of jōi changed from defense against foreign pressure to forcible expulsion of the "barbarians" then residing on Japanese soil. The proponents of that line of action were no longer daimyos or their responsible officials, but rather men such as Yoshida Shōin had been in his last year of life, men utterly cut off from institutional means to power, aliens amidst the policy setters of their own country. In the early 1860s jōi was the property of righteous lawbreakers, and the only standards of value left to them as sources of moral justification for their acts were conscience and country.

V

CONCLUSION

❋ LET US NOW consider the principal ways in which the imperial institution changed with the Meiji Restoration. Our comparison will be most meaningful if we select dates some years removed from the revolution of 1868, for the period immediately before and after that event was a transition in which the changes in the throne's condition were too rapid to permit our isolating any single instant for description. The transition may be said to have begun in 1846, with the Kyoto court's first official assertion of a political view to the world outside it. It was complete by the early 1880s, when the Satsuma-Chōshū oligarchy was in firm control of a strong national government and the broad outlines of the emperor's position in a constitutional system had already been decided.

The most striking external change that occurred between the two dates 35 years apart was the physical removal of the emperor and his court to a place in close proximity to the effective government. Had this been all, the emperor's position in the state might have been no different from what it was in the Muromachi period, when emperors were puppets of the Ashikaga shoguns and effectively isolated from political affairs. However, the Meiji Emperor was not only near the government; he was a member of it.

As described by the architects of the Meiji Restoration, the emperor was the head of the government, in a sense in which he had not been since the Heian period. That is, all major decisions of state were referred to him for ratification, and they were frequently described as having been made by him. He was kept informed of national issues, and was consulted about them. There can be little doubt that Meiji's ministers had more knowledge of affairs than he, were more decisive of temperament, had fewer inhibitions about making decisions that might later prove mistaken, and therefore had more personal "power." Still, Meiji was a ruler as his predecessors of the Tokugawa period had not been.

There were numerous institutional changes that help to account for this great change in the emperor's status. The all-embracing political power newly described as belonging to the emperor in the constitutional system which the Meiji oligarchs established was one of the most important. They made the emperor, at least in a legal sense, the head of the state, from whom all the lawful executive power of his subordinates was derived. The legal definition did not need to, and in fact did not, make the emperor an autocrat, but it did prevent the open opposition to the emperor's personal wishes that had occasionally marred the Tokugawa shogunate's treatment of the throne.

Meiji's personal authority in his government, as opposed to his constitutional position within it, must be explained by reference to other institutional changes that had taken place since the 1840s. Two of the most important of these concerned the changed character of the imperial court. First, the composition of the court had been fundamentally altered. The kuge class continued to be represented in the emperor's circle, but they no longer comprised it wholly. New men of the bushi class had personal access to the emperor of a kind that in the Tokugawa period had belonged to no one but a few favored kuge. Second, the kuge, bushi, and others who were close to the person of Emperor Meiji were figures of real political power. They were not powerful *because* they were close to the emperor. Rather, it was the other way around. Eminence in the Restoration movement, meritorious achievement in lower ranks of the government, or association with other powerful ministers lifted them to political prominence, whereupon they earned access to the throne. That, of course, conferred prestige on them, but it also gave the emperor a degree of personal influence with policy makers that sovereigns since the time of Nobunaga had lacked.

Just as the emperor's physical proximity to his government had increased, so had his closeness in law and in spirit to his subjects. After the Restoration laws were promulgated in his name, governing officials were appointed as though by him, and through the medium of imperial rescripts he spoke directly to the people on matters of broad ethical or policy significance. The public became better informed than before about the emperor's personal life and his individual qualities. Some of the pageantry of the court moved to a more public stage. For example the emperor reviewed troops, dedicated new buildings or engineering works, and (after 1890) delivered the opening address of each parliamentary session. Though ordinary subjects often averted their gaze in the presence of the imperial person, his appearance and that of other members of his family became familiar to every Japanese through the medium of photographs.

Publicity and public view went part way toward giving the emperor an aspect of greater immediacy than before with his people, but a more efficacious means to the same end was the abolition of the other offices which had primarily served as personal symbols of authority to men of the Tokugawa period. The abolition of the office of shogun had made the emperor the sole focus of national loyalties, exactly as the Restorationists of 1868 had intended that it should. The Restorationists had not initially intended that imperial loyalism should supplant the more immediate sense of obligation of a vassal to his han lord that had existed under the feudal system. The necessity of military and political modernization doomed the han system, and with it feudal loyalism as well. For a time after the

Restoration the samurai considered themselves still to be bound to their lords, whom they aided in service to the new national government, and who supported them. The creation of a new national army and the transfer of the obligation to pay samurai stipends from the domains to the central government removed the practical bonds between the samurai and daimyos; time was to accomplish even the erosion of the sentimental ties that remained when those were gone. Then only the emperor remained as a focus of the sentiments of loyalty that members of the feudal class projected beyond their own families.

The emperor's relation to commoners also changed, in part because his role in religion changed. "Emperor worship" was not new, but on the contrary of primeval antiquity. The change after the Restoration was the development known as State Shinto. From the diverse elements of earlier Shinto Meiji leaders selected those relating to the emperor, then applied the propaganda methods of the modern state to construct out of them an ethical foundation for the new program of compulsory education. This was the principal way in which the emperor cult became the property of all classes. We have seen that there had always been an emperor cult of some dimensions among commoners, manifested in the custom of pilgrimages to the Ise and other imperial-centered shrines. Whereas these Tokugawa period practices had been voluntary and had affected only part of the population, they became compulsory and universal.

Indeed, one of the most fundamental changes in the nature of the imperial institution that accompanied the transition to the Meiji state was the creation of a new national mythology including in its terms the emperor and all of the people. This new mythology incorporated much of the older loyalist mythology of the Tokugawa period, and supplanted it. It has been shown in an earlier chapter that Tokugawa period loyalism was in the most important senses an aristocratic tradition: its framers were mostly samurai, and its message was addressed in the main to other members of the feudal classes. Loyalty to the emperor was conceived of as analogous to loyalty among feudal persons. It was not the same as feudal loyalty, for it was ultimately independent of the wishes, or even the interest, of the man to whom it was directed. The similarity between feudal loyalty and loyalty to the emperor was the animating impulse that was conceived for both: not fear, but reverence. Commoner society in premodern Japan was excluded from the network of feudal loyalties, and it did not share in the political ethic of understanding, of participation, and of sympathy that was asserted for the feudality. For commoners the closest counterpart was an ethic of obedience, of blind submission to law and order. That commoners in some number had begun to embrace the other morality by the Bakumatsu period is attested by their participation in the dissident loyalist movements that accompanied the final upheavals of the shogunate. (Righteous lawbreakers are the surest possible evidence of an ethic that transcends mere obedience.) The religious and educational apparatus of the Meiji state advanced the process further by extending the code of imperial loyalism to all. Modern Japan has thereby agreed to run the risk that careers of righteous lawbreaking might appeal to some ("Taishō Restorationists" and "Shōwa Restorationists" of the twentieth century right-wing movement, for example) and that such a course of action would be argued by appeal to the imperial name. That risk was accepted for the sake of the advantages to a modernizing nation of mass acceptance of and participation in the polity.

• 2 •

In the late nineteenth and early twentieth centuries, the Japanese throne bore many of the characteristic marks of modern Western monarchies. For example, the emperor issued some laws in his own name and promulgated others passed by the loyal parliamentarians of his Imperial Diet. He was the supreme commander of an army and navy which won victories over China, Russia, and Germany and challenged Great Britain and the United States. He enjoyed equal diplomatic intercourse with heads of foreign states. He was the richest landowner in the country. The peerage, over which he presided, numbered among its members ministerial bureaucrats and party politicians, generals and admirals, chemists and sociologists, international bankers, and manufacturers of everything from breakfast cereal to battleships.

In the foregoing section, when we examined the changes in the condition of the imperial throne which were brought about by the Meiji Restoration, we tended to emphasize the alteration in its relationship to the instruments of government. We can see from the above catalogue of modern features of the recent imperial monarchy that the changes must also be described in terms of an entirely different social context from any that existed in traditional Japan. Japan's nineteenth-century revolution did not all at once make the emperor a constitutional lawgiver, a modern military commander, or a capitalist. He could not become any of those things until after the revolution had brought into being constitutionalism, a modern army and navy, and capitalism. When historians attempt to describe the imperial institution as it was before the Meiji Restoration, they must first of all see clearly that whatever its relation may have been to the other central institutions of society, the character of those institutions determined utterly the throne's condition and function.

The Meiji Restoration, by creating an entirely new element for all institutions to operate within, has tended to falsify our historical image of the imperial institution. It is as though we tried to see into the depths of a lake whose surface, both prism and mirror, distorts the contour of what it reveals beneath when it does not merely reflect what is above. The misconception that has been most far reaching of all concerns the tradition of restorationism. The fact of the Meiji Restoration plus the fact of a tradition prior to it calling for something that went by the same name should not delude one into the belief that the details of the actual historical event were fully present in the prior tradition. The combination of political and nonpolitical qualities of the imperial institution in Tokugawa times resists easy summary description, but whatever it may turn out to be it must be understood from writings of the tradition of contemporary loyalism that is our best source of information about it.

The great theme in loyalist writings is a cry for national reinvigoration through reverence for the emperor. On the level of moral philosophy, this is clear enough. It is an appeal to the values that the emperor symbolized: national independence, national historic continuity, national unity, harmony within the government, and harmony between rulers and ruled. As it applied to institutions, however, loyalist sentiment is ambiguous. On the one hand there is much nostalgia for the past vigor of the imperial court, particularly in periods when the rule of the emperor was closest to the Chinese pattern. On the other hand, there is a basic attitude of satisfaction toward existing political institutions, most notably those of the shogunate and the han. Accordingly, the loyalist program for moral regeneration is susceptible to two different interpretations. Sometimes it seems to be saying in guarded language that a restoration of ancient virtue should be accompanied by a revitalization of the atrophied functions of the imperial court. But more often it seems to say merely that the existing authorities should reform themselves and govern in the exemplary way the imperial court had once done.

The main tradition of loyalist writing clearly postulated an ideal relationship between the emperor and the government, but the emperor's part in the relationship was always passive. The government was to assume the duties of protecting the emperor, respecting him, and giving heed in its policies to the ethical values he symbolized, but of the emperor on his side nothing was expected except that he continue to be there.

The history of the imperial office, aspects of its actual condition in the Tokugawa period, and the tenor of writings about it by loyalist thinkers all hint at a tension between two contrary attitudes which Tokugawa society held on the relationship between the emperor and the government. One attitude was that the emperor had latent secular powers. The other was that his function was entirely religious or moral. Often an individual thinker held both of these views. Neither predominated to the extent that one can hold it up as the single Tokugawa theory of the state. The incompatibility between the two was not obvious until very late in the Tokugawa period; only after the Meiji Restoration was accomplished and the emperor had become a potent wielder of state power could people look back and say unequivocally that he had potentially been a secular ruler all along.

Such ambiguities are of the substance of myth, and the imperial institution was in the final analysis a thing of myth, and not of prosaic utilitarian purpose. It is certain, however, that the value which it had, though elusive to describe, was very great, for the Japanese lavished on it all their art and all their love.

CHRONOLOGY OF THE JAPANESE EMPERORS

NOTE: The early part of the list is traditional. Too much credence should not be given to the dates or even perhaps to the existence of some of the emperors. From about the nineteenth reign dates are believed to be at least approximately correct, and dates from about the twenty-fifth reign have reasonable historical certainty. Sovereigns for whom no dates of abdication are given died in office. The symbol ▲ indicates an empress regnant. The principal authorities for dates and readings are *Koji ruien*, vol. 12, pp. 1 ff; *Kokushi sōran*, Tokyo, Jimbutsu Orai-sha, 1966; Togashi Junji, *Kōshitsu jiten*, Tokyo, Mainichi Shimbun-sha, 1965.

Posthumous Name	Birth	Accession	Abdication	Death
1. Jimmu	?	660 B.C.		585
2. Suizei	632	581		549
3. Annei	577	549		511
4. Itoku	553	510		477
5. Kōshō	506	475		393
6. Kōan	427	392		291
7. Kōrei	342	290		215
8. Kōgen	273	214		158
9. Kaika	193	158		98
10. Sujin	148	98		30
11. Suinin	69	29		A.D. 70
12. Keikō	13	A.D. 71		130
13. Seimu	A.D. 84	131		190
14. Chūai	149	192		200
15. Ōjin	200	270		310

Posthumous Name	Birth	Accession	Abdication	Death
Jingū Kōgō (Regent)		201		269
16. Nintoku	257	313		399
17. Richū	319	400		405
18. Hanzei	ca. 351	406		410
19. Ingyō	ca. 376	412		453
20. Ankō	401	453		456
21. Yūryaku	418	456		479
22. Seinei	444	479		484
23. Kenzō	450	485		487
24. Ninken	449	488		498
25. Buretsu	489	498		506
26. Keitai	450	507	531	531
27. Ankan	466	531		536
28. Senka	467	536		539
29. Kimmei	509	539		571
30. Bidatsu	538	572		585
31. Yōmei	540	585		587
32. Sushun	ca. 521	587		592
▲ 33. Suiko	554	593		628
34. Jomei	593	629		641
▲ 35. Kōgyoku[1]	594	642	645	
36. Kōtoku	596	645		654
▲ 37. Saimei[1]		655		661
38. Tenji	626	668		671
39. Kōbun	648	671		672
40. Temmu	622	673		686
▲ 41. Jitō	645	690	697	702
42. Mommu	683	697		707
▲ 43. Gemmei	661	707	715	721
▲ 44. Genshō	680	715	724	748
45. Shōmu	701	724	749	756
▲ 46. Kōken[2]	718	749	758	
47. Junnin	733	758	764	765
▲ 48. Shōtoku[2]		764		770

[1] Empress Kōgyoku-Saimei has been accorded separate posthumous names for her two reign periods (nos. 35 and 37).

[2] Empress Kōken-Shōtoku has been accorded separate posthumous names for her two reign periods (nos. 46 and 48).

Posthumous Name	Birth	Accession	Abdication	Death
49. Kōnin	709	770	781	781
50. Kammu	737	781		806
51. Heizei	774	806	809	824
52. Saga	786	809	823	842
53. Junna	786	823	833	840
54. Nimmyō	810	833		850
55. Montoku	827	850		858
56. Seiwa	850	858	876	880
57. Yōzei	868	876	884	949
58. Kōkō	830	884		887
59. Uda	867	887	897	931
60. Daigo	885	897	930	930
61. Suzaku	923	930	946	952
62. Murakami	926	946		967
63. Reizei	950	967	969	1011
64. Enyū	959	969	984	991
65. Kazan	968	984	986	1008
66. Ichijō	980	986	1011	1011
67. Sanjō	976	1011	1016	1017
68. Go-Ichijō	1008	1016	1036	1036
69. Go-Suzaku	1009	1036	1045	1045
70. Go-Reizei	1025	1045		1068
71. Go-Sanjō	1034	1068	1072	1073
72. Shirakawa	1053	1072	1086	1129
73. Horikawa	1079	1086		1107
74. Toba	1103	1107	1123	1156
75. Sutoku	1119	1123	1141	1164
76. Konoe	1139	1141		1155
77. Go-Shirakawa	1127	1155	1158	1192
78. Nijō	1143	1158	1165	1165
79. Rokujō	1164	1165	1168	1176
80. Takakura	1161	1168	1180	1181
81. Antoku	1178	1180	1183	1185
82. Go-Toba	1180	1183	1198	1239
83. Tsuchimikado	1195	1198	1210	1231
84. Juntoku	1197	1210	1221	1242
85. Chūkyō	1218	1221	1221	1234
86. Go-Horikawa	1212	1221	1232	1234
87. Shijō	1231	1232		1242

Posthumous Name	Birth	Accession	Abdication	Death
88. Go-Saga	1220	1242	1246	1272
89. Go-Fukakusa	1243	1246	1259	1304
90. Kameyama	1249	1259	1274	1305
91. Go-Uda	1267	1274	1287	1324
92. Fushimi	1265	1287	1298	1317
93. Go-Fushimi	1288	1298	1301	1336
94. Go-Nijō	1285	1301		1308
95. Hanazono	1297	1308	1318	1348
96. Go-Daigo	1288	1318	1339	1339
97. Go-Murakami	1328	1339		1368
98. Chōkei	1343	1368	1383	1394
99. Go-Kameyama	1350	1383	1392	1424
100. Go-Komatsu	1377	1392	1412	1433
101. Shōkō	1401	1412		1428
102. Go-Hanazono	1419	1428	1464	1470
103. Go-Tsuchimikado	1442	1464		1500
104. Go-Kashiwabara	1464	1500		1526
105. Go-Nara	1496	1526		1557
106. Ōgimachi	1517	1557	1586	1593
107. Go-Yōzei	1571	1586	1611	1617
108. Go-Mizunoo	1596	1611	1629	1680
▲ 109. Meishō	1623	1629	1643	1696
110. Go-Kōmyō	1633	1643		1654
111. Go-Sai	1637	1654	1663	1685
112. Reigen	1654	1663	1687	1732
113. Higashiyama	1675	1687	1709	1709
114. Nakamikado	1701	1709	1735	1737
115. Sakuramachi	1720	1735	1747	1750
116. Momozono	1741	1747		1762
▲ 117. Go-Sakuramachi	1740	1762	1770	1813
118. Go-Momozono	1758	1770		1779
119. Kōkaku	1771	1779	1817	1840
120. Ninkō	1800	1817		1846
121. Kōmei	1831	1846		1866
122. Meiji	1852	1867		1912
123. Taishō	1879	1912		1926
124. (The present Emperor)	1901	1926		

Posthumous Name	Birth	Accession	Abdication	Death
Northern Dynasty				
1. Kōgon	1313	1331	1333	1364
2. Kōmyō	1321	1336	1348	1380
3. Sukō	1334	1348	1351	1398
4. Go-Kōgon	1338	1352	1371	1374
5. Go-Enyū	1358	1371	1382	1393
6. Go-Komatsu	1377	1382[3]		

[3] With the healing of the dynastic schism in 1392 the Northern Emperor Go-Komatsu became recognized as legitimate by both factions. Modern theorists count him as legitimate (no. 100) from that year.

BIBLIOGRAPHY

WORKS IN WESTERN LANGUAGES

Beasley, W. G., *Select Documents on Japanese Foreign Policy (1853–1868)*, London, Oxford University Press, 1955.

Bellah, Robert N., *Tokugawa Religion, the Values of Pre-industrial Japan*, Glencoe, Ill., Free Press, 1957.

Bohner, Hermann (trans.), *Jinnō-shōtō-ki, Buch von der Wahren Gott-kaiser-herrschafts-linie*, 2 vols., Tokyo, Japanisch-Deutschen Kultur-institut, 1935.

Borton, Hugh, *Japan's Modern Century*, New York, The Ronald Press, 1955.

Bruce, J. Percy, *Chu Hsi and His Masters*, London, Probsthain, 1923.

Craig, Albert M., *Chōshū in the Meiji Restoration*, Cambridge, Mass., Harvard University Press, 1961.

de Bary, Wm. Theodore, Wing-tsit Chan, and Burton Watson (comp.), *Sources of Chinese Tradition*, New York, Columbia University Press, 1960.

Dubs, Homer H. (trans.), *The History of the Former Han Dynasty*, 3 vols., London, Kegan Paul, 1938–1955.

Earl, David, *Emperor and Nation in Japan*, Seattle, University of Washington Press, 1964.

Eliot, Sir Charles, *Japanese Buddhism*, London, Edward Arnold, 1935.

Fang, Achilles, *The Chronicle of the Three Kingdoms (220–265)*, Cambridge, Mass., Harvard-Yenching Institute Studies, 6, 1952.

Fung Yu-lan, *A History of Chinese Philosophy*, translated by Derk Bodde, 2 vols., Princeton, Princeton University Press, 1952.

Greene, D. C., "Correspondence between William II of Holland and the Shōgun of Japan, A.D. 1844," in *Transactions of the Asiatic Society of Japan*, vol. 34, part 4, pp. 99–132.

Holtom, D. C., *The Japanese Enthronement Ceremonies*, Tokyo, The Kyo Bun Kwan, 1928.

Ishimoto, Yasuhiro, *Katsura, Tradition and Creation in Japanese Architecture*, translated by Charles S. Terry, New Haven, Yale University Press, 1960.

Japan, the Official Guide, Tokyo, Japan Travel Bureau, 1954.

Kaempfer, Engelbert, *Amoenitatum Exoticarum Politico-Physico-Medicarum Fasciculi V, Quibus Continentur Varie Relationes, Observationes, & Descriptiones Rerum Persicarum & Ulterioris Asiae*, Lemgoviae, Henrici Wilhelmi Meyeri, 1712.

Kaempfer, Engelbert, *The History of Japan, Together with a Description of the Kingdom of Siam, 1690–1692*, translated by J. G. Scheuchzer, 3 vols., Glasgow, James Mac Lehose and Sons, 1906.

Langston, Eugene, "The Seventeenth Century Hayashi, a Translation from the Sentetsu Sōdan," in John E. Lane (ed.), *Researches in the Social Sciences on Japan*, Columbia University East Asian Institute Studies No. 4, New York, 1957, pp. 1–32.

Lee, Edwin Borden, *The Political Career of Ii Naosuke*, Ph.D. dissertation, Columbia University, 1960.

Legge, James (trans.), *The Li Ki*, 2 vols., in Müller (ed.), *Sacred Books of the East*, vols. 27–28, Oxford, Clarendon Press, 1885.

Liao, W. K. (trans.), *The Complete Works of Han Fei Tzu*, vol. 1, London, Probsthain, 1939.

McCullough, Helen Craig (trans.), *The Taiheiki, a Chronicle of Medieval Japan*, New York, Columbia University Press, 1959.

Mori, Osamu, *Study on the Imperial Villa of Shugaku-in* (Nara State Institute of Cultural Materials, Monograph 2), Tenri, 1954.

Muraoka Tsunetsugu, *Studies in Shinto Thought*, translated by Delmer M. Brown and James T. Araki, Tokyo, Japanese Committee for UNESCO, 1964.

Murdoch, James, *A History of Japan*, Volume II, London, Kegan Paul, Trench, Trubner, & Co., 1925.

Nihongi, Chronicles of Japan from the Earliest Times to A.D. 697, translated by W. G. Aston, London, George Allen and Unwin, 1956.

Ponsonby-Fane, R. A. B., "Abdication in Japan," in *Transactions and Proceedings of the Japan Society, London*, vol. 32.

Ponsonby-Fane, R. A. B., "The Imperial Family and Shinto," in

Transactions and Proceedings of the Japan Society, London, vol. 27, pp. 59–72, 120–53.

Ponsonby-Fane, R. A. B., "Kōhi, Imperial Consorts in Japan," in *Transactions and Proceedings of the Japan Society*, London, vol. 33.

Ponsonby-Fane, R. A. B., *Kyoto, the Old Capital of Japan* (794–1869), Kyoto, the Ponsonby Memorial Society, 1956.

Rahder, J. "Miscellany of Personal Views of an Ignorant Fool," in *Acta Orientalia*, pp. 173–230.

Reischauer, Robert Karl, *Early Japanese History (c. 40 B.C.–A.D. 1167)*, 2 vols., Princeton, Princeton University Press, 1937.

Sadler, A. L., *The Maker of Modern Japan, the Life of Tokugawa Ieyasu*, London, George Allen & Unwin, 1937.

Sakata Yoshio and John Whitney Hall, "The Motivation of Political Leadership in the Meiji Restoration," in *The Journal of Asian Studies*, vol. xvi, no. 1, November 1956.

Sansom, George, *The Western World and Japan, a Study in the Interaction of European and Asiatic Cultures*, New York, Knopf, 1950.

Sansom, George, *A History of Japan to 1334*, Stanford, Stanford University Press, 1958.

Sansom, George, *A History of Japan, 1334–1615*, Stanford, Stanford University Press, 1961.

Sansom, George, *A History of Japan, 1615–1867*, Stanford, Stanford University Press, 1963.

Shih Ching, in James Legge (trans.), *The Chinese Classics*, 5 vols. in 8, Oxford, Clarendon Press, 1861–1872, vol. 4, part 2.

Shinoda, Minoru, *The Founding of the Kamakura Shogunate, 1180–1185*, New York, Columbia University Press, 1960.

The Tale of Genji, by Murasaki Shikibu, translated by Arthur Waley, New York, The Modern Library, 1960.

Totman, Conrad D., "The Struggle for Control of the Shogunate (1853–1858)," in *Papers on Japan*, Vol. 1, from Seminars at Harvard University, Cambridge, Mass., East Asian Research Center, Harvard University, 1961.

Tso Chuan, in James Legge (trans.), *The Chinese Classics*, 5 vols. in 8, Oxford, Clarendon Press, 1861–1872, vol. 5, part 1.

Tsunoda, Ryusaku, Wm. Theodore de Bary, and Donald Keene (comp.), *Sources of Japanese Tradition*, New York, Columbia University Press, 1958.

Van Straelen, H., *Yoshida Shōin, Forerunner of the Meiji Restoration*, Leiden, E. J. Brill, 1952.

Watson, Burton, *Ssu-ma Ch'ien, Grand Historian of China*, New York, Columbia University Press, 1958.

Webb, Herschel, "The Development of an Orthodox Attitude toward the Imperial Institution in the Nineteenth Century," in Marius B. Jansen (ed.), *Changing Japanese Attitudes Toward Modernization*, Princeton, Princeton University Press, 1965.

Webb, Herschel, *Research in Japanese Sources: A Guide*, New York, Columbia University Press, 1965.

Webb, Herschel, *The Thought and Work of the Early Mito School*, Ph.D. dissertation, Columbia University, 1958.

WORKS IN ORIENTAL LANGUAGES

Abe Yoshio, "Yamazaki Ansai to sono kyōiku," in *Kinsei Nihon no jugaku*, Tokyo, Iwanami Shoten, 1939, pp. 335–56.

Araki Toshima, *Nihon rekigakushi gaisetsu*, Kyoto, Ritsumei-kan Shuppan-bu, 1944.

Bakumatsu gaikoku kankei monjo, in *Dai Nihon komonjo*, Tokyo, Shiryō Hensan-gakari, 1910– .

Bitō Masahide, *Nihon hōken shisō-shi kenkyū*, Tokyo, Aoki Shoten, 1961.

Chūchō jijitsu, in *Kogaku sōsho*, 12 vols., Tokyo, Kōbunko Kankō-kai, 1928, vol. 12.

Dai jimmei jiten, 10 vols., Tokyo, Heibon-sha, 1954.

Dai Nihon Ishin shiryō, Tokyo, Meiji Shoin, 1938–

Dai Nihon shi, 17 vols., Tokyo, Dai Nihon Yūben-kai, 1928–1929.

Dai Nihon shi sansō, in *Mito-gaku taikei*, vol. 6.

Dai Nihon shiryō, compiled by Tōkyō Daigaku Shiryō Hansan-jo, Tokyo, published by compiler, 1901– .

Dokushi biyō, Tokyo, Naigai Shoseki k. k., 1933.

Engi-shiki, in *Kokushi taikei*, vol. 26, Tokyo, Kokushi Taikei Kankō-kai, 1938.

Fujita Motoharu, *Heian-kyō hensen-shi*, Kyoto, Suzukake Shuppan-bu, 1930.

Go-Mizunoo-in nenjū gyōji, in *Shiseki shūran*, vol. 27, pp. 191–239.

Gukanshō, in *Kokushi taikei*, vol. 19, Tokyo, Kokushi Taikei Kankō-kai, 1930.

Haisho zampitsu, in *Yamaga Sokō shū, Kinsei shakai keizai gakusetsu taikei* ed., Tokyo, Seibun-dō Shinkō-sha, 1935.

Hayashi Razan bunshū, Osaka, Kōbun-sha, 1930.

Heian tsūshi, 60 *kan*, Kyoto, Kyōto-shi Sanji-kai, 1895.

Higo Kazuo, *Tennō-shi*, Tokyo, Fuzambō, 1950.

Honchō shōin jōun-roku, in *Gunsho ruijū*, Tokyo, Naigai Shoseki k.k.,1929, vol. 3, pp. 379–498.

Inobe Shigeo, *Bakumatsu-shi gaisetsu*, Tokyo, Kigen-sha, 1927.

Inobe Shigeo, *Ishin zenshi no kenkyū*, Tokyo, Chūbun-kan Shoten, 1938.

Inoue Tetsujirō (ed.), *Nihon rinri ihen*, 10 vols., Tokyo, Ikusei-kai, 1901–1903.

Ishii Ryōsuke, *Tennō*, Tokyo, Kōbun-dō, 1951.

Ishin shi, 6 vols., Tokyo, Meiji Shoin, 1941–1943.

Itō Tasaburō, *Nihon hōken seido shi*, revised and enlarged, Tokyo, Yoshikawa Kōbun-kan, 1955.

Jinnō shōtō-ki, in *Yūhō-dō bunko*, Tokyo, Yūhō-dō, 1927.

Juraku-dai gyōkō-ki, in *Gunsho ruijū*, Tokyo, Naigai Shoseki k.k., 1929, vol. 2, pp. 468–90.

Kaei nenjū gyōji, in *Kojitsu sōsho*, 40 vols., Tokyo, Yoshikawa Kōbun-kan, 1928, vol. 3, pp. 345–489.

Kansei chōshū sho-kafu, 8 vols., Tokyo, Eishin-sha Shuppan-bu, 1917–1918.

Katsuta Katsutoshi, *Arai Hakuseki no rekishi-gaku*, Tokyo, Kōsei-sha, 1939.

Kawakami Tasuke, "Kōi no hatten to shisei seido," in *Iwanami kōza Nihon rekishi*, Tokyo, Iwanami Shoten, 1933–1935.

Koji ruien, 60 vols., Tokyo, Koji Ruien Kankō-kai, 1931–1936.

Kondō Morishige, *Go-hon nikki zokuroku*, in *Dai Nihon shiryō*, Tokyo, Tōkyō Daigaku Shiryō Hensen-jo, 1901– .

Kōya shunjū hennen shūroku, in *Dai Nihon bukkyō zensho*, vol. 131, Tokyo, Bussho Kankōkai, 1912.

Kugyō bunin, 5 vols., in *Kokushi taikei*, vols. 53–57, Tokyo, Kokushi Taikei Kankō-kai, 1934.

Kujō Hisatada monjo, 2 vols., Tokyo, Nihon Shiseki Kyōkai, 1916.

Kurita Mototsugu, *Arai Hakuseki no bunji seiji*, Tokyo, Ishizaki Shoten, 1952.

Kurita Mototsugu (comp.), *Sōgō kokushi kenkyū*, 3 vols., Tokyo, Dōbun Shoin, 1935.

Kurita Tsutomu (ed.), *Sui-han shūshi jiryaku*, Mito, Ibaraki-ken Kyōiku-kai, 1909.

Kuroita Katsumi, *Kokushi no kenkyū*, 3 vols., Tokyo, Iwanami Shoten, 1936.

Maki Kenji, "Hōsei-shi jō ni okeru tennō," in *Shin Nihon rekishi: Tennō-shi,* Tokyo, Fukumura Shoten, 1953.

Maruyama Masao, *Nihon seiji shisō-shi kenkyū,* Tokyo, Tōkyō Daigaku Shuppan-kai, 1952.

Mikami Sanji, *Sonnō-ron hattatsu-shi,* Tokyo, Fuzambō, 1941.

Mito-gaku taikei, edited by Takasu Yoshijirō, 8 vols., Tokyo, Mito-gaku Taikei Kankō-kai, 1942–1943.

Morimoto Kakuzō, *Nihon nengō taikan,* Tokyo, Meguro Shoten, 1933.

Muro Kyūsō, *Kyūsō shōsetsu,* in *Zoku shiseki shūran,* 10 vols., Tokyo, Kondō Shuppan-bu, 1930.

Naimu-shō Chiri-kyoku (comp.), *Sansei sōran,* Tokyo, Teito Shuppan-bu, 1932.

Naramoto Tatsuya, *Yoshida Shōin,* Tokyo, Iwanami Shoten, 1955.

Nihon gaishi, 2 vols., in *Yūhō-dō bunko,* Tokyo, Yūhō-dō, 1920.

Nihon hyakka dai-jiten, 1926 ed.

Nihon-shi Kenkyū-kai (comp.), *Nihon no kenkoku,* Tokyo, Tōkyō Daigaku Shuppan-kai, 1957.

Nihon shoki, in *Kokushi taikei,* vol. 1, Tokyo, Yoshikawa Kōbun-kan, 1931.

Okuno Takahiro, *Kōshitsu go-keizai-shi no kenkyū,* Tokyo, Unebi Shobō, 1942.

Ou-yang Wen-chung-Kung chi, 36 vols. *(Ssu-pu ts'ung-k'an* ed.), Shanghai, Shanghai Commercial Press, n.d.

Sakamoto Tarō, *Nihon-shi gaisetsu,* Tokyo, Shibun-dō, 1958.

Sakata Yoshio, *Meiji Ishin shi,* Tokyo, Mirai-sha, 1960.

Sanjō Sanetsumu shuroku, 2 vols., Tokyo, Nihon, Shiseki Kyōkai, 1926.

Seishi kakei dai-jiten, 3 vols., Tokyo, Seishi Kakei Dai-jiten Kankō-kai, 1934–1936.

Shōchoku-shū, 3 vols., in *Ressei zenshū,* Tokyo, Ressei Zenshū Hensan-kai, 1916.

Shoku Nihongi, in *Kokushi taikei,* vol. 2, Tokyo, Kokushi Taikei Kankō-kai, 1935.

Shōō iji, in *Shiseki shūran,* 27 vols., Tokyo, Kondō Kappan-sho, 1903.

Takashima Shūhan, *Sakuma Shōzan shū,* in *Kinsei shakai keizai gakusetsu taikei,* Tokyo, Seibun-dō Shinkō-sha, 1940.

Tanaka Sōgorō, *Tennō no kenkyū,* Tokyo, Kawade Shobō, 1951.

Teishitsu Rinya-kyoku (comp.), *Go-ryōchi shikō,* Tokyo, compiler, 1937.

Teishitsu seido-shi, 6 vols., Tokyo, Herarudo-sha, 1939– .

Tokugawa jikki, in *Kokushi taikei, vols.* 38–47, Tokyo, Kokushi Taikei Kankō-kai, 1929.

Tokugawa kinrei-kō, 6 vols., Tokyo, Yoshikawa Kōbun-kan, 1931.

Tokushige Asakichi, *Kōmei Tennō go-jiseki-ki*, Kyoto, Tōkō-sha, 1936.

Tōyama Shigeki, *Meiji Ishin*, Tokyo, Iwanami Shoten, 1951.

Tsuda Sōkichi, "*Gukanshō* oyobi *Jinnō shōtō-ki* ni okeru Shina no shigaku shisō," in *Hompō shigaku-shi ronsō*, 2 vols., Tokyo, Fuzambō, 1939, vol. 1, pp. 491–524.

Tsuji Zennosuke, *Nihon bunka-shi*, 7 vols., Tokyo, Shunjū-sha, 1952.

Tzu-chih t'ung-chien, 294 chuan (*Ssu-pu pei-yao* ed.), Shanghai, Chung-hua Shu-tien, 1918–1935.

Wada Hidematsu, *Kanshoku yōkai*, Tokyo, Meiji Shoin, 1926.

Wada Hidematsu, *Kōshitsu gosei no kenkyū*, Tokyo, Tōkyō Shoin, 1933.

Wakamori Tarō, *Kokka no seisei*, in *Shin Nihon-shi taikei*, vol. 1, Tokyo, Asakura Shoin, 1955.

Watanabe Ikujirō, *Meiji Tennō*, 2 vols., Tokyo, Meiji Tennō Shōtoku-kai, 1958.

Watanabe Yosuke, *Azuchi jidai shi*, Tokyo, Gakugei Tosho k.k., 1956.

Watsuji Tetsurō, *Sonnō shisō to sono dentō*, Tokyo, Iwanami Shoten, 1944.

Yabe Teiji, *Konoe Fumimaro*, Tokyo, Kōbun-dō, 1952.

Yamazaki Ansai zenshū, 2 vols., Tokyo, Nihon Koten Gakkai, 1936.

Yashi, compiled by Iida Tadahiko, 6 vols., Tokyo, Nihon Zuihitsu Taisei Kankō-kai, 1929.

Yoshida Shōin zenshū, 10 vols., Tokyo, Iwanami Shoten, 1934–1936.

Yoshikawa Teijirō, "Nobunaga no kinnō," in *Azuchi, Momoyama jidai shiron*, Tokyo, Jin'yū-sha, 1929.

Zoku shigushō, 3 vols., in *Kokushi taikei*, vols. 13–15, Tokyo, Kokushi Taikei Kankō-kai, 1931.

Zoku Tokugawa jikki, in *Kokushi taikei*, Tokyo, Kokushi Teikei Kankō-kai, 1932.

Zoku Yamazaki Ansai shū, 3 vols., Tokyo, Nihon Koten Gakkai, 1937.

Zoku-zoku gunsho ruijū, Tokyo, Ichijima Kenkichi, 1909.

INDEX

Abdication: and accession *(juzen)*, 103–4; ceremony, 110–14; involuntary, 110–12; voluntary, 112–14; imperial rescript (Go-Yōzei's), quoted, 114
Abe Masahiro, 230, 234, 240, 246
Abe Yoshio, "Yamazaki Ansai to sono kyōiku," cited, 144*n*
Accession, *see* Abdication; *Senso*
Administration, supplementary bodies, 40 ff.
Adviserships, extraordinary *(sangi)*, 33–34
Aesthetics, and *bun*, 6
Agricultural year, symbolized in *Daijō-sai*, 108–10
Ainu, 184
Aizawa Seishisai, 213–17, 228, 254
Amaterasu Ōmikami (Sun Goddess), progenitrix of imperial line, 13, 133, 163, 207
Analects, quoted, 194, 249–50
Ancient Studies School, 142, 146, 198–99
Appointments, imperial bestowal of, 117–18
Arai Hakuseki, 96, 143–48 *passim*; state theory, 170–71
Araki Toshima, *Nihon reki-gakushi gaisetsu*, cited, 110*nn*
Arisugawa (family), 79
Arts and pastimes, *kuge* family specialists in, 94–95
Asaka Tampaku, 147, 179–80; on Lord Takeuchi, 181; on Emperor Go-Daigo, 203

Asayama Irin'an, *see* Soshin
Ashikaga (family), 47
Ashikaga Tadayoshi, 203
Ashikaga Takauji, 46, 184, 202–3
Ashikaga Yoshiaki,.48–49
Ashikaga Yoshimasa, 55
Ashikaga Yoshimi, 55
Assistant governors *(suke)*, 30
Aston, W. G., tr., *Nihongi*, cited, 20*n*, 21*n*, 22*n*, 23*n*, 28*n*
Azuma kagami, 52–53

Bakumatsu gaikoku kankei monjo, cited, 236*n*, 238*nn*, 241*n*, 244*n*, 245*n*
Banka families, 91
Barbarians, 184–85
Beasley, W. G., *Select Documents on Japanese Foreign Policy (1853–1868)*, cited, 234*n*, 236*n*, 241*n*
Bellah, Robert N., *Tokugawa Religion, the Values of Pre-Industrial Japan*, quoted, 195; cited, 218*nn*
Bitō, Masahide, *Nihon hōken shisō-shi kenkyū*, cited, 142*n*
Board of Censors *(Danjōdai)*, 30
Bohner, Hermann, tr., *Jinnō shōtō-ki*, cited, 165*n*
Book of Odes, on King Wen and Mandate of Heaven, 200
Borton, Hugh, *Japan's Modern Century*, cited, 234*n*
Bruce, J. Percy, *Chu Hsi and His Masters*, cited, 153*n*
Bu (military government), 5

STUDIES OF THE
EAST ASIAN INSTITUTE

The Ladder of Success in Imperial China by Ping-ti Ho. New York, Columbia University Press, 1962; reprint, John Wiley, 1964.

The Chinese Inflation, 1937-1949 by Shun-hsin Chou. New York, Columbia University Press, 1963.

Reformer in Modern China: Chang Chien, 1853-1926 by Samuel Chu. New York, Columbia University Press, 1965.

Research in Japanese Sources: A Guide by Herschel Webb with the assistance of Marleigh Ryan. New York, Columbia University Press, 1965.

Society and Education in Japan by Herbert Passin. New York, Bureau of Publications, Teachers College, Columbia University, 1965.

Agricultural Production and Economic Development in Japan, 1873-1922 by James I. Nakamura. Princeton, Princeton University Press, 1966.

The Korean Communist Movement and Kim Il-Song by Dae-Sook Suh. Princeton, Princeton University Press, 1967.

The First Vietnam Crisis by Melvin Gurtov. New York, Columbia University Press, 1967.

Japan's First Modern Novel: Ukigumo *of Futabatei Shimei* by Marleigh Grayer Ryan. New York, Columbia University Press, 1967.

Cadres, Bureaucracy, and Political Power in Communist China by A. Doak Barnett with a contribution by Ezra Vogel. New York, Columbia University Press, 1967.

The Japanese Imperial Institution in the Tokugawa Period by Herschel Webb. New York, Columbia University Press, 1968.

DATE DUE

APR 30 71			
GAYLORD			PRINTED IN U.S.A.